SCANDALS IN COLLEGE SPORTS

This timely book highlights the impact that sports have on institutions of higher education and guides college leaders and educators in informed discussions of policy and practice. *Scandals in College Sports* includes 21 classic and contemporary case studies and ethical dilemmas showcasing challenges that threatened the integrity and credibility of intercollegiate sports programs at a range of institutional types across the country. Cases cover NCAA policy violations and ethical dilemmas involving student-athletes, coaches, and other stakeholders, including scandals of academic misconduct, illegal recruiting practices, sexual assault, inappropriate sexual relationships, hazing, concussions, and point shaving. Each chapter author explores the details of the specific case, presents the dilemma in a broader sociocultural context, and ultimately offers an alternative ending to help guide future practice.

Shaun R. Harper is the Clifford and Betty Allen Professor in the Rossier School of Education at the University of Southern California, USA. He is also Executive Director of the USC Race & Equity Center and President of the Association for the Study of Higher Education.

Jamel K. Donnor is Associate Professor of Education at the College of William and Mary, USA.

SCANDALS IN COLLEGE SPORTS

Edited by Shaun R. Harper and Jamel K. Donnor

Routledge
Taylor & Francis Group

NEW YORK AND LONDON

First published 2017
by Routledge
711 Third Avenue, New York, NY 10017

and by Routledge
2 Park Square, Milton Park, Abingdon, Oxon OX14 4RN

Routledge is an imprint of the Taylor & Francis Group, an informa business

British Library Cataloguing in Publication Data
A catalogue record for this book is available from the British Library

Library of Congress Cataloging in Publication Data
Names: Harper, Shaun R., 1975- author. | Donnor, Jamel K., author.
Title: Scandals in College Sports / By Shaun R. Harper and Jamel K. Donnor.
Description: New York, NY London : Routledge, 2017. | Includes index.
Identifiers: LCCN 2016039051 | ISBN 9781138830547 (hardback) |
ISBN 9781138830554 (pbk.) | ISBN 9781315737225 (ebook) |
ISBN 9781317569404 (mobi/kindle)
Subjects: LCSH: College sports--Corrupt practices–United States--History. |
College sports--Moral and ethical aspects--United States. | College athletes--
United States--Conduct of life. | National Collegiate Athletic Association--
Rules and practice.
Classification: LCC GV351 .H37 2017 | DDC 796.04/3--dc23
LC record available at https://lccn.loc.gov/2016039051

ISBN: 978-1-138-83054-7 (hbk)
ISBN: 978-1-138-83055-4 (pbk)
ISBN: 978-1-315-73722-5 (ebk)

Typeset in Bembo
by Taylor & Francis Books

To all who act with integrity, even when millions are at stake.

CONTENTS

PREFACE

This project was born of tragedy, disbelief, grief, and outrage. We immediately called each other on the telephone when news broke of the Penn State Jerry Sandusky child sex-abuse scandal. We were shocked, especially as reporters revealed that Joe Paterno knew about the situation, did nothing, and was refusing to immediately resign. We couldn't believe it. One of us had been a professor at Penn State; both of us are lovers of college football and researchers of student-athlete outcomes, and therefore had come to respect Coach Paterno's legacy of graduating players at unusually high rates. We found ourselves judging a great university for the wrongdoings of a fairly small cast of terrible actors. We were sad for Penn State and we grieved for the children victimized by its inaction. We had to do something, but were unclear at the time about what would make a difference for that institution and others like it. Hence, we carefully followed the case and engaged in several conversations about it in the ensuing weeks. While Sandusky's crimes and Penn State's neglect to address them were unacceptable and context specific, we understood the undercurrents of this situation (shame and secrecy, reputation protection, White male power and privilege, profits over principles, etc.) were more common than most sports commentators and other journalists were acknowledging in their analyses at the time.

Scandals in College Sports, unlike many other related texts, is not a broad critique of intercollegiate athletics and its myriad issues. Ours is not a restatement of all the reasons why competitive sport is bad for higher education. Instead, this is a book of 21 case studies that showcase challenges that threatened the integrity, credibility, and, in some instances, the survival of intercollegiate sports programs at a range of colleges and universities across the country. All but three chapters are devoted to a particular scandal at one college or university. The choice to commit an entire chapter to carefully unpacking and making sense of a single scandal differentiates our book from others. It is our hope that readers will find this approach educationally useful. Understanding what happened, what went wrong, why such bad decisions were made, and what alternatives various actors (e.g. coaches, athletics administrators, student-athletes, and boosters) had in each situation could be powerfully instructive for those who wish to avoid future scandals, as well as anyone staunchly committed to good sportsmanship and integrity.

CHAPTER STRUCTURE AND SECTION OVERVIEWS

In Chapter 1, we explain why scandals are so commonplace in intercollegiate athletics. Each chapter thereafter is identically structured and broken into three parts. First, authors describe each case in detail – what happened, who was involved, who was harmed, why it was so wrong, how the wrongdoing was discovered, how various stakeholders (e.g. the public, media, the NCAA, and/or the university administration) reacted, and how the individual(s) and/or institution were penalized. Cases are summarized in an engaging, quasi-journalistic fashion. As such, the overwhelming majority of references in this section are from documentary sources (newspaper and magazine articles), episodes of ESPN's *Outside the Lines* and other media coverage of the scandals, and credible websites (not Wikipedia). Second, authors place their respective cases in a broader sociocultural context: what this scandal conveys about the larger enterprise of intercollegiate athletics; what the explanatory undercurrents of this issue are (for example, greed and abuse of power); how race, gender, capitalism, culture, history, sexual orientation, college access and opportunity, exploitation of persons and systems, and/or socioeconomic status were at play in the case; and how unusual the case itself and the institution's response to it were. Traditional academic sources (namely peer-reviewed journal articles and books) are used in this part of the chapter. In the final section, authors offer an alternate ending to the scandal. They are not necessarily saying what should have occurred, but instead provide examples of a pivotal juncture in each case and forecast how the situation might have been differently handled had key actors made another set of choices in that critical moment.

Cases in this book span a range of institution types (large NCAA Division I universities, small liberal arts colleges, Christian colleges, etc.) and an array of sports (women's and men's basketball, ice hockey, wrestling, etc.). Five chapters focus exclusively on women's sports, and one on the abuse of a female student-athlete on the University of Colorado's football team. This book is organized into four parts, which we refer to as quarters. Chapters in the first quarter focus mostly on violations of NCAA player recruitment, gifts, and compensation policies that occurred throughout the 2000s. The roles boosters, sports agents, student-athletes, and coaches played are highlighted in these cases. Situations in which contest or player performance outcomes were somehow manipulated are presented in the second quarter. This section includes one chapter on an emerging, yet often-overlooked, problem that affects many collegiate sports programs: student-athletes' use of performance-enhancing drugs. Hence, authors of Chapter 12 foreshadow a scandal in the making.

Chapters in the third quarter are about coaches abusing players, student-athletes abusing each other through hazing rituals, and the harmful effects of concussions. The final section includes a collection of cases that highlight discriminatory acts against women student-athletes and coaches, as well as heterosexual men who were punished for performing sexual acts in online pornographic videos that primarily gay and bisexual men watch. Situations involving coaches having sex with players and the sexual abuse of children are also included in the fourth quarter.

Three criteria were used in selecting cases for this book. First, we attempted to pick situations that reflected a breadth of controversies and missteps in college sports. We thought it necessary, for example, to include only two cases that involved academic misconduct and tutors writing papers on behalf of student-athletes, even though all 22 chapters could have been devoted to this topic. Second, we chose cases that reflect a diversity of institutions and intercollegiate sports teams. Notwithstanding, the majority are from NCAA Division I schools and revenue-generating men's sports. And third, we attempted to pick cases that were seemingly resolved or near resolution. The Penn State Sandusky case is one noteworthy exception. At the time this book went into production, the courts had not yet ruled in the cases against former President Graham Spanier and other key administrators involved in the cover-up. We decided against including a chapter on the unionizing of student-athletes at Northwestern University; while this situation ignited much discussion and disparate viewpoints concerning the compensation of college student-athletes, it did not seem to qualify as a scandal. By the time this book is published, there will inevitably be a handful of new scandals. For instance, the scandal involving football players' sexual assaults of women at Baylor University, which resulted in the resignation of its chancellor, made national news just as this book went into production.

ACKNOWLEDGMENTS

We are incredibly indebted to the 34 friends and colleagues who wrote chapters for this book. Many are former college student-athletes; some have coached intercollegiate sports teams, served as high-level administrators in athletics departments, and played for the National Football League, Major League Baseball, and other professional sports organizations domestically and abroad; and all are scholars who care authentically about sports and student-athletes. The project benefits enormously from their expertise and thought leadership. We also thank Emily Wood and Jeffrey Frantz for their editorial and fact-checking assistance. Our spouses, Shawn K. Hill and Andrea Mitchell Donnor, are the biggest and most reliable cheerleaders of our academic work, including this book. We love and appreciate them. We are also grateful to Bailey for the joy she brought her dad while he was completing this project.

Finally, we acknowledge those who acted with integrity in the Penn State tragedy. Ultimately, it was those brave persons – not Sandusky, Paterno, and others involved in the scandal – who inspired us to undertake this important project. We continually grieve for the victims, their families, and the innocent Penn Staters who were negatively affected. We hope this project somehow helps address the source of problems in intercollegiate sports that injured these persons and others on college and university campuses across the nation.

Shaun R. Harper
Philadelphia, Pennsylvania

Jamel K. Donnor
Williamsburg, Virginia

1

BAD SPORTSMANSHIP

Why College Sports Are so Scandalous

Shaun R. Harper and Jamel K. Donnor

What about the wellness, academic performance, personal and professional development, and protection of college student-athletes? What about the sanctity and purity of sport, and love of the game? And what about the American university as sacred grounds for learning, intellectual engagement, high academic ideals, and the preparation of bright, well-educated persons for democratic citizenship? Was this not originally supposed to be about physical fitness, fun, and friendly competition among collegians? If so, how did it evolve into an enterprise that occasionally embarrasses institutions and injures innocent people? The National Collegiate Athletic Association (NCAA) exists to reduce these problems, so why does it so routinely contradict itself? Scholars, journalists, and others have posed these critical questions time and time again. Yet, there are quite possibly more scandals than there are championships in intercollegiate sports.

In his classic text, *Games Colleges Play: Scandal and Reform in Intercollegiate Athletics*, historian John Thelin masterfully documents longstanding critiques and failed attempts to effectively regulate problematic aspects of college sports over an 80-year period (1910–1990). Accordingly, most reform efforts failed to realize their intended purposes. Thelin (1996) argues that reform groups like the Knight Commission on Intercollegiate Athletics have attempted to restore something that intercollegiate athletics never had: integrity. Frederick Rudolph noted the following in his 1962 history of U.S. higher education:

> From the White House [U.S. President] Theodore Roosevelt thundered that if the colleges did not clean up football he would abolish it by executive order. And in a bit of moralism which revealed much of the temper of the age, he added: "Brutality and foul play should receive the same summary punishment given to a man who cheats at cards." (p. 376)

Problems in college sports have escalated since President Roosevelt threatened to end football in 1905.

One of the most enduring concerns is reflected in the subtitle of Murray Sperber's (2000) book, *Beer and Circus: How Big-Time College Sports Is Crippling Undergraduate Education.* Contradictions and controversies, substantiated by data and numerous examples from hundreds of intercollegiate sports programs across the nation, have been documented in several other books (e.g. Benedict & Keteyian, 2013; Bowen & Levin, 2003; Clotfelter, 2011; Duderstadt, 2000; Estler & Nelson, 2005; French, 2004; Jozsa, 2013; Lapchick, 2006; Lapchick & Slaughter, 1989; Nixon, 2014; Oriard, 2009; Shulman & Bowen, 2001; Smith, 2011; Telander, 1996; Toma, 2003; Watterson, 2000a; Yost, 2010; Zimbalist, 1999) and reports (e.g. American Association of University Professors, 1989; Desrochers, 2013; Knight Commission on Intercollegiate Athletics, 1991, 2001, 2009, 2010; Sack & Staurowsky, 1998; Savage, Bentley, McGovern, & Smiley, 1929). These authors and hundreds more offer critical insights into why competitive game play between U.S. colleges and universities has been and continues to be so scandalous. Some of these explanations are presented in the next section.

The Sociology of (Un)Sportsmanlike Conduct

Corruption in college sports is traceable back to the very first intercollegiate athletics contest in the U.S., a boat race between Harvard and Yale in 1852 on Lake Winnipesaukee in New Hampshire. James Elkins, superintendent of the Boston, Concord, Montreal Railroad, invested money into land at Lake Winnipesaukee and aspired to transform the area into an attractive tourist destination (Sperber, 2004). Elkins thought a sporting contest between the two most popular colleges in the country would attract huge crowds to the lake and garner considerable media attention. In exchange for their participation, Elkins offered a financial incentive to the Harvard and Yale boat crews. According to Sperber, it was later discovered that some men who competed in the race were not college students; they are believed to have been professional rowers who were hired for the event. He therefore observes: "even before the starting gun went off or an oar hit the water, two elements were at play: the event was totally commercial, and the participants were cheating. The history of intercollegiate athletics has gone downhill from there" (p. 18). Capitalism, greed, and enormous sums of money have since escalated myriad problems in what has become a multi-billion dollar enterprise, an industry in which per-athlete expenditures presently exceed per-student expenditures at many institutions and coaches earn the highest salaries on campus (Desrochers, 2013).

Understanding the motives of misconduct requires some acknowledgement of human participation in competitive situations. Cheating in the Yale vs. Harvard boat race most assuredly occurred because one school did not want to lose a public contest to its rival. Given the time and effort they invest into conditioning, practices, travel, and so on, student-athletes would rather win than lose. Pressures from teammates, coaches, alumni, and fans exacerbate these feelings. Student-athletes whose performances are not as great as they and others expect often aspire to do better. Furthermore, those accomplished young women and men who amass stardom and praise for their athletic prowess usually feel enormous pressure to remain at the top of their game and satisfy spectators who love them when they win. And then there are those who only view college enrollment and intercollegiate athletics participation as a vehicle to actualize their professional sports aspirations – anything short of excellence poses a serious threat to their being drafted by the NFL, NBA, or some other professional sports organization. These pressures comingle with a host of other factors that compromise integrity in intercollegiate athletics.

In addition to the excitement and personal accomplishment that student-athletes and their teammates feel, sports victories also reap enormous financial and reputational benefits for institutions. Rudolph (1962) tells of how Massachusetts Agricultural College (now University of Massachusetts Amherst) was not thought to be a "real college" until it defeated Harvard in an athletic contest in 1870; the state legislature significantly increased its appropriations to the college shortly thereafter. An institution receives considerable exposure when ESPN broadcasts *College GameDay* from its campus and when its sports teams appear in nationally televised contests. There is just so much more enthusiasm when the school wins. Plus, advancing to the conference championship, a post-season bowl game, College World Series, or the next tournament round during March Madness has serious financial implications.

The profit potential in big-time college sports, namely football and men's basketball at NCAA Division I universities, compels coaches and others to win at all costs, including occasionally breaking the law and violating policies established by their institutions, athletics conferences, and the NCAA. The University of Michigan's football stadium has 109,901 seats (University of Michigan, 2014) – surely, the goal is to fill as many of those seats as possible at every home game. However, fans are less likely to buy tickets if the Wolverines are on a losing streak; the university consequently receives less revenue when seats are empty. Moreover, alumni and boosters are more energized by a winning team. Their enthusiasm often produces profits. Conversely, losses often compel fans (some of whom are current and prospective donors) to pressure the university to make personnel changes.

Coaches who fail to fill seats, sustain back-to-back winning seasons, take their teams to post-season competitions, occasionally win championships, and stimulate giving among alumni and other enthusiasts are vulnerable for termination. People in most professions, not just college sports, would go to great lengths to save their jobs. However, it is plausible that the higher a person's salary is, the more desperate and determined she or he is to retain that high-paying job. Desperation often leads to disillusionment and dishonesty, whatever it takes to maintain one's position and corresponding lifestyle. Compensation in big-time college sports programs explains, at least in part, why corruption is so commonplace. Seventy head and three assistant football coaches, 35 head men's basketball coaches, and nine athletics directors (all men) received compensation packages that exceeded $1 million in 2013 (USA Today, 2014). The loss of a million-dollar job surely requires significant lifestyle changes – who wouldn't protect that? And doesn't it stand to reason that someone who is not yet at that compensation level would do all sorts of things to win, which, in turn, would make him (or in rare cases, her) more competitive for a multimillion-dollar coaching job?

The NCAA, the Indianapolis-based entity that creates policy and governs most intercollegiate sports programs, also has jobs to protect. While it is technically a nonprofit organization, the NCAA employs several people who earn enormously high salaries. Sander (2010) reports the association's top 14 executives earned nearly $6 million in 2009, while Solomon (2014) notes that 18 NCAA officials received total compensation packages that exceeded $240,000 in 2012. The association paid its president, Mark Emmert, a $1.36 million base salary in 2013, plus more than $200,000 in other reportable compensation and $235,700 in retirement and deferred compensation (Berkowitz, 2015). In light of the amount of money involved, Yost (2010) offers this sharp critique of the NCAA:

> The whole operation – the rules and regulations, the investigations, the seminars on balancing academics and athletics, and the ludicrous term *student-athlete* – are designed to hide the real business that the NCAA and their participating schools are engaged in: extortion . . . . they are extorting money from (the mostly poor and mostly Black) kids who provide the raw material for the sports-entertainment business that generates billions of dollars for the NCAA and participating schools every year. (pp. 159–160)

Yost further points out how profits (which are used to finance executive compensation) undermine the NCAA's willingness to more seriously regulate college sports. The same is likely true in some major athletics conferences. For instance, Big 12 Conference Commissioner Bob Bowlsby earned a $1.8 million base salary in 2013 (Berkowitz, 2015). That same year, Mike Slive, former Commissioner of the Southeastern Conference (SEC), had a total compensation package that exceeded $2.1 million.

Scandals are also explained by contradictions and governance problems on college and university campuses. On the one hand, institutions espouse in mission statements commitments to integrity, student learning, and assorted purposes that have absolutely nothing to do with winning athletic contests (Morphew & Hartley, 2006). But on the other hand, institutional leaders are seduced by revenue generated through big-time sports programs; by dollars procured via corporate sponsorships, television contracts, and alumni giving; and by the positive attention ESPN and other major networks give their institutions when competitions and championships are won. Public and private institutions, albeit for slightly different reasons, are similarly seduced by the commercialization of college sports. Over the past decade, especially during the recent economic recession, public and state-supported postsecondary institutions have experienced sharp declines in revenues from their state and local governments (State Higher Education Executive Officers, 2014). Budget cuts demand diversifying revenue streams, quite possibly making corporate sponsorships, television contracts, and championship payouts more enticing than ever before.

Rudolph (1962) and Thelin (2011) describe eras in the history of American higher education when professors were in charge, when faculty owned admissions and the curriculum, and when they often made important decisions about the institution. Watterson (2000b) points to several instances in the early 1900s in which faculty attempted to keep athletics, particularly football, from spiraling out of control. He notes that, at the University of Chicago in 1905, "the faculty openly defied their ailing president, William Harper, as well as domineering coach and Director of Physical Culture Amos Alonzo Stagg. They refused to allow students to play football unless 'the moral and physical evils' were remedied" (p. 293). Watterson also quotes an academic dean at Chicago who characterized football as "a social obsession – a boy killing, education-prostituting, gladiatorial sport" (p. 293). Football at Chicago was eventually banned from 1939 to 1969 in large part because of concerns faculty repeatedly expressed about its threat to the institution's soul.

Statements such as the one the American Association of University Professors (AAUP) crafted in 1989, as well as many of the previously cited reports from the Knight Commission on Intercollegiate Athletics, spotlight longstanding governance tensions between faculty and athletics departments. In sum, as sport became more popularized and profitable in the university, professors were less able to control its unsportsmanlike features, which has allowed scandals to flourish. These governance problems – especially the question of who is in charge of intercollegiate athletics – are worsened by current shifts in the professoriate. Faculties at many institutions have changed from primarily full-time, tenure-track professors to mostly part-time, adjunct, and clinical/contingent faculty; the latter presently comprises the majority in U.S. higher education (Kezar, 2012). This shift signifies an erosion of faculty leadership, including the ability to limit the corporatization of the university and regulate problematic activities within its athletics department (e.g. lowering admission standards for underqualified recruits). With fewer full-time tenured professors on campus, college sports are almost guaranteed to become more scandalous.

At many institutions, athletics departments are seemingly on the outskirts, even when they are physically situated in or near the center of campus. Buildings in which they are located are usually perceived to be only for coaches, athletics personnel, and student-athletes; few others find reasons to visit, many have no idea what occurs therein. Atmospheres of exclusion, even those not deliberately fostered or sustained, can be places susceptible to scandal. With no (or few) outsiders watching, misconduct and secrecy are more easily sustained. These spaces also tend to be structurally and culturally masculine, oftentimes with men possessing considerably more power and being compensated at much higher rates than women. Harper and Harris (2010) argue that masculine norms and gendered ideologies that privilege men were historically woven into the structure, architecture, and character of most colleges and universities; the same is true of athletics departments at many institutions, including those that women presently lead. We are not suggesting that men and masculinities are bad; we both are men who know countless other men, like us, who are good. Our point here, though, is that settings in which wealthy men are overrepresented and power is inequitably distributed are particularly susceptible to scandals.

In addition to its masculine cultural features, many athletics departments with high-profile football and men's basketball teams preserve a problematic racial paradox year after year: the majority of student-athletes on those teams are Black men, yet the overwhelming majority of staff and well-compensated leaders are White. Coaches and administrators of color are terribly underrepresented, which also contributes to cultural norms in which opportunity, power, and wealth are inequitably distributed. In 2010, Black men comprised just 6.6 percent of head coaches and 7.4 percent of athletics directors in NCAA Division I (Lapchick, Hoff, & Kaiser, 2010), but were 57.1 percent and 64.3 percent of student-athletes on Division I football and men's basketball teams, respectively (Harper, Williams, & Blackman, 2013). Workplace settings that lack diversity also tend to lack certain forms of transparency and accountability. To be sure, it is not our position that White athletics directors and coaches are genetically corrupt; we don't believe this. However, in our view, big-time sports programs that earn millions on the backs of Black male student-athletes (many of whom they fail to graduate), yet refuse to find qualified people of color for coaching and top leadership positions, lack integrity. As made clear throughout this book, scandals occur more routinely in organizations and environments that lack integrity. In each chapter that follows, authors masterfully show how the scandal itself is almost always a manifestation of larger structural and cultural problems such as those we have described in this section.

Not All Bad: An Anti-Deficit Acknowledgment

In his 2013 book, *Fourth and Long: The Fight for the Soul of College Football*, John U. Bacon presents powerfully refreshing insights from the time he spent observing football teams at the University of Michigan, Ohio State, Northwestern, and Penn State. He physically immersed himself in locker rooms, practices, team meetings, and other spaces in which student-athletes and coaches were interacting, strategizing, and sometimes disagreeing. Bacon tells several inspiring stories of good sportsmanship, teamwork, and accountability – features of big-time college sports programs not often highlighted in the media. Like him, we, too, acknowledge there is much goodness that occurs within intercollegiate sports programs. For instance, student-athletes are afforded substantive opportunities to develop teamwork skills, their rates of participation in community-service projects tend to be higher than rates for non-athletes, and in most sports they are far likelier than are non-athletes to interact meaningfully with peers from a range of races/ethnicities, sexual orientations, and socioeconomic statuses. Additionally, on lots of campuses, coaches are extraordinary mentors and role models for student-athletes with whom they work; they invest richly into students' development and learning beyond the field, pool, or court. Likewise, professionals in athletics departments do much that is praiseworthy to honestly facilitate student-athletes' academic success, wellness, and holistic development. These staff persons also work to ensure the department complies with NCAA, conference, and institutional policies.

In a letter on the NCAA website, President Mark Emmert notes, "more than eight in 10 student-athletes earn their bachelor's degrees, and more than 35 percent of Division I student-athletes go on to earn postgraduate degrees. Additionally, the graduation rates of student-athletes are consistently higher than those of the general student population." This is good and mostly true (although Black men in major Division I football and basketball programs actually graduate at rates lower than undergraduates in the general student body, other student-athletes, and Black men who do not play on intercollegiate sports teams). Notwithstanding the racial inequities that are masked when NCAA officials talk about data in aggregate terms, that student-athletes generally graduate at higher rates should be celebrated and we should endeavor to learn more about how athletics departments achieve such impressive results. In this way, U.S. higher education, broadly, has something to learn from athletics.

We know for sure that not every person or athletics department is corrupt. We therefore believe that much can be learned from coaches, athletics directors, student-athletes and others who cling unflinchingly to their principles – we do not hear enough about what inspires them to resist the temptations to win at any cost. We both are seriously loyal and longtime college sports enthusiasts. We love games so much that we desperately want them to be fair. Offering a sociological explanation for unsportsmanlike conduct earlier in this chapter was our way of acknowledging that people involved in college sports are not bad, per se, but there are certain incentives, pressures, expectations, and cultural norms that sometimes compel otherwise good-behaving people to do inexcusably bad things. Despite the goodness evidenced in athletics departments across the country, bad sportsmanship occurs more often than it should.

References

American Association of University Professors. (1989). *The role of the faculty in the governance of college athletics*. Washington, DC: Author.

Bacon, J. U. (2013). *Fourth and long: The fight for the soul of college football*. New York: Simon & Schuster.

Benedict, J., & Keteyian, A. (2013). *The system: The glory and scandal of big-time college football*. New York: Doubleday.

Berkowitz, S. (2015, June 30). NCAA's Mark Emmert made more than $1.8 million in 2013. Retrieved July 16, 2015 from www.usatoday.com/story/sports/college/2015/06/30/ncaa-mark-emmert-compensation-tax-return-990-form/29516401

Bowen, W. G., & Levin, S. A. (2003). *Reclaiming the game: College sports and educational values*. Princeton, NJ: Princeton University Press.

Clotfelter, C. T. (2011). *Big-time sports in American universities*. New York: Cambridge University Press.

Desrochers, D. M. (2013). *Academic spending versus athletics spending: Who wins?* Washington, DC: American Institutes for Research, Delta Cost Project.

Duderstadt, J. J. (2000). *Intercollegiate athletics and the American university: A university president's perspective*. Ann Arbor: University of Michigan Press.

Estler, S. E., & Nelson, L. J. (2005). Who calls the shots? Sports and university leadership, culture, and decision making. *ASHE Higher Education Report*, 30(5).

French, P. A. (2004). *Ethics and college sports: Ethics, sports, and the university*. Lanham, MD: Rowman & Littlefield.

Harper, S. R., & Harris III, F. (Eds.). (2010). *College men and masculinities: Theory, research, and implications for practice*. San Francisco: Jossey-Bass.

Harper, S. R., Williams Jr., C. D., & Blackman, H. W. (2013). *Black male student-athletes and racial inequities in NCAA Division I college sports*. Philadelphia: University of Pennsylvania, Center for the Study of Race and Equity in Education.

Jozsa Jr., F. P. (2013). *College sports Inc.: How commercialism influences intercollegiate athletics*. New York: Springer.

Kezar, A. J. (Ed.). (2012). *Embracing non-tenure track faculty: Changing campuses for the new faculty majority*. New York: Routledge.

Knight Commission on Intercollegiate Athletics. (1991). *Keeping faith with the student-athlete: A new model for intercollegiate athletics*. Charlotte, NC: Author.

Knight Commission on Intercollegiate Athletics. (2001). *A call to action: Reconnecting college sports and higher education*. Miami, FL: Author.

Knight Commission on Intercollegiate Athletics. (2009). *College sports 101: A primer on money, athletics, and higher education in the 21st century*. Miami, FL: Author.

Knight Commission on Intercollegiate Athletics. (2010). *Restoring the balance: Dollars, values, and the future of college sports*. Miami, FL: Author.

Lapchick, R. E. (Ed.). (2006). *New game plan for college sport*. Westport, CT: Praeger.

Lapchick, R. E., Hoff, B., & Kaiser, C. (2010). *The 2010 racial and gender report card: College sport*. Orlando: University of Central Florida, The Institute for Diversity and Ethics in Sport.

Lapchick, R. E., & Slaughter, J. B. (Eds.). (1989). *The rules of the game: Ethics in college sport*. New York: Macmillan.

Morphew, C., & Hartley, M. (2006). Mission statements: A thematic analysis of rhetoric across institutional type. *The Journal of Higher Education*, 77(3), 456–471.

Nixon II, H. L. (2014). *The athletic trap: How college sports corrupted the academy*. Baltimore, MD: Johns Hopkins University Press.

Oriard, M. (2009). *Bowled over: Big-time college football from the sixties to the BCS era*. Chapel Hill: University of North Carolina Press.

Rudolph, F. (1962). *The American college and university: A history*. New York: Alfred A. Knopf.

Sack, A. L., & Staurowsky, E. J. (1998). *College athletes for hire: The evolution and legacy of the NCAA's amateur myth*. Westport, CT: Praeger.

Sander, L. (2010). Pay for top 14 NCAA executives totaled nearly $6-million last year. Retrieved July 31, 2014 from http://chronicle.com/article/Pay-for-Top-14-NCAA-Executives/124358

Savage, H. J., Bentley, H. W., McGovern, J. T., & Smiley, D. F. (1929). *American college athletics bulletin number twenty-three*. New York: The Carnegie Foundation for the Advancement of Teaching.

Shulman, J., & Bowen, W. (2001). *The game of life: College sports and educational values*. Princeton, NJ: Princeton University Press.

Smith, R. A. (2011). *Pay for play: A history of big-time college athletic reform*. Champaign: University of Illinois Press.

Solomon, J. (2014). NCAA president Mark Emmert was paid $1.7 million in 2012. Retrieved July 31, 2014 from www.cbssports.com/collegefootball/writer/jon-solomon/24620900/ncaa-president-mark-emmert-was-paid-17-million-in-2012

Sperber, M. (2000). *Beer and circus: How big-time college sports is crippling undergraduate education.* New York: Henry Holt.

Sperber, M. (2004). College sports, Inc.: How big-time athletic departments run interference for college, Inc. In D. G. Stein (Ed.), *Buying in or selling out? The commercialization of the American research university* (pp. 17–31). Piscataway, NJ: Rutgers University Press.

State Higher Education Executive Officers. (2014). *State higher education finance, FY 2013.* Boulder, CO: Author.

Telander, R. (1996). *The hundred yard lie: The corruption of college football and what we can do to stop it.* Champaign: University of Illinois Press.

Thelin, J. R. (1996). *Games colleges play: Scandal and reform in intercollegiate athletics.* Baltimore, MD: Johns Hopkins University Press.

Thelin, J. R. (2011). *A history of American higher education* (2nd ed.). Baltimore, MD: Johns Hopkins University Press.

Toma, J. D. (2003). *Football U: Spectator sports in the life of the American university.* Ann Arbor: University of Michigan Press.

University of Michigan. (2014). Facilities: Michigan Stadium. Retrieved July 29, 2014 from www.mgoblue.com/facilities/michigan-stadium.html

USA Today. (2014). NCAAF coaches salaries, 2013. Retrieved July 29, 2014 from www.usatoday.com/sports/college/salaries

Watterson, J. S. (2000a). *College football: History, spectacle, controversy.* Baltimore, MD: Johns Hopkins University Press.

Watterson, J. S. (2000b). The gridiron crisis of 1905: Was it really a crisis? *Journal of Sport History, 27*(2), 291–298.

Yost, M. (2010). *Varsity green: A behind the scenes look at culture and corruption in college athletics.* Stanford, CA: Stanford University Press.

Zimbalist, A. (1999). *Unpaid professionals: Commercialism and conflict in big-time college sports.* Princeton, NJ: Princeton University Press.

Recruitment and Compensation Scandals

2

TILL DEATH DO US PART

The Rise and Fall of Mustang Mania at Southern Methodist University

David Horton Jr. and Justin L. Davis

When David Berst, former chairman of the NCAA Committee on Infractions, announced that the NCAA had decided to impose what has become so affectionately known as the "death penalty" on Southern Methodist University's (SMU) football program in 1987, it was the collegiate athletics equivalent of the 1775 "shot heard 'round the world." Though not the official term used by the NCAA, the "death penalty" refers to the sanction the NCAA gives member institutions that repeatedly violate policies and regulations. According to the NCAA, an institution is a repeat violator "if a second major violation occurs within five years of the start date of the penalty from the first case" (2010). Sanctions associated with this particular penalty can include, but are not limited to, the elimination of the involved sport for at least one year and the elimination of athletics aid (scholarships) in that sport for two years. Prior to SMU, never before had such a bold and catastrophic penalty been placed on a top-tier, nationally recognized collegiate athletics program, and it is very likely that no one will ever witness a top-rated collegiate athletics program handed such a penalty again because of the long-term, systemic impact.

In this chapter, we discuss the events and activities involving the Southern Methodist University Mustang's administrators, coaches, players, and boosters that led to the death of "Mustang Mania" in 1987 and provide commentary on the implications of these events and activities for SMU as an institution and collegiate athletics as a whole. Mustang Mania refers to a promotion program used by the athletics program to create increased excitement within Dallas and the state of Texas for the SMU football program, beginning in the late 1970s. Additionally, the authors provide questions for current and future higher education and collegiate athletics administrators to critically consider within the context of the SMU case.

The Case

SMU, with its rich college football history – including a national championship (1935), a Heisman Trophy winner (Doak Walker, 1949), and multiple Southwest Conference (SWC) titles (9) and bowl game appearances (13) – established itself as a David among the numerous college football Goliaths. Sustaining such success, however, proved to be increasingly difficult for SMU. As one of four private institutions in the SWC, their small size and the growing popularity (both economically and athletically) of college football during the 1970s and 1980s made it extremely difficult for SMU to compete with their public school conference peers (University of Arkansas, University of Texas, Texas A&M University, Texas Tech University, and University of Houston). To level the playing field, SMU found a way to consistently straddle the line between ethical and unethical behavior as it sought to overcome its unshakable underdog status. This Texas two-step eventually led to the fall of SMU as a prominent football power. It has been three decades since the death penalty, and SMU has yet to fully recover from its death sentence.

The journey leading to SMU's ultimate destruction began a decade earlier with the signing of a new football head coach, Ron Meyer, in 1975. Meyer (1976–1981), a former assistant coach and scout for the Dallas Cowboys, brought experience, passion, and competitiveness to SMU. Respected as one of the most effective and convincing football recruiters in college football during that time, Meyer was able to quickly improve the quality of high school players that signed athletic scholarships with SMU. Coincidentally, his ability to bring top recruits to the small, private Methodist university in Dallas, Texas, and to compete with the bigger state colleges in the SWC, also drew uninvited attention and raised eyebrows from his colleagues within and outside the state.

Many analysts and commentators have chronicled Meyer's recruiting methods (Whitford, 1989). Among his many recruiting accomplishments, his most notable was demonstrated in 1979 when he got last-minute commitments from two of the top-rated high school recruits in the country, Eric Dickerson and Craig James. The recruitment of these two blue-chip athletes, along with numerous other top high school recruits that year and throughout his tenure, positioned SMU as the football powerhouse of the early 1980s. For example, between 1980 and 1985, SMU posted a record of 55–14–1 (under Meyer and Bobby Collins [1982–1986]). This was a vast improvement over the 26–31–1 record the program posted during the preceding six-year span. For targeted blue-chip athletes during the glory days of SMU football, receiving a phone call or home visit from a member of the SMU football coaching staff became the equivalent of hitting the college sports jackpot, as recruits knew that SMU was willing and able to pay more than others to get star athletes. One former SMU football player stated that he received an offer of $40,000 and a car from Texas Christian University (TCU). He continued, "I might have considered except that the offer from SMU was a whole lot better."

The infamous recruiting practices of SMU prior to receiving the death penalty involved a general "slush fund," which was used for providing incentives to top recruits. Envisioned by Meyer and funded primarily by top contributing booster Sherwood Blunt Jr., a wealthy real-estate mogul and former SMU player, this underground fund was used for sweetening the deal for potential players. Incentives offered to recruits included things such as moving expenses, paying rent for a player or his family, and monthly cash payments ranging from $50 to $750. In fact, the NCAA found that, during the 1985–1986 season alone, $61,000 was used to provide various cash and non-cash incentives to a group of thirteen players on the SMU roster (Matula, 2010). This financial support for recruits and players was one of many questionable practices that took place during Meyer's and Collins' coaching tenure, and ultimately led to the demise of the SMU football program.

Indeed, SMU was consistently under NCAA investigation during the eleven-year period between 1974 and 1985. During this time period, the football program accumulated countless violations and five different probation penalties. A turning point in the SMU scandal came in 1985 when a former player, Sean Stopperich, spoke publicly and on record about the inappropriate recruiting practices that SMU used during his recruitment. Stopperich admitted to receiving an undisclosed amount of cash in 1983 to back out of his oral commitment to the University of Pittsburgh and commit formally to SMU. As indicated in the recent documentary directed by Thaddeus Matula, *Pony Excess* (2010), the violations that Stopperich described took place with the knowledge and consent of various SMU administrators. Stopperich's comments resulted in the NCAA imposing a three-year probationary period on the SMU football program. Additionally, football games were not allowed to be broadcast live for one year (1986), and the program was not permitted to compete in a bowl game during the 1985 or 1986 seasons.

Future investigations uncovered that the payments to players from boosters and others did not cease, even after SMU had completed its NCAA probation in 1985. The final straw came in 1986 when David Stanley, a former linebacker (1983–1984) who was terminated from the team due to psychological and substance abuse issues, claimed that he had been paid $25,000 to sign with SMU in 1983. Stanley further stated that he had received payments after being removed from the team and was still receiving payments at the time of his interview. Stanley's claims indicated that, even after the NCAA put SMU on probation in 1985, payments and incentives had continued to be provided to players. This particular infraction made SMU a repeat violator and subject to receive the death penalty, as it ultimately did. Following Stanley's comments, several current and former administrators, boosters, and board members who knew about the continued cash payments to players, including former chairman of the SMU Board of Governors and Governor of Texas, Bill Clements, tried to explain the continued payments. Clements claimed that they had committed to pay the students and that they had decided to phase out the payments over the upcoming few years as those players receiving the incentives would be leaving the institution soon. Ironically, at the height of the scandal, those involved in making payments actually felt an ethical obligation to fulfill their agreements to the students.

In a watershed moment during the scandal, John Sparks and Dale Hansen from the Dallas-Fort Worth affiliate of ABC (WFAA-TV) conducted a live interview with SMU Athletics Director Bob Hitch, the head coach of football at the time, Bobby Collins, and SMU recruiting coordinator Henry Parker. In the 1985 interview, Hansen directly confronted the men about the allegations from Stanley. Hansen produced a postmarked envelope that was handwritten and addressed to Stanley. The allegation was that the letter contained a check for $350. Parker first stated he had addressed the letter but then quickly changed direction, suggesting the document was printed and the handwriting was not his. Incidentally, a handwriting expert later confirmed, with absolute confidence, that it was indeed Parker's handwriting on the envelope. The widespread knowledge within the football program of the continued payments is believed to have been the primary factor in the NCAA's decision to take such drastic action against SMU.

On February 25, 1987, the chair of the NCAA Committee on Infractions, David Berst, announced in a press conference at SMU that the committee had voted unanimously to hand down its most extreme actions against the SMU football program. Because of the numerous violations, SMU would not be allowed to compete in the 1987 season. In addition, the football program lost 55 scholarships over the course of four years, had its initial probation extended to 1990, and was limited in the number of assistant coaches it was able to hire. Further, existing players were formally released from their athletic scholarships, thus giving them freedom to stay and continue their education at SMU or to transfer to another university without penalty. The result was mass exodus by the players as top football programs from around the country hotly recruited them. The exodus led to the SMU administration's choice to cancel the 1988 season since it would not be able to field a competitive team. The long-term effects of this scandal are still being felt at SMU. Since 1989, it has had only four winning seasons (1997, 2009, 2011, 2012). Three of these four winning seasons have come since 2009, suggesting recovery even to an average level of competition took over 20 years.

Sociocultural Context

As noted by the former president of Harvard, Derek Bok, college athletics and the passion and fanfare such competitions induce "create a constant tendency toward excess, pushing the search for winning teams to extremes that threaten to harm the lives of student-athletes and compromise the integrity of universities as serious educational institutions" (Staudohar & Zepel, 2004, p. 38). It is our belief that the series of events that led to SMU receiving the death penalty, and the unethical and illegal activities other institutions, coaches, boosters, and players have and currently participate in, is the product of an extremely flawed collegiate athletics system. This system, which fuels and encourages the doctrine that the team that wins is the team with the highest-paid coaches, newest facilities, and largest apparel and television contract (Lapchick, 2006), begs for competitive individuals (coaches and administrators) to tiptoe the line between what activities are legal and those that are not to gain the slightest advantage over their competition. What happened at SMU brought to light major sociocultural issues concerning college athletics – in particular, the desire to win at any cost. The issues discussed below are couched within the context of the events at SMU during the 1970s and '80s. However, it is our intent that these discussion points should be considered within the context of numerous other past NCAA athletics violations and will help to better consider the implications of past actions and regulations and the opportunities for advancement of effective policies.

College Athletics: The Uncontrollable Beast

What happened at SMU illustrates a message about the larger enterprise of intercollegiate athletics. More specifically, this particular scandal illuminates the fact that athletic programs with substantial revenues and prestige shape the enterprise of athletics (Schwartz, 2009). Institutions that are overmatched within their athletic conference are often at the mercy, especially financially, of these larger programs. Within the SWC, Rice, Baylor, TCU, and SMU were four private schools that were overmatched and competing against conference mates that included some of the best football schools in the Southwest, each of which received national exposure and were able to attract large crowds and revenues. These smaller market teams were not only competing on the field against stronger teams but also competing for the best athletes in the state; they felt it necessary, if not obligated, to do whatever it took to field a competitive team. The SMU scandal illustrates, both at the macro and micro levels, how difficult it is to truly monitor what athletics programs and institutions are doing. While measures have been put in place since SMU received the death penalty to better monitor and catch infractions violators, the system is only as good as those that monitor it.

Friends Matter, Choose Wisely

The athletic conference with which a university is associated carries significant financial influence. In other words, success begets success, and more success begets large financial gains. As a member of a conference that had larger teams that were nationally televised and could bring in large revenues, SMU, and the other private institutions in the conference, benefitted. However, the larger institutions understood that, if they joined conferences that could attract similar or larger crowds, they would become a benefactor of additional funds instead of a majority contributor. This is partly the reason that, in 1991, the University of Arkansas left the SWC to join the more visible and powerful Southeastern Conference (SEC), and in 1996 the SWC dissolved, with a majority of the schools forming what is now the Big XII conference.

What's Underneath?

Many times when individuals examine issues concerning college athletics, particularly college football, they have a difficult time separating what the symptoms or undercurrents of the problem are from the actual problem. We argue that the power and influence of alumni to make decisions and the presence of capitalism disguised as a system of charity are the actual problems of big-time college football.

Power and Influence of Alumni

A columnist once noted that SMU has "always been the place that Dallas elite send their children" (McCollough, 2007). During the glory days of SMU football, however, SMU was the place that wealthy donors sent others' children, particularly those children with high athletic skills. Wealthy boosters, alumni, and friends of SMU primarily supported the slush fund that was created in the 1970s and maintained through the 1980s to recruit and support SMU football players. Many of these individuals made their fortunes in Dallas and Houston as CEOs of banks and oil companies, and as real-estate developers and brokers. They were well-connected, influential, and powerful members of their respective communities. Collectively, they believed that their financial contributions to the football program and players were just and necessary and entitled them to a seat at the decision-making table – whether it was making a decision on which athlete to recruit, how much they would be paid, or which play would be called on First and Ten. It was this sense of power that the boosters felt that eventually led to SMU's troubles; after all, regardless of what the institution or NCAA said, they still "had a payroll to meet" and they were going to meet it. Even today, boosters will donate millions of dollars to athletic programs to be welcomed into the inner circle (NCAA punishes university, 2013; Fish, 2006).

Charity... by Any Other Name Is Still Illegal

Athletic programs oftentimes use their prestige and money to attract individuals from minority and low-income households and those that have no academic goals beyond using college football as a platform to play professional football (Horton, 2012). During the early years of Meyer's career at SMU, he and his coaching staff were committed to recruiting the best players in Texas, regardless of race, when other SWC institutions overlooked talented Black athletes. Meyer understood and took advantage of what many schools in the Midwest and East had already realized: there was an untapped reserve of talented Black athletes in Texas. During the 1960s and 1970s, SMU could not compete with the larger state schools to get the most talented White players in Texas. As a result, in 1965 Meyer recruited and signed Jerry LeVias, the first Black scholarship athlete in the SWC. LeVias, a five-foot-ten running back from Beaumont, Texas, would go on to become an All-American at SMU. With this signing, SMU solidified a relationship with predominantly Black and inner-city high schools in Texas (Whitford, 1989). Meyer not only changed the way SMU recruited but the way other schools in the SWC recruited prospective student-athletes as well.

When examined with a critical eye, SMU's willingness to recruit and pay star athletes from minority and low-income communities (though not exclusively) was a business decision, though often presented as a social justice initiative or charitable act. Those who supported this practice at SMU knew that they were investing in a commodity that would reap great returns. The sentiments of one SMU booster epitomized this: "There is no way on God's green earth that a football coach is gonna let a valuable *commodity* be screwed up in the head because he's having an outside [financial] problem" (Whitford, 1989, p. 45). Today, student-athletes, scholars, and journalists, among others, still banter and discuss this idea that student-athletes should be paid, and many have made strong arguments for and against this issue (Mahler, 2014). However, whether money is given to players with a charitable heart or for purely selfish reasons, it is still illegal. This is a lesson SMU learned the hard way.

The Exception Was the Rule

The SMU case is both unusual and the norm. Let us explain. To begin, this case is unusual in that the SMU football program was given the death penalty – the first and last time such a harsh penalty has been given to a top-rated football program. However, at one point, five of the nine SWC institutions were on probation for committing NCAA infractions. So, the activities that led to SMU receiving the death penalty were not uncommon then, and they are not uncommon now (Ridpath, 2012). There are plenty of examples of institutions making inappropriate payments to college athletes such as payments made to St. Johns University (2000–2004) and University of Missouri (2003) basketball players, and football players from the University of Miami (1990s), to name a few. More recent examples of improper payments or benefits are seen at major institutions such as Ohio State University (2010), Oklahoma State University (2013), and various SEC football programs (2013) – including the recently dominant University of Alabama.

The NCAA has had to put extensive rules in place defining what a "proper" relationship is between an institution and a student-athlete because incidents have taken place over the years that necessitate such standards. Further, the distinction between what an amateur athlete and professional athlete is has been made very clear (Staudohar & Zepel, 2004). However, from the beginning of college sports, amateur athletes have not only encountered individuals that are willing and able to pay for their services but have accepted payments, small and large. Again, this is a symptom, not the problem.

Alternate Ending

Commenting on the decision to impose the death penalty on SMU football in 1987, David Berst, former chairman of the NCAA Committee on Infractions, poignantly stated, "there simply didn't seem to be any option left." That SMU was guilty of multiple major NCAA rules violations is undisputed. The fraudulent activity that continued to take place among coaches and administrators from the late 1970s through the mid-1980s was calculated, blatant, and without remorse.

However, in retrospect some might second-guess the decision of the NCAA's Committee on Infractions to assess a penalty that would have such long-term, far-reaching implications.

The fact that such a harsh penalty has not been assessed on a top athletics program since SMU (despite schools such as Kentucky and Baylor being equally qualified candidates for such a penalty) speaks to the regret that the NCAA feels. However, the NCAA had rules in place that stipulated how a situation such as SMU's would be handled. Rather than question the NCAA's decision to cancel SMU's 1987 season, we prefer to look at how SMU might have instituted different internal managerial and organizational policies and processes to avoid finding itself in such a situation.

At the most fundamental level, the implementation of broader hierarchical decision-making and more appropriate hiring practices would have made such unethical actions less likely. Under the leadership of former head coach Ron Meyer, SMU developed a deep culture of disregard for rules, faulty and unethical recruiting practices, and inappropriate player/booster relationships. With a culture in place that supported such behaviors, the SMU program's defiance for rules and regulations only became more embedded with time, even after Meyer resigned as head coach. A more formal hierarchy of decision-making and self-auditing, in combination with intentional turnover within the system, would have made such behavior difficult.

Players, coaches, boosters, and administrators at SMU knew about this behavior. The policies in place at SMU allowed for this practice to become a coordinated effort. If, for example, there were a requirement for turnover in positions integral to the functioning of the recruitment of players and player/booster involvement, it would have been much more difficult for such behavior to take place over an extended period of time. Such monitoring mechanisms, while costly to the organization, would ensure that the actions within the system are continuously exposed to individuals outside the "inner circle." Of course, the implementation of such policies would be unpopular with players and coaches alike.

As collegiate athletics continue to account for large revenue streams, many university administrators neglect to remember that universities are educational, not athletic, institutions. Their primary responsibility is to the various educational stakeholders in their institution (i.e. students, faculty, and alumni). The fact is, collegiate athletics, particularly at institutions with leading football and basketball programs, have become the street-level equivalent of the prostitute working for her pimp (the media and sports fan). However, expecting schools that see such high revenues from these programs to monitor themselves and discourage unethical behavior and rules violations is unrealistic. Thus, it is up to the larger systems (NCAA) to create and enforce policies and regulations that reduce the level of competition and the extreme incentives for unethical behavior.

However, such changes are extremely difficult to implement when a system has so many influential stakeholders. These components include multibillion dollar contracts with media outlets, large and influential leading athletics programs, and rules and regulations that continue to separate top programs from the rest and give a greater amount of power to those top universities. The current structure for collegiate athletics, as dictated by the NCAA, encourages cutthroat recruiting, a disregard for ethical standards, and escalating pressure for athlete compensation. In fact, the NCAA has formally considered allowing institutions to legally pay players a stipend (Dodd, 2014). That the NCAA is considering this attests to the blurring of lines between amateurism and professionalism. Again and again we see major programs being found guilty of rules violations (e.g. Ohio State, 2010) and receiving a slap on the wrist in comparison to the sanctions placed on SMU in 1987 (e.g. University of Kentucky, 1989). Perhaps the most provocative explanation for this is the financial implications to those universities and the NCAA if the universities were to incur such a harsh penalty. Without changing the monitoring and enforcement practices of the NCAA, we will continue to see significant violations at major public (and private) institutions. In addition, by behaving this way, the NCAA and universities are instilling the idea that cheating the system is acceptable, that ethics are optional, and that integrity is situational into the very students they are entrusted to educate and mold.

In the case of SMU, we see a program that was continuously under investigation and on probation for more than a decade. Administrators, boosters, and coaches were so involved in the practices that even making ethical changes (i.e. stopping payments to players) was seemingly impossible. As one former player stated, "once Collins started a payroll, the SMU Mustangs program was finished." SMU had gone so far outside the ethical standard that they actually codified the illegal activities that were taking place. Even board members of the university continued to ignore the NCAA's threats. When considering all this, the NCAA's decision seems more than substantiated. SMU should have instantly made sweeping changes at the first sight of fraudulent activity within the organization.

One example of a school that took swift action is the University of Kentucky. In 1989, when the men's basketball program was found to have violated major NCAA recruiting and eligibility violations, Kentucky's president, David Roselle, took quick and decisive action to get the program under control. The NCAA Committee on Infractions stated that Kentucky's violations were worthy of the "death penalty," but it elected not to assess such a major penalty because of President Roselle's actions. This example might confirm the importance of recognizing unethical activity within a university system and taking actions once aware of it to ensure sweeping change takes place. However, from an athletics perspective, this example might be telling a different story. The Kentucky Wildcats basketball team won the 2012 NCAA Basketball Tournament and became the national champions that year. This came less than two years after the program was investigated for violating recruiting rules. Thus, current NCAA policies and enforcement may not be harsh enough if coaches feel they can simply skirt as many rules as possible until they get caught and then respond with quick sweeping change and requests for forgiveness by the coach and university officials.

References

Dodd, D. (2014). Schools closer to paying players, but how much say will players have?. Retrieved from www.cbssports.com/collegefootball/writer/dennis-dodd/24412886/schools-closer-to-paying-players-but-how-much-say-will-players-have

Fish, M. (2006, January). Most powerful boosters. Retrieved from http://sports.espn.go.com/ncf/news/story?id=2285986

Horton Jr., D. (2012). '"Man-to-man": An exploratory study of coaches" impact on Black male student-athlete success at HBCUs. In R. T. Palmer & J. L. Wood (Eds.), *Black men in college: Implications for HBCUs and beyond* (138–147). New York: Routledge.

Lapchick, R. E.. (Ed.). (2006). *New game plan for college sport.* Westport, CT: American Council on Education/Praeger.

Mahler, J. (2014, January). College athletes should be paid exactly this much. Retrieved from www.businessweek.com/articles/2014-01-02/how-much-should-college-athletes-get-paid

Matula, Thaddeus D. (Director). (2010). *Pony Excess* [Television documentary]. Bristol, CT: ESPN.

McCollough, J. B. (2007, September). Once-powerful SMU program still struggles to regain relevance. Retrieved from www.ncaatop25.com/smu.htm

National Collegiate Athletic Association (NCAA). (2010). Glossary of terms. Retrieved from www.ncaa.org

NCAA punishes university of South Carolina for booster, recruiting violations. (2013, April). Retrieved from www.huffingtonpost.com/2012/04/30/ncaa-punishes-university-of-south-carolina_n_1464455.html?view=print&comm_ref=false

Ridpath, B. D. (2012). *Tainted glory: Marshal University, the NCAA, and one man's fight for justice.* Bloomington, IN: iUniverse.

Schwartz, P. J. (2009). College football's most valuable teams. Retrieved from www.forbes.com.

Staudohar, P. D., & Zepel, B. (2004). The impact on higher education of corruption in big-time college sports. In J. Fizel and R. Fort (Eds.), *Economics of College Sports* (35–50). Westport, CT: Praeger.

Whitford, D. (1989). *A payroll to meet: A story of greed, corruption, and football at SMU.* New York: Macmillan Publishing Company.

3

NEVIN SHAPIRO'S $930 MILLION PONZI SCHEME AT THE UNIVERSITY OF MIAMI

C. Keith Harrison and Scott Bukstein

Nevin Shapiro is currently serving a 20-year sentence in federal prison for orchestrating and overseeing a $930 million Ponzi scheme linked to a phony wholesale grocery distribution business, Capitol Investments USA, Inc. Companies in the grocery-diverting industry typically purchase lower-priced groceries in one region and then resell those groceries in another region where prices are higher. Nevin Shapiro sought investors for Capitol Investments to help grow the business. According to the official complaint filed by the U.S. Securities and Exchange Commission (SEC) in April 2010:

> [Shapiro] promised to refund prospective investors' principal within thirty days and pay 10% to 26% annual returns on their investment. Shapiro told prospective investors this was a risk-free investment in Capitol's grocery business. . . . . Shapiro assured prospective investors Capitol's purchase contracts and accounts receivable secured their investments.

To induce investors, Shapiro fabricated invoices and purchase orders for nonexistent sales; he also helped to create fraudulent and misleading financial statements and tax returns (Securities and Exchange Commission [SEC], 2010; FBI, 2011).

By late 2004, Capitol Investments was operating at a loss. As explained in the SEC complaint, Capitol Investments' sales were less than $300,000 in 2005 and 2006, and the company had no sales from 2007 through 2009. According to the litigation release published by the SEC in August 2010, from January 2005 through November 2009 Shapiro operated a Ponzi scheme in which he used new investor funds to pay principal and interest to earlier investors. Shapiro paid existing investors approximately $769 million from about $880 million in new investor funds, and Shapiro also siphoned at least $38 million of investor funds to fund his lavish lifestyle and finance outside business ventures unrelated to the grocery business (SEC,

2010). In addition to using more than $400,000 in investor funds for courtside seats at Miami Heat basketball games and approximately $4,700 per month for the lease of a Mercedes-Benz S65 AMG, Shapiro also became heavily involved with the athletics program at the University of Miami.

The Case

On August 16, 2011 – approximately two months after Shapiro had been sentenced to 20 years in prison for pleading guilty to securities fraud and money laundering – Yahoo!Sports broke a story that detailed the extent of Shapiro's involvement with the University of Miami athletics program. In 2001, Shapiro paid $12,000 to become a "booster" of the University of Miami athletics program. The Yahoo! Sports report (Robinson, 2011) details allegations that Shapiro provided thousands of impermissible benefits to at least 72 student-athletes at the University of Miami from 2002 to 2010. As detailed in the FBI press release (2011), payments to student-athletes at the University of Miami included "cash in amounts up to $10,000 and gifts such as jewelry and entertainment at nightclubs and restaurants." For example, Shapiro allegedly paid for prostitutes to be available to players and paid money to help secure commitments from high school student-athletes who were being recruited to play football or basketball at the University of Miami (Robinson, 2011). Shapiro explained:

> I became a booster in late 2001, and by early 2002, I was giving kids gifts. From the start, I wasn't really challenged. And once I got going, it just got bigger and bigger. I just did what I wanted and didn't pay much mind toward the potential repercussions. . . . . I did it because I could [and] because nobody stepped in to stop me.
>
> *(Robinson, 2011)*[1]

Shapiro's involvement with and influence over the University of Miami athletics department did not end with his providing impermissible benefits to prospective and current student-athletes. Shapiro pledged to donate $150,000 in exchange for the University of Miami naming a student-athlete lounge in his honor, and he pledged to donate $50,000 to the University's basketball program in 2008 (Robinson, 2011; United States of America v. Nevin Shapiro, 2010). Shapiro was also part owner of a sports agency, Axcess Sports, which represented several former University of Miami football players. According to the Yahoo!Sports report (Robinson, 2011), Shapiro paid $1.5 million for 30 percent ownership of the sports agency, with the implicit goal of transforming his relationships with the student-athletes into a successful athlete-representation business owned and operated by him and his business partner Michael Huyghue.

Yahoo!Sports conducted almost 100 interviews related to this scandal and audited approximately 20,000 pages of financial and business records from Shapiro's bankruptcy case along with more than 5,000 pages of cell phone records. Yahoo!Sports also interviewed nine former University of Miami football players or recruits and one former coach who verified and corroborated the accuracy of allegations against Shapiro and Shapiro's assertions. On the other hand, when asked about this scandal, University of Miami senior associate athletic director of communications, marketing, and sales, Chris Freet, stated:

> When Shapiro made his allegations nearly a year ago, he and his attorneys refused to provide any facts to the university. . . . . We notified the NCAA enforcement officials of these allegations. We are fully cooperating with the NCAA and are conducting a joint investigation. We take these matters very seriously.
>
> *(Robinson, 2011)*

In a news release from the University of Miami in August 2011, the school explained that:

> [The university] has the highest standards in all of our academic and athletic endeavors. We will remain steadfast in our commitment to continue to build winning programs with the utmost of integrity. We will be more vigilant in our compliance and continue to work with the NCAA on the joint investigation to determine the facts.
>
> *(University of Miami, 2011)*

Pending the conclusion of the NCAA investigation and the issuance of anticipated additional severe sanctions/penalties, the University of Miami decided to "self-impose" penalties related to the NCAA inquiry. The university declared its football team ineligible for selection to a bowl game for a two-year period, forfeited the opportunity to participate in an Atlantic Coast Conference (ACC) football championship game, and also agreed to give back $83,000 received "directly and indirectly" from Shapiro (Reynolds, 2011). In addition, the University of Miami declared a number of its football players ineligible, only to see the NCAA reinstate eight of the players; as explained by former University of Miami Director of Athletics, Shawn Eichorst:

> The NCAA has informed the University of Miami of their decisions regarding the reinstatement of eight student-athletes who were declared ineligible by the University last week. . . . . The student-athletes involved have acknowledged receiving improper benefits and will now be responsible for restitution and, in some cases, the student-athletes will also serve game suspensions.
>
> *(University of Miami, 2011)*

Finally, in January 2012 the compliance office within the University of Miami athletics department announced new policies that prohibited boosters from providing occasional meals or hosting student-athletes at their homes, even though those acts are typically permitted under NCAA rules and regulations (University of Miami, 2012).

Throughout 2012, the NCAA continued to interview current and former coaches, student-athletes, and University of Miami administrators, as well as other individuals connected with the investigation. The NCAA conducted more than 70 interviews (NCAA, 2013b). In January 2013, the NCAA uncovered an issue of improper conduct within its internal enforcement program that occurred during the investigation (NCAA, 2013a). The NCAA hired a law firm, Cadwalader, Wickersham & Taft LLP, to conduct an external review of the NCAA's internal enforcement program. An extensive report by the law firm concluded that the NCAA enforcement staff "had paid a source's attorney to insert herself into an ongoing bankruptcy proceeding and to use its subpoena power to compel depositions from uncooperative witnesses" (Wainstein et al., 2013). The authors of the report recognized that this incident "raised understandable doubts in the minds of many about the management, integrity and effectiveness of the NCAA's Enforcement operations" (Wainstein et al., 2013). NCAA President Mark Emmert addressed this situation:

> To say the least, I am angered and saddened by this situation. Trust and credibility are essential to our regulatory tasks. My intent is to insure our investigatory functions operate with integrity and are fair and consistent with our member schools, athletics staff and most importantly our student-athletes.
>
> *(NCAA, 2013a)*

In February 2013, the University of Miami received a notice of allegations from the NCAA. The notice of allegations accused the university of having a "lack of institutional control" for failing to monitor the conduct of Shapiro as well as failing to monitor university coaching staff members and student-athletes (NCAA, 2013b). In response to the notice of allegations, University of Miami President Donna E. Shalala stated:

> Many of the charges brought forth are based on the word of a man who made a fortune by lying. . . . . The NCAA enforcement staff failed, even after repeated requests, to interview many essential witnesses of great integrity who could have provided first hand testimony.
>
> *(University of Miami, 2013a)*

Shalala further explained:

> For any rule violation – substantiated and proven with facts – that the University, its employees, or student-athletes committed, we have been and should be held accountable. We have worked hard to improve our compliance oversight, and we have already self-imposed harsh sanctions. We deeply regret any violations, but we have suffered enough.
>
> *(University of Miami, 2013a)*

After several additional months of interviews and hearings, which included an attempt by the University of Miami to have the entire case dismissed, the NCAA released its final findings in a 102-page document titled "University of Miami Public Infractions Report." The NCAA Division I Committee on Infractions acknowledged and accepted "the extensive and significant self-imposed penalties" by the university, and imposed the following principal penalties: "three years of probation, a reduction in the maximum number of athletics awards in football and men's basketball, restrictions on unofficial visits, a five-game suspension for the former head men's basketball coach, and two-year show-cause orders for former assistant [coaches]" (NCAA Committee on Infractions, 2013). The Committee on Infractions found violations in the following areas: involvement by boosters such as Nevin Shapiro in the men's basketball and football programs, telephone and text messaging violations in multiple sport programs, and violations relating to the university's administration and overall control of its athletics programs and commitment to rules education, monitoring, and compliance (NCAA Committee on Infractions, 2013). The University of Miami "accept[ed] the findings and the additional penalties as detailed in the Committee on Infractions report and will not appeal" (University of Miami, 2013b). Current University of Miami Director of Athletics, Blake James, stated:

> Our honest and committed efforts to address these allegations have made us stronger. We have already taken many proactive steps to ameliorate any concerns, and we will continue to improve in all areas. Now it is time we look ahead and work diligently to support our student-athletes.
>
> *(University of Miami, 2013b)*

Sociocultural Context

During the 2012 NCAA Men's Basketball Tournament ("March Madness"), Jim Nantz interviewed Mark Emmert during halftime of the University of Kentucky vs. Baylor University game. There were four major issues that were addressed during this brief interview: (1) improper benefits to student-athletes; (2) underclassmen and the "one and done" phenomenon; (3) policy and disincentives with graduation rates; and (4) policy and incentives with the Academic Progress Rate (APR). These four themes and constructs are harbingers of the broader sociocultural context of college athletics. Further investigation and analysis on the enterprise and "system" of intercollegiate athletics should continue to make transparent the current realities of college athletics that lead to these four key issues mentioned by Mark Emmert: the pressure to win, media rights deals, presence of corporate sponsors, gate receipts, product licensing, and other revenue streams connected to college sports, especially the revenue-generating sports of football and men's basketball. Numerous scholars have previously examined the contradiction between higher education and big-time athletics (e.g. Boyd, 2003; Byers, 1995; Kissinger & Miller, 2009; Smith, 1988, 2011; Toma, 2003; Yost, 2010; Watterson, 2000). For example, Byers (1995) explained that:

> This system is so biased . . . in light of today's high-dollar, commercialized college marketplace that the ever-increasing number of primary and secondary NCAA infractions cases . . . emerge in the current environment as mostly an indictment of the system itself.
>
> *(p. 3)*

Future examinations of intercollegiate athletics should focus on practical and realistic policy proposals with respect to NCAA governance and enforcement as well as academic standards for student-athletes and economic support of student-athletes.

Unfortunately, cases like that of University of Miami are not uncommon. These issues existed in the early 1900s, when university presidents and athletics administrators threatened to end college football due to scandals and the deterioration of educational integrity (Thelin, 1996). The response by the University of Miami mirrors the corruption and hypocrisy of society; sport is simply a microcosm of the broader culture that benefits off the backs of individuals labeled as student-athletes. This is how someone such as Nevin Shapiro can "get in" and have so much influence so fast on the ballplayers. According to Sack (2008):

> Probably the most significant finding of my study, from my perspective, concerned the athlete's perceptions of the propriety of accepting under-the-table benefits and the adequacy of their financial aid packages. Overall, 53 percent of those responding said they saw nothing wrong with accepting under-the-table payments for living expenses, with the number rising to 72 percent among black players. And 78 percent of all respondents said that athletes deserve greater compensation than NCAA rules allow.
>
> *(p. 125)*

Dr. Harry Edwards coined the phrase that "there are no final victories" in terms of the cultural forces of oppression that systemically face today's student-athlete (Edwards, 2000; Johnson & Masucci, 2009). The University of Miami incident involved a White male, heterosexual activity, hyper-masculinity, sex and women, and several African American males on athletic scholarship at a predominantly White university. The undercurrents of the Miami situation are booster influence, recruiting of some entitled players, and institutional laziness – things that should not point the finger at the campus in Coral Gables, Florida, but to a system that perpetuates irrational behaviors and a lack of integrity. The response by the University of Miami is the status quo – institutions react and are rarely proactive while protecting their turf and framing the incidents as isolated acts by individuals versus the norm of a capitalistic system of control and power.

One college football coach has shed some light on the behaviors of college athletes off the field and the current system of accountability that is arbitrary in terms of disciplinary actions and decisions. On April 10, 2012, on the ESPN show *College GameDay* (five months before the football season actually started), University of Georgia head football coach Mark Richt was asked about his leadership role given student-athlete behavior, particularly in football. Coach Richt responded: "We are attempting to do those things that are in the best interest of our young men both short- and long-term." When asked, "Should the NCAA institute a universal policy for ill off-the-field behaviors by college athletes?", Coach Richt was less assertive in his comments. He stated: "I think it would be an interesting discussion." The discussion will continue, but when will the proper actions take place that minimize scandals and maximize the true spirit of college academics and athletics?

Alternate Ending

Why was the University of Miami not more vigilant in their compliance before Yahoo!Sports broke the story about this scandal in August 2011? In the words of Shapiro:

> [If the University of Miami] had hired a private investigator for a day, it would have been the easiest job that guy ever had. It would have been over in five minutes. You would have had all the information you needed. Follow me to a nightclub or a strip club. Lunches. Dinners. The boat. Hotels for parties. All the outings at Lucky Strike. These guys were at my house . . . . Gambling. Pool tournaments. Prostitution. Drinking.
>
> *(Robinson, 2011)*

The University of Miami appears to have intentionally ignored many red flags and bases for caution with respect to Shapiro's ties to its athletics program. For example, reports indicate that in 2007 former head football coach Randy Shannon told his coaching staff to avoid Shapiro and routinely explained to student-athletes on the football team about the importance of staying away from boosters such as Shapiro (Ferman, 2011). Shapiro's claims demonstrate an ostensible overall lack of institutional control on the part of the University of Miami that led to apparent violations of numerous NCAA rules and regulations relating to recruiting prospective student-athletes, providing extra benefits to student-athletes, and providing impermissible compensation to coaches and other staff members within the university's athletics department.

Had the University of Miami intervened earlier and spent a little more time learning about Shapiro, the outcome of this scandal may have been drastically different. As described by University of Miami head football coach Al Golden, "Certainly if [our players] were exposed to Mr. Shapiro, we have to prevent that from happening again moving forward. . . . . We have to get the facts. If this guy was around our players, how did it get to that?" (Patterson, 2011). The culture of college athletics likely also led to the University of Miami's complacency and inaction in this particular situation. When asked about Shapiro, Larry Coker, who was the head coach of the Hurricanes football team from 2001 to 2006, stated that he would not recognize Shapiro if he saw him. However, Coker clearly recognized the problems associated with the commercialization of collegiate athletics. In August 2011, Coker told ESPN:

> If [Shapiro] walked up to me right now I wouldn't know it. . . . . He was "around the program." I certainly wasn't aware of any improprieties. Now, when you look at college athletics today, would it surprise me if somebody gave gifts to players? No, it wouldn't.
>
> *(ESPN, 2011)*

NCAA President Mark Emmert expounded: "If the assertions are true, the alleged conduct at the University of Miami is an illustration of the need for serious and fundamental change in many critical aspects of college sports" (NCAA, 2011).

Note

1 It is important to note that some of Nevin Shapiro's comments and allegations may be self-serving and have not been confirmed with respect to accuracy by an uninvolved, independent source. In late 2011 and early 2012, Shapiro sent a series of e-mails to the *Miami Herald* that demonstrated his frustrations and his intent to continue to "take down" the University of Miami athletics program. In these e-mails, Shapiro opined that he is "more of a victim than a Ponzi schemer and assailant" and that "[t]he public is going to hate [him] worse in the next coming months. ... It's going to be severe and catastrophic ... I'm coming for them both [University of Miami and former players] and I'm going to be successful" (Jackson, 2012).

References

Boyd, T. (2003). *Young, black, rich, and famous: The rise of the NBA, the Hip Hop invasion and the transformation of American culture.* Lincoln: University of Nebraska Press.

Byers, W. (1995). *Unsportsmanlike conduct: Exploiting college athletes.* Ann Arbor: University of Michigan Press.

Edwards, H. (2000). Crisis of black athletes on the eve of the 21st century. *Society, 37*(3), 9–12.

ESPN. (2011). NCAA Investigation Miami, Lawyer Says. Retrieved from http://espn.go.com

FBI. (2011). CEO of Capitol Investments USA, Inc. sentenced to 20 years in prison for $930 million ponzi scheme based on phony grocery business. Retrieved from www.fbi.gov

Ferman, G. (2011, August). Sources: Shannon warned team about Shapiro. Retrieved from http://miami.rivals.com/content.asp?CID=1253198

Jackson, B. (2012, February). NCAA investigation update: Nevin Shapiro rants from prison; UM optimistic. Retrieved from http://miamiherald.typepad.com

Johnson, J., & Masucci, M. A. (2009). No final victories forty years on the frontlines of race, sport, and culture an interview with scholar/activist Dr. Harry Edwards. *Journal for the study of sports and athletes in education, 3*(2), 233–251.

Kissinger, D. B., & Miller, M. T. (2009). *College student-athletes.* Charlotte, NC: Information Age Publishing Inc.

NCAA. (2011). NCAA President Mark Emmert responds to Miami allegations. Retrieved from www.ncaa.org

NCAA. (2013a). NCAA launches external review of enforcement program. Retrieved from www.ncaa.org

NCAA. (2013b). University of Miami lacked institutional control resulting in a decade of violations. Retrieved from www.ncaa.org

NCAA Committee on Infractions. (2013). University of Miami public infractions report. Retrieved from www.ncaa.org

Patterson, C. (2011). Al Golden feels he should have been informed. Retrieved from http://eye-on-collegefootball.blogs.cbssports.com/mcc/blogs/entry/24156338/31372057

Reynolds, T. (2011, December). Miami repaying $83,000 in Shapiro donations. Retrieved from http://news.yahoo.com/miami-repaying-83-000-shapiro-donations-234259050-spt.html

Robinson, C. (2011, August). Renegade Miami Football booster spells out illicit benefits to players. Retrieved from http://sports.yahoo.com

Sack, A. L. (2008). *Counterfeit amateurs: An athlete's journey through the sixties to the age of academic capitalism.* University Park, PA: Penn State Press.

Securities and Exchange Commission (SEC). (2010). SEC charges prominent Miami Beach businessman Nevin K. Shapiro with operating a $900 million fraud and Ponzi scheme. Litigation Release No. 21495.

Smith, R. A. (1988). *Sports and freedom.* New York: Oxford University Press.

Smith, R. A. (2011). *Pay for play.* Champaign: University of Illinois Press.

Thelin, J. R. (1996). *Games colleges play.* Baltimore, MD: Johns Hopkins University Press.

Toma, J. D. (2003). *Football U.* Ann Arbor: University of Michigan Press.

United States of America v. Nevin Shapiro. (2010). 28 U.S.C. § 2461.

University of Miami. (2011). UM notified of NCAA penalties, clearances. Retrieved from www.miami.edu

University of Miami. (2012). Athletic representative rules compliance newsletter. Retrieved from http://issuu.com/miamihurricanes/docs/booster_newsletter_spring_2012

University of Miami. (2013a). Statement from President Donna E. Shalala. Retrieved from www.miami.edu

University of Miami. (2013b). University of Miami leadership address NCAA report. Retrieved from www.miami.edu

Wainstein, K. L., Jay III, A. J., Guerin, T. M., Kukowski, C. D., Gerver, K. M. & Dreilinger, S. A. (2013). *Report on the NCAA's engagement of a source's counsel and use of the bankruptcy process in its University of Miami investigation.* New York: Cadwalader, Wickersham & Taft LLP.

Watterson, J. S. (2000). *College football.* Baltimore, MD: The John Hopkins University Press.

Yost, M. (2010). *Varsity green: A behind the scenes look at the culture and corruption in college athletics.* Stanford, CA: Stanford University Press.

4

UNIVERSITY OF ALABAMA ALBERT MEANS COLLEGE RECRUITING SCANDAL

Louis Harrison Jr., Albert Y. Bimper Jr., Langston Clark, and Martin Smith

Logan Young was found dead in a Memphis, Tennessee, mansion on April 11, 2006. It remains unknown if this former big-time booster died as the result of a brutal homicide or by some other means (USA Today, 2006a, 2006b; Curtis, 2006). Young's death is fraught with questions and conspiracy theories. His story in no way resembles a Shakespearean tale of a virtuous hero who had fallen from grace (Red, 2006); rather, Logan is part of a larger story, one of power brokers and pawns that played the game known as collegiate football recruiting.

The Case

The story preceding the epilogue is a tale with intricate details, a complex context with interesting characters. In February 2002, the renowned University of Alabama football program narrowly escaped "the death penalty" (the complete abolishment of an athletic program) following the highly publicized illegal recruitment of one of the nation's most coveted high school prospects, defensive lineman Albert Means (Layden, 2002). As a result of this recruitment infraction, the University of Alabama was given five years' probation, a two-year post-season eligibility sanction, and lost 21 scholarships over three seasons. Alabama's football program was no stranger in this arena of NCAA violations. In 1992, Antonio Langham signed with a sports agent after winning an NCAA championship with Alabama, ending his amateur status. But he then decided to return to Alabama for another collegiate season. As a result, Alabama lost 26 scholarships and was forced to vacate eight games from the 1993 season. In 1999 then head coach Mike Dubose provided false information about his involvement in the sexual harassment of a former secretary and resigned in 2000, a year after winning the SEC football title (Columbus Ledger Enquirer, 2009).

In the midst of the Dubose scandal, Albert Means was signing to play with the Crimson Tide at the University of Alabama. Means was highly touted as one of the top two defensive line prospects in the nation. As a player at Trezvant High School in Memphis, his accolades included being named to the *Parade, USA Today*, Tom Lemming, and Super Prep All-American selections (The University of Memphis Athletics, n.d.). Like others in similar positions, he was coveted by many football programs. Perhaps what made Albert most attractive, however, was his background. His biography reads like that of the stereotypical Black male super athlete. Physically gifted, born to a single mother with six children, academically inept, and his only sources of fatherly guidance were his football coaches (Rubin, 2002). All of these factors made Albert more than just the perfect lynchpin for the defensive line, it made him the perfect pawn to be manipulated in the interests of those who would attempt to be the architects of his athletic destiny.

Lynn Lang was supposed to be Albert Means's father figure, high school coach, confidant, and mentor. Instead he turned out to be an intermediary for those who would be willing to pay top dollar for a top player. The scandal began to unravel as Coach Lang was attempting to broker a deal with the University of Tennessee's assistant coach, Pat Washington. In exchange for Means signing with Tennessee, Lang requested a home and vehicle for Means's mother, $50,000 for himself, and additional money for his assistant coach. In a later conversation with Washington, Lang indicated, "another school had already made an offer for $80,000" (USA Today, 2005a). Lang was unaware this phone call was part of a setup that would cause his and Assistant Coach Milton Kirk's downfall. Washington was actually an informant for law enforcement officials (USA Today, 2005a; Fish, 2005).

It is important to note that Memphis is a major recruiting territory for the University of Tennessee and the University of Memphis. Lang was eventually found to have steered Albert Means to the University of Alabama for $150,000 (Fish, 2005; Curtis, 2006; USA Today, 2006a, 2005b; Branston, 2005). Lang and Kirk had been working together to sell the athletic services of Albert Means to the highest bidder. Unfortunately for Lang, Kirk (his sidekick-turned-snitch) revealed back-door dealings after reportedly not receiving his portion of the bribe (Branston, 2005). Kirk supplied critical evidence for the NCAA case by providing firsthand knowledge of the plan to collect payment for the signing of Means to Alabama.

During the investigation, Kirk stated, "Here's a kid that had done everything we asked him to do . . . . Here's a grown person who's going to take advantage of a kid who is already coming from a disadvantaged situation. I couldn't live with that" (Rubin, 2002). Nevertheless, both Lang and Kirk were indicted, but given relatively lenient sentences. Lang pled guilty to racketeering and was sentenced to two years of supervised release, community service, and $2,600 in fines (Roberts, 2009). Kirk received six months in a halfway house, three years' probation, community service, and a $1,000 fine for conspiracy (Roberts, 2009). Unsurprisingly, Lang agreed to testify against Logan Young, the benefactor behind the bribe.

Young was the millionaire son of a Tennessee businessman. Known for his boisterous behavior and lavish life style, Young was perhaps one of the most influential football boosters in Memphis, if not the entire country (USA Today, 2006b; Fish, 2005). He was known for bragging about his relationship with the legendary Bear Bryant. Supposedly, Young learned his recruiting tactics from Bryant and Young's father. Logan Young Sr. was a close friend of legendary Alabama coach Bear Bryant. At a time when the NCAA did not restrict the influence of boosters in college recruiting, Logan Young Sr. facilitated the recruitment of top athletes from west Tennessee and east Arkansas to the University of Alabama. When Logan Young Sr. passed away, Logan Young Jr. inherited not only his father's beverage company, but also his relationship with Bryant (Curtis, 2006).

While it appears that Young was simply living up to his reputation as a broker of gridiron talent, the influence of fellow boosters and the actions of other powerful individuals and institutions cannot be ignored in this football odyssey. The original informant, Pat Washington, was assistant coach to then University of Tennessee head coach Phillip Fulmer. Fulmer was said to have been upset about losing top players in Memphis and called upon University of Tennessee fans to find some dirt on Young and hand it over to SEC and NCAA investigators. This would ultimately lead to the charges brought by the U.S. Attorney's office (Fish, 2005). After sending various documents to SEC commissioner Roy Kramer, Fulmer tipped the first domino that sparked both NCAA and Federal investigations (Fish, 2005). But these actions were not so much about the integrity of collegiate athletics as they were about protecting coveted recruiting territory. Another informant in the case was former University of Memphis head football coach Rip Scherer. Scherer served as a secret witness in the case against Young (Fish, 2005). Scherer was upset about not being able to recruit Means and indicated that Lynn would not divulge any contact information for Means, stating that it was a waste of his time. But Lynn did allegedly tell another Memphis coach that they could possibly have a chance at Means if they were "willing to deal" (Rubin, 2002).

Throughout this story, at one point or another, all of the brokers (coaches, mentors, boosters, etc.) sought to profit from the athletic talent of Albert Means. Lang and Milton would have unapologetically supplemented their incomes if their plan had been successful. If Kirk had not blown the whistle on his former boss, he would have likely not been a key witness. Ultimately, all of the informants, coaches, and representatives from rival universities sought to protect their own recruiting ground. Logan was interested in maintaining his status among the booster elite at The University of Alabama. Even the University of Memphis benefitted from the scandal, as Means was permitted to transfer there in the midst of the scandal. Surprisingly, the NCAA did not question Means's athletic or academic eligibility, even though his former coach claimed to have paid a teammate $30 to take the college entrance exam for Means (Fish, 2005).

But what about Albert Means, the student-athlete in this case? Throughout the entire scandal Means remained virtually innocuous, and the NCAA found him to be innocent of any wrongdoing (USA Today, 2006b). During the trial, Means testified that he depended on Lang to handle college recruiters (ESPN, 2005). While Lang and others sought to profit from Means's talents, Means himself was left with little (Branston, 2005). Although some news outlets suggested that the Means family was given about $60,000 (Baird, 2005b; outsidethesidelines, 2011), it is likely that Means never received anything close to what others were making off of him.

Means had been declared academically ineligible before the 2003 season (The University of Memphis Athletics, n.d.), but he went on to graduate from the University of Memphis with bachelor's and master's degrees. Means is now an educated educator. As recently as 2011, he was a coach at a Memphis High School. Unlike his former coaches, Means warns his student-athletes about the downfalls of pay for play.

Sociocultural Context

The University of Alabama recruiting scandal, in many ways, illuminates how intercollegiate athletics has evolved far beyond competitive entertainment. This case brings to light how intercollegiate athletics is an industry clearly aimed at producing an economic commodity (i.e. the student-athlete) to be showcased on the field or court. The aim is not just to provide entertainment for an overzealous following of spectators but to produce monetary profits and institutional prestige. There are several stakeholders within the enterprise of college sports, including the athletics administration, coaches, the affiliated academic institutions, athletic/institutional boosters, marketing groups, and the athletic support staff. However, the most powerless stakeholder functions at the core of this industry. Student-athletes, such as Albert Means, are the most vulnerable stakeholders, as they tend to gain the least while having the most at stake (their bodies, education, promising lucrative careers, etc.). As evident in the University of Alabama scandal, the magnitude of the present-day industry of college athletics can entice opportunists to seek to exploit the product and systems of college athletics for their own financial gain. The University of Alabama case exposes how opportunists exploit the persistent social issues of race, class, access, gender (i.e. African American males), and the systemic free-market recruiting of young, talented high school athletes.

This scandal underscores the need to have a broader understanding of the complexity by which the culture of intercollegiate sports affects race relations in society, influences the allocation and use of power, and precipitates a systemic structure that can be easily manipulated to exploit a student-athlete. Reflecting upon the circumstances and outcome of the Albert Means case, there are three pertinent issues that surface, which shed light on the effects of the enterprise of intercollegiate athletics.

First, dependency materializes as a concern in this case. Means was quite dependent on others (i.e. Lynn Lang) to a level that rendered him a complacent participant in the process of his college recruitment. He displayed a high degree of trust in his high school coach to guide him throughout the overwhelming and often daunting process of being recruited. Unfortunately, Lang negotiated with his own self-interests in mind. Based on his testimony, Means relied on and trusted Lang to "deal with college recruiters" because he "took care of everything" (Baird, 2005a). Lang capitalized on the dependency of Means by manipulating his decision to attend the University of Alabama. Conceivably, Means may have had a limited sense of human agency to even question the use of a stand-in to take an entrance exam based on his dependence on his high school coach.

Second, this case unveils the commodification of the student-athlete, particularly the disproportionate number of Black student athletes in revenue-generating intercollegiate sports (Lapchick, 2010; Harper, Williams, & Blackman, 2013). In a broader sense, the Black collegiate student-athlete has been virtually reduced to an expendable commodity fueling the industry and self-serving interests of NCAA intercollegiate athletics. Sports scholars have employed the analytical lens and affiliated principles of Critical Race Theory (Delgado, 2001; Bell, 1992a, 1992b; Donnor, 2005; Tate, 1997) to examine race as a social construct situated in socio-cultural and sociopolitical institutions such as universities and the industry of sport. Critical race sports scholars have argued that the commodification of the disproportionately over-represented Black athlete in high-profile sports at pre-dominately White academic institutions signals a deeply inscribed systemic structure of contemporary, institutional racism (Donnor, 2005; Singer, 2005, 2008).

Means was recognized as a prized catch for any football program and was recruited nationwide. According to testimony, Lang engaged in "shopping Means around" and "bidding on Means" with coaches and boosters, including the affiliated Alabama booster, Logan Young. The process and culture of free-market college recruiting, including this case, reduces a person (i.e. a student-athlete) to property. Viewing athletes, particularly Black male student-athletes, as property permits a White-dominated industry – at the institutional, administrative, and coaching levels – to do business in its own interest and remain separated from a historically marginalized group. Lang's actions speak to the fact that the free-market structure of intercollegiate sports can entice and enable members of a historically marginalized group to engage as passive actors in the exploitation of the Black male athlete for their own social mobility and financial gain.

Last, a critique of the outcomes of this case uncovers the issue of bypassing due process. The accusations against Means were significant enough to prompt NCAA investigations, which led to subsequent firings, sanctions, and court deliberations. But because of the public accusations and investigations, Means, without legal representation, was essentially forced to transfer from Alabama with the remainder of his collegiate eligibility in question and at the hands of the NCAA. Although he eventually transferred to the University of Memphis, was Means aware of his rights as a student-athlete in the midst of these accusations and investigations? Generally, there has been a dearth of progress in appropriately outlining student-athletes' rights as an "amateur." Without appropriate representation, much like was the case in the Means scandal, student-athletes will have to disprove their guilt rather than be presumed innocent until proven otherwise.

When there was information to suggest that violations of NCAA policy had occurred in the recruitment of Albert Means, the university appeared to react relatively swiftly. However, their response was not without negative implications for those who often bear the brunt of such actions, the student-athlete. Albert Means was dismissed from the football program based on the accusations. His dismissal did not convey his victimization but cast him in the media and court of public opinion as a corroborating player and another athlete trying to swindle the system even before the facts of the case had unfolded. The university also decided to suspend recruitment of all players in the Memphis area until the conclusion of all investigations. Decisions such as these cast unyielding doubt about the values of the people in the Memphis area and limited the opportunities for a number of talented athletes in the area. Although the University of Alabama and its athletic program suffered as a result of the scandal, the university's response negated the possibility that Means was a victim in the case and simultaneously communicated distorted and negative beliefs about the communities from which student-athletes emerge.

This case is unique in the fact that there are hundreds (perhaps thousands) of high school student-athletes recruited every year to play in high-profile inter-collegiate athletics across the country without similar incident. This scandal showcases a blatant, dismissive regard of the mores and safeguarding rules of the NCAA and trivializes a person – Albert Means. The players in this case, from Logan Young to the University of Alabama, who attempted to skirt NCAA policy and the law, illustrate the uniqueness of this case. However, the scandal is arguably more com-monplace than unique if one views this case beyond the sole context of sports and instead views it through a complex sociocultural lens considering the social factors of race, class, and power.

The industry of intercollegiate athletics has not and will not have immunity to the socially constructed issues of race, class, gender, equity, and power that are influential at the core of society. In this realm there is no truly level playing field. The University of Alabama case underscores these issues embedded in society and in the industry of college sports. This recruiting scandal took shape because there were opportunists who recognized that Albert Means was unique because of his talent but easily exploitable because he represented the ideal commodity that the industry of sport thrives upon. In this sense, Albert Means was not unique. If anything, he was as common and expendable as every young Black boy with the talent and aspirations to continue playing the game they love for an industry they have yet to fully understand. At some point all stakeholders must come to recognize that these young men are human beings and not just economic commodities (Harrison, 2011).

Alternate Ending

Looking back on this case it is rather obvious that it could have been handled in a way that would have better served Albert Means and all high-profile student-athletes. Refocusing on the rights and wellness of student-athletes would yield more equitable outcomes in college recruiting. Developing honest language and practices that reflect the realities of college athletics and the true roles and responsi-bilities of student-athletes would aid in dispelling the hypocrisy of revenue-generating college sports.

If Albert Means existed in a collegiate environment where players are paid to play, this would have significantly changed the dynamics of this case. Albert could have signed a four-year athletic contract to play for the University of Alabama that stipulated that all of his educational and living expenses would be paid for the duration of the contract. To protect the interests of student-athletes, there could have also been a players' union that consisted of former and current players to advise fellow players on their rights as students and athletes. This players' union would provide lawyers, and players would be provided due process and assumed innocent until proven guilty. The NCAA and individual universities would not have the unilateral ability to decide how to punish athletes.

Here we propose a change in the discourse to halt the exploitation of student-athletes such as Means. Student-athletes are in need of representation from impartial individuals that have the ability to see these situations from the student-athletes' perspective. Because of the short tenure of collegiate athletes there is a revolving door of athletes that does not allow for the development of student-athlete power. Student-athletes are in need of education regarding their rights and a forum to voice concerns without being penalized by coaches or their institutions. An advocacy group can address issues that a high-profile athlete will face.

The fallacy of amateurism continues to drive the compensation of student-athletes in revenue-producing sports underground. Taking bargaining power from the hands of people such as Lynn Lang or Logan Young and placing it in the hands of student-athletes and their parents is a first step in preventing scandals such as this from occurring again. Some might suggest that placing this responsibility in the hands of inexperienced young men or low-income, uneducated parents would provide an environment for even greater exploitation and corruption. This paternalistic view suggests that the current system that bred Lang and Young is a better alternative. Placing the bargaining power in the hands of student-athletes and their parents would also open the possibility of brokering deals that include the education of siblings, relatives, or friends who would not normally have the resources to attend such universities. The student-athlete might also choose to negotiate for additional years of education to pursue graduate degrees or the right to pursue an area of study often not available to student-athletes because of class time and practice time conflicts. Placing this power in the hands of student-athletes may prove to increase their awareness and agency in the educational process and raise their levels of responsibility for their own education.

If we compare college students to student-athletes, we can see a stark contrast. Academically gifted students can decide which college to attend based on the best financial assistance and scholarship packages they can receive. To supplement an academic scholarship, these students can work as many hours as they can fit into their academic schedule to earn funds in addition to their scholarship. If they have special skills or can secure good-paying positions, they can earn significant salaries to supplement their scholarships. While their scholarships are often contingent on maintenance of a certain grade point average, they are not required to work for their scholarship. However, student-athletes are required to work for their scholarship. Though symbolic rules indicate that they are not to exceed twenty hours, the enforcement of this rule is rare.

If the NCAA looks the other way regarding enforcement of rules designed to protect student-athletes while ignoring due process for rules allegedly broken by student-athletes, the NCAA is complicit in the exploitation of student-athletes. In this way, the NCAA is no different than Lang or Young. All are attempting to cash in on student-athletes' athletic ability. The hypocrisy of the NCAA is ubiquitous in the revenue-producing sports of basketball and football. The exorbitant revenues garnered from these players through media contracts, endorsement deals, and ticket revenue rival that of professional sports, yet the NCAA stamps amateur status onto the industry to protect its interest. To enact an alternate ending in the Albert Means case, a change of paradigm and discourse is necessary. A discourse and perspective change that no longer portrays athletes as benefactors of benevolence of the university is necessary for authentic change to take place. Athletes would function more like paid employees on work-study, required to attend practice, film sessions, weights, and team meetings. They would function on an enforced time schedule that would eliminate "voluntary mandatory" off-season workouts. The realization of a paradigm shift such as this would precipitate an alternate ending to this and other cases like it.

References

Baird, W. (2005a, January 25). Former coach says he took payoff in Alabama recruiting scandal. Retrieved from www.usatoday.com

Baird, W. (2005b, June 13). Ex-Alabama booster Young gets 6-month prison term. Retrieved from www.usatoday.com

Bell, D. (1992a). *Faces at the bottom of the well: The permanence of racism*. New York: Basic Books.

Bell, D. (1992b). *Race, racism and American law*. Boston, MA: Little Brown & Company.

Branston, J. (2005, January 21). Kickoff, at last. Retrieved from www.memphisflyer.com

Columbus Ledger Enquirer. (2009, June 12). A timeline of Alabama's NCAA problems. Retrieved from www.ledger-enquirer.com

Curtis, D. (2006, April 23). The odd life & death of Logan Young. Retrieved from http://articles. orlandosentinel.com/2006-04-23/sports/YOUNG23_1_logan-young-memphis-police-higgins

Delgado, R. (2001). *Critical Race Theory: An introduction*. New York: New York University Press.

Donnor, J. K. (2005). Towards an interest-convergence in the education of African-American football student athletes in major college sports. *Race Ethnicity and Education*, 8(1), 45–67.

ESPN. (2005, January 5). Tide booster charged with paying 150k. Retrieved from http://sports. espn.go.com

Fish, M. (2005). The crimson hide: How Vols boosters dug up the dirt that sent 'Bama's biggest braggart to the big house. Retrieved from http://sports.espn.go.com

Harper, S. R., Williams, C. D., & Blackman, H. W. (2013). *Black male student-athletes and racial inequities in NCAA Division I College Sports*. Philadelphia: University of Pennsylvania, Center for the Study of Race and Equity in Education.

Harrison Jr., L. (2011). Athletes' rights and justice issues: Its not business, its personal. *Journal of Intercollegiate Sport, 4*(1), 14–17.

Lapchick, R. E. (2010). The 2010 racial and gender report card: College sport. Retrieved from http://web.bus.ucf.edu/sportbusiness/?page=1445

Layden, T. (2002, November 18). The loneliest losers. Retrieved from http://sportsillustrated.cnn.com

Outsidethesidelines. (2011). Albert Means: Born Again Victim. Retrieved February 4, 2014 from www.rollbamaroll.com/2011/2/6/1979284/albert-means-born-again-victim

Red, C. (2006, April 16). A bloody ending at 'Bama. Booster's death an accident. Retrieved from http://articles.nydailynews.com

Roberts, J. (2009, November 28). Milton Kirk sues city schools for pay. Retrieved from www.commercialappeal.com/news/2009/nov/28/kirk-sues-city-schools-for-pay

Rubin, A. (2002, August 25). Coaches pay price for peddling prep star Albert Means. Retrieved from http://articles.nydailynews.com

Singer, J. N. (2005). Understanding racism through the eyes of African American male student-athletes. *Race Ethnicity and Education, 8*(4), 365–386.

Singer, J. N. (2008). Benefits and detriments of African American male athletes' participation in a big time college football program. *International Review of Sociology of Sport, 43*(4), 399–408.

Tate IV, W. F. (1997). Critical Race Theory and education: History, theory and implications. *Review of research in education, 22*(1),195–247.

The University of Memphis Athletics. (n.d.). Albert Means player biography. Retrieved February 3, 2014 from www.gotigersgo.com/sports/m-footbl/mtt/means_albert00.html

USA Today. (2005a, June 25). Memos show sec ware coach was shopping player. Retrieved from www.usatoday.com

USA Today. (2005b, July 6). Convicted ex-Alabama booster denies buying player, rips Fulmer. Retrieved from www.usatoday.com

USA Today. (2006a, April 12). Alabama booster convicted in recruiting scandal found dead. Retrieved from www.usatoday.com

USA Today. (2006b, April 12). Coroner examining brutal death of Alabama booster Young. Retrieved from www.usatoday.com

5

SPORTS AGENTS AND THE RECRUITMENT OF REGGIE BUSH TO THE UNIVERSITY OF SOUTHERN CALIFORNIA

Timothy Davis and Kenneth L. Shropshire

Coming out of high school, Reggie Bush was a highly touted and sought-after football player. Football scouts and athlete-rating agencies predicted a stellar collegiate career for Reggie Bush. As predicted, Bush would have a fantastic career as the featured running back for the legendary football program at the University of Southern California (USC). However, the competition to secure Bush as a player did not end when he matriculated at USC. Rather, to the surprise of the public – but not to those familiar with efforts by sports agents to curry favor with elite college athletes – the intense recruitment of Bush continued during his career at USC. Bush's relationship with individuals who hoped to represent him as a professional athlete shone a spotlight on the elite college athlete/sports agent recruitment culture. These relationships, and the events surrounding them, caused college sports constituents at least momentary and perhaps long-term reflection on the effectiveness of the NCAA's rules that attempt to regulate interactions between college athletes and sports agents, on the NCAA's amateurism principle on which these rules are premised, and on questions relating to equity and fairness within big-time intercollegiate athletics.

This chapter examines the multiple dimensions of sports agents' alleged improper recruitment of Reggie Bush. Part I provides a summary of the factual allegations that led the NCAA to conclude that, as a result of his interaction with persons that the NCAA characterized as sports agents, Reggie Bush committed multiple NCAA violations. Part I also provides a glimpse into the NCAA penalty structure, in place when Bush committed NCAA rules violations, through a discussion of the penalties that the NCAA imposed directly on USC and indirectly on Reggie Bush and a USC assistant coach. Part II discusses the broader implications of these events and how they speak to the current state of intercollegiate sports within academic, economic and social contexts. Part III presents an alternative narrative, as we consider how events might have been recast if an open market were a feature of the relationship between colleges and athletes, the latter being primary producers of revenues for financially successful intercollegiate football programs.

The Case

Just days before the 2006 NFL rookie draft, press reports surfaced indicating that, during his collegiate career at USC, Reggie Bush and his family had received gifts that violated NCAA regulations. Bush reportedly received these gifts from individuals (hereafter described as "agents," the term that the NCAA assigned to them) who sought an advantage over others vying to represent Bush, who was projected to be a top NFL draft pick. Negotiating Bush's contract with the NFL team that drafted him was no doubt seen as only the beginning of a profitable agent/athlete relationship. Bush's prospective agents also anticipated the significant representation fees that would accrue from promoting the athlete's interests in other endeavors, including endorsement deals with merchandisers. In addition, having a prominent athlete such as Bush on the agent's client roster would aid his/her recruitment of other, future NFL draft picks. At a minimum, they anticipated three percent of Bush's multiyear, multimillion-dollar NFL contract. As is common, however, Bush signed a representation agreement with an agency other than those who had lavished him with gifts. Bush's decision invoked an unpleasant and public reaction from the agents who had provided gifts to Bush and his family. This prompted the NCAA's enforcement staff to initiate an investigation into whether Bush had violated NCAA agent and amateurism regulations.

An NCAA investigative report and media accounts, including a Yahoo! Sports investigation, revealed that agents had offered gifts to Bush and his family, and at other times Bush and his family had requested gifts (Robinson & Cole, 2006). According to these sources, Bush and his family received multiple gifts from Michael Michaels and Lloyd Lake, sports agents with New Era Sports and Entertainment who sought to form a sports agency and marketing company with Bush and his father. Bush also received gifts from Mike Orenstein and his associates, via Orenstein's marketing agency, which also hired the athlete as an intern (Banowsky et al., 2010). The NCAA's fact-finding and sanctioning body, the Division I Committee on Infractions (COI), found that Bush began receiving gifts as early as December 2004 and as late as December 2005, when the agents provided Bush with a suit to wear and a limousine ride to the Heisman trophy presentation in New York City.

Focusing on Bush's relationship with Michaels and Lake, the COI report stated that "in the course of this relationship," the agents gave gifts to Bush and his family including: 1) airline and other transportation expenses (e.g. limousine services), which were often requested by Bush or his parents; 2) cash requested by Bush to enable him to purchase a car and to accessorize it; 3) cash to cover lodging expenses for out-of-town travel by Bush and his family; 4) the purchase of a home for use by Bush's parents (in this arrangement, Bush's parents paid the agents only $1,400 of the approximately $4,500 monthly mortgage); 5) $10,000 in cash to facilitate Bush's family to purchase furniture for the house; and 6) substantial cash payments to Bush, often at the athlete's request (Banowsky et al., 2010).

Based on these and other factual findings, the COI accused Bush and a USC assistant coach of violating several NCAA regulations. The COI concluded that Bush had violated an NCAA rule prohibiting college athletes, their friends, or relatives from accepting transportation and other benefits from agents if the benefits were not available to the student body in general (National Collegiate Athletic Association [NCAA], 2011). The COI also concluded that Bush had violated an NCAA rule that prohibits student-athletes from entering into representation agreements with agents (Banowsky et al., 2010). By violating these rules, Bush also ran afoul of one of the NCAA's fundamental principles: the preservation of amateurism. Therefore, Bush's conduct was problematic because of both the value of the gifts received and the nature of his interaction with agents. The NCAA's amateurism rules stipulate, among other things, that student-athletes are not permitted to receive any level of compensation beyond the room, board, tuition, and educational expenses designated by those regulations. As the amateurism bylaw denotes, Bush's behavior cost him his amateur status and rendered him ineligible to participate in intercollegiate athletics. NCAA Division I Bylaw 12.01.1 states: "Only an amateur student-athlete is eligible for intercollegiate athletics participation in a particular sport" (NCAA, 2011).

With respect to the USC assistant football coach, the COI found that the coach knew of Bush's relationship with the agents and that Bush had violated NCAA rules. Consequently, the assistant coach violated NCAA rules by not conveying his knowledge to USC's athletic compliance staff. NCAA rules promote self-reporting at the earliest opportunities. The coach was also found to have engaged in unethical conduct for providing false and misleading information during the NCAA's investigation (Banowsky et al., 2010).

During the same time frame that Bush and the assistant coach had committed NCAA rules violations, similar violations were occurring in the men's basketball program with star player O. J. Mayo. These violations included Mayo's receipt of extra benefits (e.g. cash, airline tickets, and merchandise) from a person affiliated with a sports agency. Violations also had occurred in the women's tennis program, where a tennis player used an athletic department long-distance access code to make over $7,500 in unauthorized calls. Therefore, Bush's and the assistant football coach's conduct, in conjunction with these problems, resulted in the COI's finding of a lack of institutional control at USC.

One of the NCAA's fundamental governing principles is institutional control. According to the NCAA Principle of Institutional Control and Responsibility, "it is the responsibility of each member institution to control its intercollegiate athletics program in compliance with the rules and regulations of the Association" (NCAA, 2011, p. 3). Under this bylaw, an institution is responsible for developing compliance measures, including monitoring procedures, that facilitate NCAA rules compliance by all those involved in intercollegiate athletics (i.e. athletes, athletic department representatives, boosters, and university administrators). In regard to USC, the COI concluded: "The institution exhibited a lack of control over its department of athletics by its failure to have in place procedures to effectively monitor the violations of NCAA amateurism, recruiting and extra-benefit legislation in the sports of football, men's basketball and women's tennis" (Banowsky et al., 2010, p. 45).

Applying its rule of restitution (NCAA, 2011, Bylaw 19.7), the COI vacated all of USC's football team's victories in which Reggie Bush had played when he was ineligible for intercollegiate athletic competition for having violated the NCAA rules discussed. Consequently, the NCAA vacated the football team's last two victories of the 2004 football season, which included the team's January 2005 Orange Bowl win, and all of its wins during the 2005 season (Banowsky et al., 2010, p. 57). The Orange Bowl victory was notable because it resulted in USC being designated as the BCS Championship winner.

Other notable penalties imposed on USC were: a two-year ban on post-season play (i.e. the football team was prohibited from participating in bowl games during the 2010 and 2011 seasons); a loss of a total of 30 football scholarships for the 2011–2014 academic years; four years of probation from June 2010 through June 9, 2014 (Zinser, 2010); and vacation of all the individual records of Reggie Bush for contests in which he competed while ineligible (Banowsky et al., 2010, p. 57–58). USC had to, therefore, remove memorabilia related to Bush, including his jerseys and the replica Heisman Trophy that was once showcased at the school. USC self-imposed a penalty of disassociation with Bush, which forbade USC from receiving any financial, recruiting, or other assistance from the athlete (Banowsky et al., 2010, p. 59).

It is important to understand that only NCAA member institutions have direct contractual relationships with the NCAA. Consequently, only the NCAA can take direct action against an institution. The NCAA nevertheless expects institutions to act in accordance with NCAA findings regarding rules violations by student-athletes, coaches, and other athletic department personnel. A failure of the institution to do so could result in the NCAA imposing harsher sanctions on the institution.

The penalties that the NCAA imposed on USC were regarded as some of the most severe since Southern Methodist University (SMU) received the so-called death penalty in 1986. The NCAA prohibited SMU's football program from intercollegiate competition for two years. Notwithstanding their severity, the penalties assessed against USC could have been harsher. The COI considered imposing one of the most severe penalties that can be imposed – a television ban. It declined to do so, however, citing USC's cooperation, the severity of the other penalties imposed, and the consequences suffered by those involved (Banowsky et al., 2010, p. 56). Interestingly, and contrary to what may have been predicted, USC's football program had a relatively successful record during the seasons immediately following the imposition of the sanctions. The scholarship restrictions and post-season ban did not appear to have a negative impact on the football program's recruiting efforts. The academic year following the imposition of sanctions, USC's football team's incoming freshman recruiting class of 2011 was ranked in the top five by all of the major services evaluating collegiate football recruits (Peszko, 2011).

After Bush failed to sign a representation agreement with Lake and Michaels, the prospective agents filed a lawsuit against the athlete in which they sought to recover the value of the gifts they had given to Bush and his family. Those civil lawsuits were settled privately. The Michaels suit settled in April 2007 for an amount reportedly between $200,000 and $300,000, and the Lake case was settled for an undisclosed amount in April 2010 (Robinson & Cole, 2010).

Following the COI decision, Bush sought to rehabilitate his reputation and standing with the following statement:

> I have a great love for the University of Southern California and I very much regret the turn that this matter has taken, not only for USC, but for the fans and players. I am disappointed by [the] decision and disagree with the NCAA's findings. If the University decides to appeal, I will continue to cooperate with the NCAA and USC, as I did during the investigation. In the meantime, I will continue to focus on making a positive impact for the University and for the community where I live.
>
> *(ESPN.com, 2010)*

USC appealed the penalties that the COI imposed, arguing that the penalties were excessive and not supported by factual evidence (Griffin, Friedenthal, Hoye, Ohlendorf & Williams, 2011, p.16). The NCAA's Division I Infractions Appeals Committee rejected USC's arguments and upheld all penalties that the COI had imposed (Griffin et al., 2011, p. 22).

Sociocultural Context

Many of the elements in the Reggie Bush case are not unique. Indeed, the case presents a replay of the oft-told story of an aspiring sports agency seeking to secure a world-class athlete as a client. To do so, agents may provide benefits to the athlete, believing that this is the formula for successfully engendering the loyalty of the star collegiate athlete. Rather than ensuring loyalty, the agent's efforts create a web that entangles the agents, athlete, and the athlete's family, friends, coaches, and university. What then follows is a narrative in which the agent, the athlete, and the athletes' parents are depicted as selfish and greedy individuals who knowingly violated NCAA rules and damaged the interests and image of the athlete's college or university. Some of this sentiment was captured in the Bush decision, wherein the COI stated: "This case is a window onto a landscape of elite college athletes and certain individuals close to them who, in the course of their relationships, disregard NCAA rules and regulations" (Mandel, 2010, p. 1).

NCAA infractions decisions, such as in the Bush case, can certainly be viewed through such a narrow lens. On the other hand, such incidents can be viewed through a broader prism that demands consideration of the extant economic and social order that resides within college sports. Such reconsideration necessarily begins with a critical assessment of the NCAA's conceptualization of amateurism, on which its agent, and other, rules are premised in part. An examination of the amateurism concept, in turn, requires inquiry into the very nature of the student-athlete's relationship with his or her college or university. This is particularly true in regard to Division I's revenue-producing sports – football and men's basketball. Questions that have emerged from an examination of these specific relationships include whether: 1) limitations imposed on the financial benefits that student-athletes can receive from their institutions exploit men's football and basketball players given the revenues and other benefits, tangible and intangible, that universities accrue from these athletes' services; 2) the NCAA's regulatory scheme does more to perpetuate this imbalance in the student-athlete/university relationship than it does to promote student-athlete welfare (another core NCAA principle); 3) coaches and others have benefited financially from artificial market restraints on the compensation that student-athletes could receive from their institutions in a more open market; 4) student-athletes' willingness to disregard NCAA agent restrictions and violate other rules are borne of financial necessity, greed, or disrespect for a regulatory system the athletes view as disconnected from social realities and as the protector of a system that exploits them; and 5) issues of race reside within the current structure given the racial demographics of NCAA Division I football and men's basketball teams. Discussion of these issues is beyond the scope of this chapter. But consideration of them demonstrates the danger of viewing the Reggie Bush case myopically.

Alternate Ending

Would a different NCAA regulatory structure or other changes within college sports have produced a different outcome in the Reggie Bush matter? Imagine the following alternative narrative, in which the economics of college sports are premised on a free market, not only for coaches and athletic administrators but also for student-athletes.

The year is 2004, and USC star running back Reggie Bush has entered into a contract in which he has agreed to be represented by sports agents Michael Michaels and Lloyd Lake of New Era Sports and Entertainment. Pursuant to this agreement, the agents will represent Bush after he leaves USC, but will also provide representation services, including advice on a range of pre- and post-collegiate career matters, prior to Bush's departure from USC. For example, prior to his leaving USC, Reggie Bush's agents will provide him with advice that allows Bush to make more informed decisions relative to when to enter the NFL draft and his value to an NFL club.

This representation agreement, one of the first of its kind, is sanctioned under revised NCAA rules governing the relationship between sports agents and college athletes. Under the revised rules, student-athletes evaluate sports agents as part of a process established by the NCAA that is implemented at the university/college level. Similar rules have been fashioned for athletes in other sports that take into account the peculiarities of those sports, such as when a particular sport's professional draft occurs. Bush and his agents sign a standard form representation agreement that is developed jointly by the NCAA and the National Football League Players Association (the entity that regulates agents who negotiate contracts between their player clients and NFL clubs). The standardized agreement was developed to ensure a balanced relationship between agents and athletes.

Under this alternative regime and subject to limitations proscribing fraud, over-reaching, and other forms of improper behavior, agents openly recruit college athletes. Agent abuses would be, as they are now, regulated by the players' associations for the four major team sports in the United States; each players' association would modify its regulations in accordance with NCAA bylaw changes and also would enhance their enforcement efforts. Consonant with their open recruitment of athletes, agents would evaluate the risks associated with investing in a prospective professional athlete.

This open market framework permits any agent to invest as much as he or she desires in the recruitment of an athlete. In other words, agents will provide a level of compensation to athletes based upon the agent's perception of the athlete's worth. These recruiting enticements can include cash, automobiles, jewelry, and even a home for the athlete's parents. Once the student-athlete commits to the agent, however, that commitment becomes contractually binding.

The alternative path, in which there would have been an open market for Bush's services and any payments, gifts, and other compensation could have been made to him openly, has been championed by advocates of college sports reform. The outcome in the Bush case, however, makes it clear that we are not yet in this alternative space. As we are not in this space, we return to our discussion of the foundation for the NCAA's "no agent" rule and the notion of amateurism.

David C. Young's *The Olympic Myth of Greek Amateur Athletics* provides the most in-depth analysis of the concept of amateurism that we know of (1985). Young persuasively makes the case that amateurism, both as a word and a concept, did not even exist for the ancient Greeks. For the concept's origin, Young points us to Victorian England and then to the modern Olympiad, which only slightly precedes the creation of organized collegiate sports in the United States. In short, there is no glamorous history of amateurism, as NCAA rules and proponents of amateurism in college sports suggest. There is certainly, for many, a philosophical basis for the current professional/amateur dichotomy. What should not be ignored, however, are the economic foundations of amateurism: a sporting event or any activity with free labor is likely to be more profitable for the organizers than one where labor is paid for.

Numerous questions emerge in regard to a market-driven approach to college athletics. Would human nature propel an athlete to seek more compensation, perhaps under the table, even if the level of compensation provided under an open-market system were fair? Is there always an agent willing to pay one dollar more than the previous agent to stop by a student-athlete's dorm room or violate players' association regulations to secure a client? How willing would an athlete be to switch alliances for that additional dollar? Some of these, and other, issues could be addressed within the standardized contracts between agents and athletes and modifications to existing players' association regulations that govern agents. Open market theory suggests that, at some point, all would balance out and agents would pay no more than an athlete is worth. Under an open-market structure, as regulated by players' associations, the agent who obtains the best contract and other results for an athlete would ultimately prevail in the competition for athletes as clients.

References

Banowsky, B., Black, J.S., Conboy, M., Dee, P.T., Hallaron, B., Myers, E.W., Potuto, J., & Thomas, D.E. (2010). University of Southern California Public Infractions Report. Retrieved from http://i.usatoday.net/sports/college/2010-06-10-usc-ncaa-report.pdf

ESPN.com. (2010, Jun. 11). NCAA delivers postseason football ban. Retrieved on May 3, 2012 from http://sports.espn.go.com/los-angeles/ncf/news/story?id=5272615

Griffin, C., Friedenthal, J., Hoye, W., Ohlendorf, P., & Williams, D. (2011) Report of the National Collegiate Athletics Association Division I Infractions Appeals Committee. Retrieved from http://fs.ncaa.org/Docs/PressArchive/2011/Infractions/20110526_USC_Final

Mandel, S. (2010, Jun. 10). With harsh USC penalties, NCAA sends warning to all elite programs. Retrieved on May 3, 2012 from http://sportsillustrated.cnn.com/2010/wri ters/stewart_mandel/06/10/usc.penalties/index.html

National Collegiate Athletic Association. (2011). *2011–12 NCAA Division 1 Manual.* Indianapolis, IN: Author.

Peszko, P. (2011, Feb. 3). USC football recruiting: grading the Trojans' 2011 class. Retrieved on May 15, 2012 from http://bleacherreport.com/articles/595247-usc-footba ll-recruiting-grading-the-trojans-2011-class#/articles/595247-usc-football-recruiting-gra ding-the-trojans-2011-class

Robinson, C., & Cole, J. (2006, Sept. 15). Cash and carry. Retrieved on May 3, 2012 from http://sports.yahoo.com/ncaa/football/news?slug=ys-bushprobe

Robinson, C., & Cole, J. (2010, Apr. 21). Settlement reached in Bush civil case. Retrieved on May 13, 2012 from http://sports.yahoo.com/ncaa/football/news?slug=ys-bushca se042110

Young, D. C. (1985). *The Olympic Myth of Greek Amateur Athletics.* Chicago: Ares Publishers.

Zinser, L. (2010, Jun. 10). U.S.C. Sports Receive Harsh Penalties. Retrieved on May 3, 2012 from www.nytimes.com/2010/06/11/sports/ncaafootball/11usc.html?_r=1

6

FOOTBALL MEMORABILIA, TATTOOS, AND THE FALL OF JIM TRESSEL AT OHIO STATE

Jamel K. Donnor and Collin D. Williams Jr.

Colloquially referred to as the "senator" because of his calculated responses to the media and trademark sweater vests, Jim Tressel, the former head football coach for The Ohio State University (OSU), tendered his resignation on May 30, 2011, citing that the "recent situation has been a distraction for our great university" (Tressel, 2011, p. 1). The "recent situation" Tressel was referring to was a story posted on Yahoo!Sports, an online sports newspaper, which stated that for approximately eight months he (Tressel) had failed to inform the university's athletics compliance department that five members of the football team, including starting quarterback Terrelle Pryor, had sold or exchanged OSU sports memorabilia for tattoos to Mr. Edward Rife, the owner of Fine Line Ink Tattoo, a tattoo parlor in Columbus, Ohio. A violation of the NCAA's amateurism policy regarding extra benefits and preferential treatment, Tressel – the most successful coach at Ohio State since Woody Hayes – knew that reporting the student-athletes' infractions would result in their immediate disqualification, and for all intents and purposes preclude the team from contending in a Bowl Championship Series (BCS) postseason bowl game.

Perhaps what was most troubling about the situation was Tressel's behavior upon learning of the violations and his actions once the matter became public. For example, upon initial notification of the student-athletes' infractions by Christopher Cicero, a local attorney and former football player at Ohio State, Tressel stated to Cicero by email that he would "investigate the matter and take appropriate action" (Robinson & Wetzel, 2011, p. 2). While there is very little information to determine whether Tressel conducted an investigation as stated, it was clear, according to Tressel's Ohio State email account, that he chose to handle the matter personally rather than notify the university's compliance department, athletic director (Gene Smith), or president (E. Gordon Gee), as stipulated in his employment contract. Similarly, once the university began an internal investigation into the situation,

Tressel falsely attested that he had reported any knowledge of NCAA violations to the university.

Tressel's conduct is symptomatic of the commercial forces and competitive pressures to win in major college football (Oriard, 2009; Clotfelter, 2011). For example, despite being a nonprofit organization, the NCAA (2010) reported that its total revenue generated from big-time college football alone was $14,841,000; a $5,632,000 increase from $9,209,000 reported in 2004 (NCAA, 2010, p. 27). Similarly, universities with high-profile teams, such as Ohio State, generate millions of dollars in revenue through ticket and merchandise sales, corporate sponsors, and television contracts. Likewise, the compensation packages for head (and assistant coaches) at many of the top football programs currently exceed $1 million (Upton, Gillum, & Berkowitz, 2010). Consider, for example, that Tressel's contract at the time of his resignation was worth approximately $17.4 million over seven years. In addition to a base salary of $550,000, a "longevity bonus" of $450,000, and the use of a private jet for recruiting visits, Tressel's contract stipulated that he receive a $25,000 raise per year, and an annual contribution of $40,000 toward his retirement from the university (Upton et al., 2010). In essence, the money in major college football is exorbitant.

The goal of this chapter is threefold. The first is to describe the situation that involved Tressel and OSU's football program in-depth. The second goal is to situate the Tressel scandal (and major college football) within a larger sociocultural and political economic context. Specifically, by explaining what the former head coach's and the student-athletes' actions convey regarding the commercialization of intercollegiate football, power, and wrongful benefice. The final goal is to provide an alternative ending to the OSU scandal – a counter-narrative, if you will. In particular, we consider whether Tressel would have had to resign if his student-athletes had been paid to play.

The Case

On April 2, 2010, former Ohio State head football coach Jim Tressel received the first of a string of emails from Christopher Cicero, a local attorney, indicating that several members of the OSU football team had received preferential treatment at a Columbus tattoo parlor as a result of selling their athletics trophies, awards, apparel, and equipment to Mr. Edward Rife, the owner of the parlor, who was also a convicted felon. According to Cicero's email, the U.S. Department of Justice (DOJ) raided Rife's home related to drug trafficking. In addition, Cicero indicated to Tressel that the student-athletes should "stay away from this guy [Rife] . . . quite frankly for their safety" (NCAA, 2011a, pp. 6–7). In response, Tressel thanked Cicero and remarked that he would "get on it ASAP" (NCAA, 2011a, p. 7). According to the NCAA's (2011a) infractions report, rather than notify campus officials of Cicero's email, Tressel forwarded the email to Terrelle Pryor's mentor in Jeannette, Pennsylvania, to apprise him of the "situation."

In a subsequent email sent on April 16, 2010, Cicero informed Tressel that Rife confirmed his interactions with some of the current members of the football team, and Cicero asked that the email "be treated as confidential" (NCAA, 2011a, p. 7). In addition to thanking Cicero, Tressel said, "Keep me posted as to what I need to do if anything. I will keep pounding these kids hoping they grow up" (NCAA, 2011a, p. 7). The next correspondence between Tressel and Cicero occurred on April 19, 2010, when Tressel sent an email to Cicero stating that "I told [the student-athletes] to steer clear . . . is there any way I can get all the ring names. . . . . I have a little plan once this year's rings arrive" (NCAA, 2011a, p. 8). The "ring names" Tressel was referring to were the names of the student-athletes other than Terrelle Pryor and DeVier Posey who had sold their Big Ten Conference championship rings to Rife. The next day (April 20, 2010), Cicero replied to Tressel that he would contact the Columbus district attorney to inquire about the names of additional student-athletes who might have sold their conference rings to Rife (NCAA, 2011a). For nearly three weeks, Tressel did not notify university officials of the infractions or forward Cicero's emails to any university officials. In fact, the next correspondence between Tressel and Cicero did not occur until June 10, 2010, when Tressel sent an email inquiring about the additional ring names to which Cicero replied "no more names" (NCAA, 2011a, p. 8). For more than two months, Tressel failed to inform the university's compliance department, athletic director, or president of the violations.

Incidentally, Tressel and Cicero did not have additional communication until December 2010 – the same time at which OSU's Office of Legal Affairs received a letter from the DOJ informing Ohio State of the DOJ's criminal investigation of Rife, during which DOJ officials seized "a significant amount of OSU sports memorabilia" (U.S. Department of Justice [U.S. DOJ], 2010, p. 1). According to the U.S. Department of Justice (2010), while "many of the items seized were acquired from Ebay and autographed at various signing events . . . several of the items seized appear to have belonged to Ohio State football players and/or The Ohio State University at some point in time" (p.1). Among the items seized were several Big Ten Conference Championship rings, trophies, and Ohio State football uniforms (U.S. DOJ, 2010). In response, Ohio State conducted an investigation of the violations, during which the student-athletes named in the DOJ's letter admitted to wrongdoing. From this investigation, the university uncovered additional violations (NCAA, 2011a, p. 4).

Among the additional violations uncovered from the internal institutional investigation were "payment to several student-athletes for work not performed at a private company, improper sale or exchange of institutional equipment or apparel for cash, or reduced-cost/free tattoos from Mr. Rife's tattoo parlor" (Ohio State Athletics, 2012, p. 1). According to the infractions report, between spring 2009 and summer 2011, Rife, without the university's knowledge or approval, arranged for the five football student-athletes to receive compensation for "work not performed" (Ohio State Athletics, 2012, p. 1).

Sociocultural Context

A major policy dilemma surrounding the Tressel scandal is the NCAA's amateurism policy, which, among other things, prohibits student-athletes from receiving compensation for their involvement in college athletics. According to the NCAA (2010), "student-athlete participation in intercollegiate athletics is an avocation" (NCAA Bylaw, Article 2.9). What this means is that a student who participates in NCAA-sanctioned athletic activities does so solely for its intrinsic value and functional purpose, such as learning the value of hard work and working within a team setting. Indeed, the sheer volume of "pay-for-play" infractions involving former elite student-athletes and institutions, such as Reggie Bush, Cam Newton, and the University of Miami, suggests that college athletes should be allowed to profit from their labors. Further, not only have critics of major college sports considered these bylaws unnecessary and exploitive (Glicksman, 2012; Wilbon, 2011; Sack, 2009), some have even likened them to apartheid (McCormick & McCormick, 2010) and slavery (Rhoden, 2007). Though he cautions against slavery comparisons, leading civil rights historian Taylor Branch (2011) argues that the current college sports regime is more analogous to colonialism as "two of the noble principles on which the NCAA justifies its existence – 'amateurism' and the 'student-athlete' – are cynical hoaxes, legalistic confections propagated by the universities so they can exploit the skills and fame of young athletes" (Branch, 2011, p. 3). In *The Shame of College Sports* (2011), Branch states that "the real scandal is not that students are getting illegally paid or recruited" (p. 3). This section provides further insight into the controversy surrounding amateurism, more closely examining the rules, the context in which they were created, the racial dynamics in college football and basketball, and the extent to which various stakeholders profit from intercollegiate athletics.

The Rules

Article 2 of the NCAA manual for Division 1 athletics lists 16 Principles for Conduct of Intercollegiate Athletics. The Principle of Amateurism, or Bylaw Article 2.9, states:

> Student-athletes shall be amateurs in an intercollegiate sport, and their participation should be motivated primarily by education and by the physical, mental and social benefits to be derived. Student participation in intercollegiate athletics is an avocation, and student-athletes should be protected from exploitation by professional and commercial enterprises.
>
> *(NCAA, 2011b, p. 4)*

Thus, the NCAA forbids students-athletes from receiving compensation for participation in college athletics beyond the cost of attending college. Under Article 15, the NCAA requires that an institution "shall not award financial aid to a student-athlete that exceeds the cost of attendance that normally is incurred by students enrolled in a comparable program at the institution" (NCAA, 2011b, p. 192) and "is an amount calculated by an institutional financial aid office" (NCAA, 2011b, p. 192). The bylaw violated by the OSU football players was 15.01.3: "Any student who receives financial aid other than that administered by the student-athlete's institution shall not be eligible for intercollegiate athletics competition" (NCAA, 2011b, p. 191). By receiving money and tattoos in exchange for autographs, jerseys, and other athletic memorabilia, the OSU football players terminated their amateur status as student-athletes and became ineligible to compete.

So-Called Student-Athletes

The term "student-athlete" endorses the wholesome virtue of amateurism in college sports as well as the idealistic notion of academics over athletics. In reality, though, the phrase was created to protect the NCAA from adequately compensating its athletes by focusing on their status as students and preventing them from being identified as employees. When Ray Dennison died of a head injury in Colorado in the 1950s while playing football in Colorado for the Fort Lewis A&M Aggies, his wife filed for workers'-compensation death benefits. According to the then-president of the NCAA, Walter Byers, "the threat was the dreaded notion that athletes could be identified as employees by state industrial commissions and the courts" (Byers and Hammer, 1997, p. 69). Thus, in a rapid, yet calculated, response, the NCAA "crafted the term student-athlete, and soon it was embedded in all NCAA rules and interpretations as a mandated substitute for words as players and athletes" (Byers and Hammer, 1997, p. 69). In conjunction with the amateurism rules, the term student-athlete preserves the image of college athletes as being students first, athletes second, but never employees. Since its creation, the NCAA and its member institutions have won several liability cases, successfully circumventing potentially large payouts. Evidently, the ambiguous term has been an exclusive shield for the NCAA, both promoting the falsified noble ideals of amateurism and serving as an effective legal defense (Branch, 2011). In *State Compensation Insurance Fund v. Industrial Commission* (1957), the Colorado Supreme Court ruled that neither Dennison nor his wife was eligible for benefits since the college was "not in the football business."

Profits

It is no longer feasible to deny that college sports has evolved into big business (Berkowitz & Upton, 2011a, 2011b; Greenberg & Smith, 2007; Upton, Gillum, & Berkowitz, 2010; Wilson, Schrager, Burke, Hawkins & Gauntt, 2011). The growing popularity of the major revenue-generating sports of basketball and football has been evidenced by enormous price tags on television rights packages, athletic department spending, and coaching salaries. In 2008, ESPN contracted to pay the NCAA $500 million to broadcast four of the five major BCS games (Wilbon, 2011). Just the appearance of a team in a single BCS football game earned its respective conference $18 million as well as an extra $4.5 million for each team beyond the first (Bakalar, 2009). By 2011, four individual conferences – the Big 12, Pac 12, SEC, and ACC – had all signed football TV deals valued at more than a billion dollars each (Thamel, 2011). In 2010, the NCAA entered into a 14-year, $10.8 billion dollar agreement with Turner/CBS sports to broadcast the Division I Men's Basketball Championship (Sandomir & Thamel, 2010). In a study of athletic departments' total expenditures, Berkowitz and Upton (2011b) found that 228 athletic departments had spent a total of $6.8 billion in 2010. In the same year, the University of Alabama Athletics Department alone brought in $26.6 million in revenue.

Coaches, too, have seen much of this profit. Other high-profile basketball and football coaches such as Rick Pitino, Nick Saban, and John Calipari eclipse even the $3.5 million that Tressel made in 2011 — in the same year, each brought in $7.5, $5.9, and $3.8 million, respectively (Berkowitz & Upton, 2011a; Wilbon, 2011). In 2011, the coaches of approximately half of the 68 teams that made it to the 2011 NCAA Men's Basketball Tournament and 58 of the 120 FBS football schools earned salaries greater than $1 million dollars (O'Neil, 2011). In contrast, players see menial amounts of this revenue. In fact, a joint study conducted by the National College Players Association (NCPA) and the Drexel University Department of Sport Management found that the average student-athlete at an FBS school on full scholarship has total earnings below the federal poverty line (Huma & Staurowsky, 2011). The comparisons to apartheid, colonialism, and slavery become clearer by understanding the racial disparities between teams and coaches.

Race

When intercollegiate athletics were racially segregated and minority students were barred from participation, college teams, regardless of the sport, were exclusively White. Since their integration, though, the racial composition of college basketball and football teams has grown to become overwhelmingly Black, while the racial composition of the managers of the sports (coaches, athletic directors, university officials, NCAA or conference officials, and so on) has remained overwhelmingly White (McCormick & McCormick, 2010, 2012). In 2010, for example, the top 25 basketball and football teams were 66 and 61 percent Black, respectively, while the administrators for those same teams were 91 and 96 percent White, respectively (McCormick & McCormick, 2012). While it is blatant that Black men are the majority in these sports and that their talent and labor have generated income for their schools, the revenue has been disproportionately distributed. What is interesting, though, is that the amateurism laws that the NCAA put in place apply solely to the athletes. As McCormick and McCormick (2012) explain, "amateurism reserves the vast financial rewards for the managers of college sports who are almost exclusively of European descent" (p. 18).

Alternate Ending

In late 2011, after being rocked by a bevy of scandals, the NCAA convened with conference representatives, member institution officials, and a variety of sports personalities who had demonstrated an acute interest in the compensation of college athletes to amend their amateurism rules. By the close of the weekend-long conference, the NCAA had agreed, in principle, "to amend Article 12 on amateurism, Article 15 on financial aid, and Article 16 on awards, benefits, and expenses" and "allow student-athletes the opportunity to open additional streams of income by signing endorsement agreements and selling items associated with their athletic achievements without losing their eligibility to compete" (Glicksman, 2012, p. 7). Long-time proponents of the free-market view of college sports, ESPN columnist and tenured sports journalist Michael Wilbon, and Allen Sack, a professor at the College of Business at the University of New Haven and member of the 1966 University of Notre Dame national championship football team, were voted the most valuable players (MVPs) for presenting compelling arguments in favor of paying student-athletes. The passage below summarizes the free-market view as explained by Sack (2009):

> No good reason exists for preventing athletes from engaging in the same entrepreneurial activities as their celebrity coaches. Big-time college athletes should be able to endorse products, get paid for speaking engagements and be compensated for the use of their likenesses on licensed products. They should be allowed to negotiate an actual contract with the N.B.A. as part of a final project in a finance class, and have an agent. These athletes are working their way through college by playing professional college sports. It is time to accept this reality and move on.

In addressing the audience, Wilbon (2011) confessed, "he used to argue vehemently against paying college athletes," believing "tuition, room, board and books were compensation enough." However, after the NCAA began receiving "$11 billion dollars for three weekends of television per year," he admittedly became interested not in "distributing the funds equitably or even paying every college athlete," but rather "in seeing the people who produce the revenue share a teeny, tiny slice of it." His stance is based in capitalism where "not everything is equal" or "fair." For example, "the most distinguished professor at the University of Alabama won't make $5.9 million in his entire tenure in Tuscaloosa," but "Nick Saban will make that this year." Accordingly, he supports a system where "the football and men's basketball players get paid," while "lacrosse, field hockey, softball, baseball, soccer players get nothing." In fact, a particularly convincing aspect of Wilbon's argument is his rebuttal for those who were not in favor of paying athletes because of the inability to do so "fairly":

> Using the inability to distribute the funds equally as an impediment is an excuse, a rather intellectually lazy one at that. Nothing about the way hundreds of millions of dollars is distributed is equitable or even fair. . . . . Of the $174 million distributed from five bowl games, 83.4 percent went to six conferences in 2011. . . . . So, the equitable-application excuse for not paying

athletes doesn't hold water; at the very least there's a level of hypocrisy here that ought to make the opponents of paying athletes uncomfortable.

(Wilbon, 2011)

To further illustrate his point, not only does Wilbon refute the claims of unfairness, but he also continues on to reframe the University of Georgia "scandal" in which the wide receiver on the football team sold his jersey for $1,000:

> If somebody is willing to give A. J. Green $750 or $1,000 or even $2,500 for his Georgia Bulldogs jersey, fine, good. If one of his teammates, a tackle, can fetch only $50 for his jersey, then it'll be a good marketing lesson for both of them. It's called supply and demand, and if both men are fortunate enough to reach the NFL it'll be a lesson worth learning because that dynamic will exist their entire careers. If a soccer player can't get a dime for his jersey, well, there's a realization in that, too.
>
> *(Wilbon, 2011)*

Here, Wilbon (2011), like Sack, alludes to the added value of engaging in a free market for student-athletes beyond their getting paid to play. As Ben Glicksman (2012) posits in *Game Change: Letting Student-Athletes Earn a Living*, allowing student-athletes to endorse products and use their fame to earn money would "teach them valuable lessons about economics" and "help keep players in school," by encouraging "more students to complete their degrees instead of leaving early to play professionally." Thus, he concludes, "if the NCAA truly puts the student first in student-athlete, then a change must be made to help keep players in school" (Glicksman, 2012, p. 13). Unfortunately, no such change was made.

The end of the OSU scandal makes an interesting case for why things remain as is. Though the NCAA alleges that the five OSU football players who violated the amateurism rules were allowed to postpone their suspension and play in the Sugar Bowl because they "did not receive adequate rules education during the time period the violations occurred" (NCAA, 2010), few believe these claims. Take, for instance, the response of Bob Hunter, a writer for the *Columbus Dispatch*:

> No columnist or commentator I've found can see the logic in the NCAA ruling permitting the Ohio State players to play in New Orleans and then sit out five games next season. The message that both instances send is that rules are interpreted differently when it means protecting TV and bowl partners that have become so lucrative for its member schools.
>
> *(Hunter, 2011)*

It would seem that the NCAA's stance around amateurism is hypocritical: while they continue to impose these outdated and exploitative rules on their student-athletes, they themselves are unwilling to prioritize these rules when ratings and profits are at stake. To be clear, the argument here is not whether profit should be the end goal, but rather for transparency around the revenue distribution model. If profit is indeed the end goal, then those creating the profits undoubtedly deserve to see, at minimum, a "teeny, tiny slice of it."

References

Bakalar, N. (2009, January 3). In BCS, dollars are the only relevant numbers. Retrieved from http://nyti.ms/2cNeJtm

Berkowitz, S., & Upton, J. (2011a, March 30). An analysis of salaries for college basketball coaches. Retrieved from http://usatoday30.usatoday.com/sports/college/mensbasketball/2011-coaches-salary-database.htm

Berkowitz, S., & Upton, J. (2011b, June 16). Money flows to college sports: Spending up amid schools' tight times. Retrieved from www.pressreader.com/usa/usa-today-international-edition/20110617/textview

Branch, T. (2011). The shame of college sports. *The Atlantic*, 308(3), 80–110.

Byers, W., & Hammer, C. (1997). *Unsportsmanlike conduct: Exploiting college athletes*. Ann Arbor: University of Michigan Press.

Clotfelter, C. T. (2011). *Big-time sports in American universities*. New York: Cambridge University Press.

Glicksman, B. (2012). Game change: Letting student-athletes earn a living. *Sports & Entertainment Law Journal*, 2(1), 1–25.

Greenberg, M. J., & Smith, J. S. (2007). A study of Division I assistant football and men's basketball coaches' contracts. *Marquette Sports Law Review*, 18(1), 25–99.

Huma, R., & Staurowsky, E. J. (2011). *The price of poverty in big time college sport*. Riverside, CA: National College Players Association.

Hunter, B. (2011, January 9). Delaying players' suspensions still seems dicey. Retrieved from www.dispatch.com/content/stories/sports/2011/01/09/delaying-players-suspensions-still-seems-dicey.html

McCormick, A., & McCormick, R. (2012). Race and interest convergence in NCAA sports. *Wake Forest Journal of Law & Policy*, 2(1), 17–43.

McCormick, R., & McCormick, A. (2010). Major college sports: A modern apartheid. *Texas Review of Entertainment & Sports Law*, 12(1), 12–51.

National Collegiate Athletic Association. (2010). NCAA requires loss of contests for six Ohio State football student-athletes. Retrieved from www.ncaa.org

National Collegiate Athletic Association. (2011a). *2012 NCAA Division I Manual: Constitution, operating bylaws, administrative bylaws*. Indianapolis, IN: Author.

National Collegiate Athletic Association. (2011b). The Ohio State University Public Infractions Report. Retrieved from www.ncaa.org

Ohio State Athletics. (2012). *The Ohio State University annual report concerning compliance and education program (Case No. M352)*. Columbus, OH: The Ohio State University.

O'Neil, D. (2011, October 25). Student-athletes ask: Will NCAA listen. Retrieved from www.espn.com/college-sports/story/_/id/7148175/ncaa-student-athletes-ask-cut-television-revenue-cover-school-costs

Oriard, M. (2009). *Bowled over: Big-time college football from the sixties to the BCS*. Chapel Hill: University of North Carolina Press.

Rhoden, W. C. (2007). *Forty million dollar slaves: The rise, fall, and redemption of the black athlete*. New York: Three Rivers Press.

Robinson, C., & Wetzel, D. (2011). Tressel knew of gear scheme last April. Retrieved from www.rivals.yahoo.com/ncaa/football/news

Sack, A. (2009, March 18). March money madness. Retrieved from http://roomfordebate.blogs.nytimes.com/2009/03/18/march-money-madness

Sandomir, R., & Thamel, P. (2010, April 22). TV deal pushes NCAA closer to 68-team tournament. Retrieved from http://nyti.ms/2cNfuCy

State Compensation Insurance Fund v. Industrial Commission, 314 P.2d 288, 135 Colo. 570(1957).

Thamel, P. (2011, September 9). With big paydays at stake, college teams scramble for a spot. Retrieved from http://nyti.ms/2cNffHQ

Tressel, J. (2011). Letter of resignation. Retrieved from http://media.cleveland.com/osu_impact/other/Tressel-resignation-letter.pdf

Upton, J., Gillum, J., & Berkowitz, S. (2010, April 12). Rising salaries of coaches force colleges to seek budget patch. Retrieved from http://usatoday30.usatoday.com/sports/college/mensbasketball/2010-04-01-coaches-salaries-cover_N.htm

U.S. Department of Justice. (2010). Letter to The Ohio State University Office of Legal Affairs. Retrieved from http://media.cleveland.com/osu_impact/other/OhioStateDOJletter.pdf

Wilbon, M. (2011). College athletes deserve to be paid. Retrieved from www.espn.com

Wilson, M. J., Schrager, M., Burke, K. L., Hawkins, B. J., & Gauntt, L. (2011). NCAA Division I men's basketball coaching contracts: A comparative analysis of incentives for athletic and academic team performance. *Journal of Issues in Intercollegiate Athletics*, 4(1), 396–410.

7

SUSPECT RECRUITING

The SUNY Binghamton Basketball Scandal

Collin D. Williams Jr.

During the tenures of University President Lois B. DeFleur and Athletics Director Dr. Joel Thirer, the State University of New York (SUNY) Binghamton men's basketball team became a full member of the National Collegiate Athletic Association (NCAA) Division I (DI). Despite other university officials' concerns about the financial impact of the transition and the potential effect on the institution's academic mission, the Bearcats entered into an affiliation with the America East Conference (AEC) in the 2001–2002 academic year. In 2004, continuing their pursuit of athletic prowess, Binghamton (BU) opened the Events Center, its $33.1 million facility that seats nearly 5,500 people. With it came increased pressure on the basketball program to compete at a high level and win. When the head coach, Al Walker, failed to do so in 2007, getting eliminated from the AEC quarterfinals, he was relieved of his coaching duties. As Georgetown's men's basketball team was on its way to its first Final Four appearance in more than twenty years, a press conference was held on March 26, 2007, to announce the hiring of one of its assistant coaches, Kevin Broadus, as the new BU head coach. Four days later, Pete Thamel, a *New York Times* writer, released an article detailing Broadus's role in recruiting a Georgetown basketball player who had been severely underprepared for college. After 12 failing grades and transferring to a school that the NCAA no longer recognizes, he barely received a diploma. Despite this allegation and the subsequent concerns expressed by other members of the AEC, Dr. Thirer assured the commissioner, Patrick Nero, that its reputation as SUNY's strongest academic institution would not be compromised, as he would personally supervise Coach Broadus and the men's basketball team. Just two years after being hired, Broadus helped his team tie the school record of 23 wins in a season. Tying for first place in the AEC, Broadus received the 2009 AEC Coach of the Year Award. The team, led by Emanuel Mayben, D.J. Rivera, and Reggie Fuller, defeated the University of Maryland, Baltimore County (UMBC) Retrievers 61–51 to capture their first conference tournament title in 63 years and secured a bid to the NCAA Tournament. Though they would go on to lose to second-seeded Duke in the first round, the Bearcats were AEC champions. They had won in dramatic fashion at the Events Center, and thousands of exuberant fans stormed their home court in support; however, celebration was soon met with clamor as, over the course of the next several months, the means through which Broadus and his coaching staff had achieved this seemingly miraculous success came to light (Thamel, 2009a).

The Case

The incessant unethical compromises that the BU administration made in their quest of athletic glory were exposed on February 11, 2010, when Judge Judith S. Kaye of Skadden, Arps, Slate, Meagher & Flom, LLP released a 99-page investigative report, chronicling in detail the suspect series of events that occurred between the 2007 and 2009 seasons (Kaye, 2010). The audit (Thamel, 2009f), lasting more than four months and costing more than $900,000, unveiled that several university officials – most notably President DeFleur, Athletic Director Thirer, and Coach Broadus and his coaching staff – had drastically lowered BU's admission criteria and thus jeopardized its academic pedigree as they readily recruited, admitted, and poorly advised a number of athletes who exhibited illicit behaviors and severe academic inadequacy (Kaye, 2010; Thamel, 2010a). The litany of academic and criminal infractions raises the question whether the administration was merely engaging in suspect recruiting or recruiting suspects (Moltz, 2010).

Suspect Recruiting

The first signs of Coach Broadus's dubious recruiting decisions came in fall 2007, when two talented but troubled guards were signed to letters of intent. The first, Emanuel Mayben, was an extremely successful high school player and a top college recruit; however, due to strong concerns about his scholastic underperformance and numerous suspensions, major programs like Syracuse, rumored to be pursuing him, lost interest. After a year at the University of Massachusetts, followed by a transfer to Hudson Valley Community College, Mayben signed with the Bearcats despite the potential risk. The second of these guards, Malik Alvin, also played at two different institutions – Chipola College and University of Texas, El Paso – eventually leaving the latter because of academic problems. When he landed at BU, the whispers in the AEC that arose after Mayben's signing loudened.

When Theus Davis, a Canadian transfer from Gonzaga who was dismissed from the university because of substance abuse, signed with BU in January 2008, the rumblings in the AEC turned into legitimate concern. Several coaches and athletic directors in the AEC called Commissioner Nero who, after questioning Athletic Director Thirer, was assured that the testing mechanisms in place at BU were more than capable of handling drug-related issues.

A month later, BU was again the subject of concerned discussion within the AEC when, after a game, Broadus himself was involved in an altercation with Will Brown, an assistant coach from the University of Albany. While in the hand-shaking line, the two coaches exchanged words that led to a brief physical altercation; Broadus instigated the incident, which was caught on video and quickly made public via YouTube. For his actions, Binghamton suspended Broadus for one game.

The spotlight of skepticism was again on BU's program in May 2008, when another controversial player was admitted. Transfer D.J. Rivera was another guard and top high school recruit who, during his two years of play at St. Joseph's in Philadelphia, PA, had to forego a semester because of academic issues. When Rivera became immediately eligible to play for BU without sitting out the standard year, some in the AEC were cynical about how this decision was made and were again critical of the Bearcats program.

Amid the external scrutiny, BU also faced internal conflict, as many of the players, several not mentioned above, were seen as undesirable by the admissions personnel. Despite the admissions office's reluctance and, at times, outright refusal, Broadus found discrete ways to get his recruits in the door through innovative arrangements such as "conditional admittances." Admitting a student but only allowing said student to be fully enrolled after demonstrating adequate classroom performance may have been a novel idea, but such action would only be advantageous to the student and university were the proper infrastructure in place to nurture the student's academic development. In actuality, this probationary program served as a way to ease the concerns of the admissions office. Once students entered the door, little structure existed and, consequently, struggling athletes only persisted because of preferential treatment and academic favoritism. These recruiting tactics would prove to be a win for the basketball team but not the individuals on it.

In early 2009, BU was again in the press. On February 22, Pete Thamel, the *New York Times* writer who authored the cautionary piece just days after Broadus's hiring, released an even more caustic article that delved deep into the suspect activity at BU. It addressed the cost of BU's move to DI, the lowering of their admission criteria to the NCAA minimum requirement, the pressure placed on academics as a result, Coach Broadus's questionable recruiting, and the suspect academic and behavioral problems of a number of BU's talented players. On March 16th, ESPN's *Outside the Lines* aired a special episode, "Binghamton in the Big Time" (2009), to examine the recent occurrences, featuring a three-person panel – Thamel, Thirer, and Tom Brennan, an ESPN analyst – facilitated by host Bob Ley. A month later, Broadus signed another academically underprepared student, initially deemed inadmissible, with a GPA well below a 2.0. Growing concerned, the director of compliance, David Eagan, expressed his discomfort with the team's operations in August, pressuring Thirer to rein in Coach Broadus. Thirer agreed to address it. Within the next two weeks though, Corey Chandler, a recruit suspended from another DI program because of academic issues, joined BU's team. That year, after claiming the AEC championship and regularly circumventing critique seemingly unscathed (Thamel, 2010c), the Bearcats appeared to be winning on all levels; however, the team's streak came to an end in September, when, in less than a month, four incidents led to the dismissal of six of its players.

Recruiting Suspects

In fall 2009, a frightening series of events finally signaled to various BU stakeholders that the Bearcats program was out of control. While the recruiting activity chronicled above shines light on the rampant academic issues related to many of the student-athletes who Broadus recruited, what follows summarizes the delinquent and criminal behavior of a number of BU student-athletes.

Prior to the fall of 2009, incidents involving BU basketball players left several people seriously injured. First, on May 4, 2008, a BU basketball player, Miladin Kovacevic, was arrested for leaving a fellow BU student in a coma after assaulting him at a bar in downtown Binghamton. After Kovacevic fled the country and returned to his native Serbia, the university had little to no means to properly discipline him (Barron, 2010). He was a fugitive; however, the same cannot be said about Malik Alvin. On October 26, 2008, Alvin – signed by Coach Broadus the year before – collided with and injured a 66-year-old woman while attempting to steal condoms from a Wal-Mart. This scenario provided the first setting in which Broadus and his coaching staff could, through appropriate discipline, set a precedent for what types of behavior would and would not be condoned; this did not happen. After a three-game suspension, Alvin was fully reinstated. There is no evidence of any other punishment. Despite those two incidents, little attention was paid to the behavior problems of many Bearcats players (Kaye, 2010).

On September 7, 2009, after responding to complaints about marijuana odor, BU police found David Fine, a BU basketball player, high in his dorm room with remnants of a marijuana cigarette and two additional grams of the drug. Fine was reported but not arrested. Less than a week later, on September 13, a BU police officer pulled over Fine's teammate, Emanuel Mayben, for speeding and discovered a marijuana cigarette in the car as well as a baggie with more marijuana on Mayben. When questioned, Mayben alleged that the car belonged to Fine. Mayben was issued a speeding ticket and a court appearance for illegal possession. The very next day, a BU student reported that her debit card had been stolen and used to make unauthorized purchases. The investigation revealed that BU basketball players D.J. Rivera, Malik Alvin, Paul Crosby, and Corey Chandler were the culprits (Kaye, 2010). The players involved had conspired to have Rivera take the fall for the whole thing; however, due to discrepancies in their initial accounts, the police did not believe any of their claims. Kaye (2010) later discovered that the players involved in this incident, and Mayben, after his ticket, had received prohibited legal counsel from members of the coaching staff. Though President DeFleur was notified of all of these occurrences, none of the involved players were dismissed, only subjected to varying suspensions. This changed hastily on September 23, 2009, when police arrested Emanuel Mayben for selling crack cocaine in Troy, NY (Thamel, 2009c). The institution was now forced to act quickly and forcibly. Both President

DeFleur and Dr. Thirer, the parties arguably most responsible for the persistence of these behaviors (Thamel, 2010a), issued two separate statements, both of which declared that BU "[would] not tolerate this type of behavior" (Thamel, 2009d). On September 24, Mayben was permanently dismissed from the team for his infraction (Thamel, 2009d). To further send a message that such behavior was unacceptable, BU also permanently dismissed D.J. Rivera, Malik Alvin, Paul Crosby, Corey Chandler, and David Fine on September 25 (Thamel, 2009b; 2009e). Their infractions, however, were not disclosed and BU personnel made no further comment after Broadus announced their dismissal. Interestingly, the next comment to be made about the Bearcat program came from Sally Dear, a lecturer in human development at BU. On September 29, she alleged that the university was letting her go because she had refused to give preferential treatment to athletes in her classroom (Kaye, 2010). By the end of September, the BU team and those who governed it were shrouded in controversy and turmoil.

The Aftermath

On October 2, BU hired Judge Kaye and her firm to conduct an audit of the program and the resignations of various university administrators (Thamel, 2009f). In her investigation, Kaye found that there were differing accounts of how Thirer's resignation came about, but two things were certain: On September 30, he was reassigned to the Office of the Provost, and he was not the last administrator to suffer repercussions for what Kaye (2010) dubbed "a lack of oversight" (Sander, 2010). Coach Broadus, on October 14, was suspended indefinitely with pay before ultimately resigning two weeks later, on October 29. Assistant coaches Hsu and Allen, allegedly responsible for some combination of providing legal counsel, conspiring in lies to BU police, and providing transportation and cash for players, were fired midseason (Kaye, 2010). In January, President DeFleur also announced her retirement (O'Neil, 2010). With a decimated coaching staff and player roster, the Bearcats ultimately forfeited postseason play in 2010 (Thamel, 2010b).

Sociocultural Context

> For almost a century, big-time college sport has been a wildly popular but consistently problematic part of American higher education. The challenges it poses to traditional academic values have been recognized from the start, but they have grown more ominous in recent decades, as cable television has become ubiquitous, commercial opportunities have proliferated and athletic budgets have ballooned.
>
> *(Clotfelter, 2011)*

To understand the ethical and academic compromises that occurred at BU, one must understand that, within the enterprise of revenue generating, or "big-time," DI basketball and football programs, behavior similar to what occurred in the BU scandal is neither uncharacteristic nor unprecedented.

Scandals in college sports both predated the NCAA's formation and would continue after it. For example, the very first intercollegiate match was an 1852 independently sponsored boat race in which Harvard attempted to best its academic rival Yale by fielding a player who was not a student (Smith, 2000). In 1929, a report by Carnegie Foundation exposed 81 of 112 schools surveyed were paying their athletes (Savage, Bentley, McGovern, & Smiley, 1929). By 1948, embarrassed of its failure to control the rampant corruption in college sports, the NCAA enacted a "Sanity Code," prohibiting schools from paying these academically suspect athletes beyond tuition, room, and board, providing the framework for what is now known as the athletic scholarship (Branch, 2011). The term student-athlete would be created in the following decade to further prevent players from being identified as employees as well as emphasize their questionable statuses as students. In response to "the dreaded notion that athletes could be identified as employees by state industrial commissions and the courts," Walter Byers, the former executive director of the NCAA, "crafted the term student-athlete, and soon it was embedded in all NCAA rules and interpretations as a mandated substitute for words as players and athletes" (Byers & Hammer, 1997, p. 69).

Much of the literature on big-time sports in American colleges and universities has addressed the bevy of extant academic and ethical compromises (Axthelm, 1980; Pappano, 2012; Underwood, 1980). These include falsified transcripts by colleges, athletes receiving credit for courses not taken, and the financial and academic exploitation of athletes (Hanford, 1979). In their study at a western university, accounting for more than 2,000 athletes over the course of ten years, Purdy, Eitzen, and Hufnagel (1982) found that scholarship holders, Blacks, and participants in the major revenue-producing sports of football and basketball had the poorest academic potential and performance. As scholarship-holding Black males are the largest demographic in big-time college sports, the regularly cited exploitation of college athletes most frequently refers to them.

Black Male Student-Athletes and Racial Inequities in NCAA Division I College Sports (Harper, Williams, & Blackman, 2013) juxtaposes the graduation rates and representation of Black male student-athletes with those of student-athletes overall, undergraduate students overall, and Black undergraduate men overall to make transparent the racial disparities within the NCAA's six most lucrative and competitive conferences. At these 76 institutions, Harper, Williams and Blackman (2013) found that, between 2007 and 2010, Black male student-athletes only represented 2.7 percent of full-time, degree-seeking undergraduate students, but 57.1 percent of football teams and 64.3 percent of basketball teams. Disaggregating the data by sport, race, and gender, the report also revealed that, across four cohorts, only 50.2 percent of Black male student-athletes graduated within six years, compared to 66.9 percent of student-athletes overall, 72.8 percent of undergraduate students overall, and 55.5 percent of Black undergraduate men overall. Recognizing the problems of the underrepresentation of Black men in the undergraduate student population at predominantly White colleges and universities, their overrepresentation on revenue-generating NCAA Division I sports teams, and their comparatively lower six-year graduation rates are pervasive, Harper (2006) asserts, "Perhaps nowhere in higher education is the disenfranchisement of Black male students more insidious than in college athletics" (p. 6). Despite the appallingly preferential treatment athletes receive – tutors, attendance waivers, extensions, and grade curving – many still struggle to acquire college credentials.

Purdy et al. (1982) posited that inherent in this issue is that the policing body, the NCAA, focuses more on payment of athletes and amateurism infractions than inferior education matters, reiterating Hanford's (1978) argument that we are amid "an educational dilemma concerning the place and mission of athletics within our intellectual estates by mixing dollar values with educational ones" (p. 232). Clotfelter (2011 in Barnes, 2011, p. 1) agrees, claiming, "The biggest source of trouble for college sports is the NCAA's insistence that athletes remain unpaid amateurs." He continues, "Coaches desperate for stars to keep programs competitive will, with the help of eager alumni, do almost anything to sign players and keep them happy. New cars, rent-free apartments and no-show jobs are some of the inducements" (Clotfelter, 2011 in Barnes, 2011, p. 1). While revenue generation is the source of much of the controversy in college sports, there is more to the story.

Beyond issues of commercialism, Lindo, Swensen, and Waddell (2011) discovered a negative correlation between collegiate football success and non-athlete academic performance. They found that males, more significantly than females, respond to winning teams with high levels of partying and alcohol consumption and less studying. Accordingly, some have concluded that, in universities with major sports programs, the corruption of academic ideals is endemic (Eitzen & Sage, 1982).

At the end of the investigation, Kaye (2010) submitted several principal findings and recommendations, examining the most salient problems within the Bearcats program under Broadus's leadership. These included the lowering of admission standards, the lack of timely and effective academic support services, insufficient responses to allegations of misbehavior, the mishandling of the Sally Dear allegation, and the general lack of oversight of the basketball program (Sander, 2010).

The increased pressure to compete at a winning level within DI athletics helped to cultivate a culture in which Coach Broadus could reduce BU's admissions standards to the NCAA minimum for the basketball team. The minimum is principally meant for less academically rigorous institutions and, at BU, the admissions criteria were traditionally only broken on occasion. Broadus, with the "experimental" approval of Thirer and DeFleur, claimed complete autonomy over admissions decisions, repeatedly resisting decisions made by the admissions office, enlisting other administrators to assist in overturning admissions office decisions, circumventing the admissions liaison with whom they were to communicate about all such matters, and essentially doing whatever it took to enroll the underprepared athletes he desired. With lowered admissions standards came an influx of athletes who were not prepared for the academic rigor of most AEC schools, much less that of a standout like BU. Though steps were taken to assist in the remediation of these athletes, these steps were all reactionary rather than preemptive and implemented too late to achieve the desired academic outcomes.

Perhaps the most salient issue in the entire scandal is the way in which the institutional leaders responded to the allegations of misbehavior. Forcibly procured texts and emails revealed that the coaching staff assisted in, and in some cases coordinated, the corroboration of false accounts of events, and intervened in criminal cases. In Kaye's words, they "contributed to a culture in which damage control was emphasized at the expense of constructive discipline and personal responsibility" (Kaye, 2010, p. 93).

The investigation found that Sally Dear was the only lecturer to report having been pressured by the athletic department, though not enough evidence was found to hold either party culpable for any unapproved behaviors. However, that nothing was done, even after Ms. Dear's allegation of near harassment by the athletic department, shows that there was a lack of appropriate institutional procedures. In fact, one administrator went as far as to review emails and documents and conclude that Ms. Dear's allegations were unfounded without ever speaking to her directly. Despite the potentially dubious claims of Ms. Dear, an appropriate response would have at least included a conversation with her to address and alleviate concerns.

The above points converge to indicate a general lack of oversight within the Bearcats program (Kaye, 2010; Sander, 2010). They demonstrate a lack of checks and balances inside and outside of the athletic department. For these reasons, Kaye recommended that BU establish a more active role for the Intercollegiate Athletic Committee (IAC) and Intercollegiate Athletic Board (IAB) in oversight and control of the athletics program as well as the appointment of an athletic oversight officer (Barr, 2010). Still, when considering the rate at which these types of infractions occur across big-time sports programs, BU seems uncomfortably normal.

Alternate Ending

With a contextualized understanding of the larger enterprise of revenue-generating college sports and its myriad problems, rewriting an ethically sound end to the BU case would involve a holistic remodeling of the entire athletic landscape. Primary considerations, for example, would ideally include consistent admissions standards for student-athletes, greater compensation for participation in intercollegiate athletics, and a set of accountability measures that would maintain the espoused balance between academics and athletics. As these lofty goals are improbable, I offer a set of chronological recommendations of how the situation, within the existing sociocultural context, might have been handled differently.

Recognizing BU's rational desire to compete within DI and win, as well as the necessity of lowering admissions standards to recruit and admit elite talent, the first recommendation would be for the institutional agents to be forthright about athletes' lack of preparation and provide the academic structures required to get them on par with their non-athlete peers. As amateurism prevents student-athletes from receiving compensation beyond athletic scholarships – despite them garnering publicity, fostering school pride, providing entertainment, and generating billions of dollars in revenue (Sylwester & Witosky, 2004) – the institutions they attend should make access to and actualization of the lifelong benefits of a quality education the primary form of payment for athletes' efforts. As Figler (1981 in Leonard, 1986, p. 40) asserts, a college athlete is exploited when "he is recruited into the college setting without possessing the necessary abilities or background to have a reasonable chance of succeeding academically."

Beyond providing timely and effective academic support, another recommendation is timely and effective discipline for behavioral infractions, for players, coaches and others involved in athletics. For each infraction leading up to the peddling of crack cocaine – violence, drug use, speeding, and theft – BU staff not only missed opportunity after opportunity to hold students accountable but also, by covering much of it up, contributed to a culture of misbehavior without repercussion.

Similarly, only one player, Emanuel Mayben, should have been permanently expelled from the university; the sale of crack cocaine is simply inexcusable. Though all guilty of criminal acts, the other five athletes suffered penalties worse than the institutional leaders who enabled them. Before their teammate's arrest, there was no indication of any punishment for the other men involved in the slew of events that took place in September 2009, which supports two of the literature's claims, namely that athletes do in fact receive preferential treatment, and misbehavior is commonplace among them. If their behavior was not such a big deal at first, why did it ultimately result in the academic death penalty for these athletes? Removal from the team, even if severe, was warranted, but expulsion was unnecessary and, arguably, even more problematic, strategically reactionary. Their dismissals were used as examples of enforcing programmatic boundaries that clearly never existed before and were really a last-minute effort to cover the tracks of the stakeholders – DeFleur, Thirer, and Broadus – who had handled the program sloppily for two years and knew that the gavel would ultimately fall on them.

Whereas the players were all expelled, severely limiting their chances to ever receive another opportunity at a postsecondary education or actualize their academic or athletic aspirations, DeFleur, Thirer, and Broadus were all allowed to resign. Clearly, there is a stark disparity in college sports in who gets treated with consideration and who does not. The central issue in the handling of this case, I contend, is that disparate amounts of blame were placed on the actors. Ironically, the suspects are seemingly the victims as well. Oftentimes, the administrators who actively engage in unethical behaviors and those who turn their heads the other way – all of whom should be held accountable – go insufficiently punished, when and if disciplined at all. This further illustrates that athletic departments, even when committing what appear to be inexcusable infractions, are actually acting on behalf of one of the universities' competing interests, achieving greater success in revenue-generating sports programs. Only when these behaviors become blatant, specifically, when they have become public, does it seem that universities choose to be committed to their academic and ethical ideals by thoroughly reprimanding administrators who behaved unethically. With such suspect standards in place for practitioners, those employed to uphold and enforce institutions' missions, it comes as little surprise that the students conduct themselves in the ways that they do.

References

Axthelm, P. (1980, September 22). The shame of college sports. *Newsweek*, pp. 54–59.

Barnes, F. (2011, April 23). Calculating the Score. Retrieved from https://sites.duke.edu/bigtimesports/2011/04/fred-barnes-the-wall-street-journal

Barr, J. (2010, February 12). Report recommends "oversight officer". Retrieved from http://sports.espn.go.com

Barron, J. (2010, September 13). Guilty plea is expected in beating of classmate. Retrieved from http://www.nytimes.com

Branch, T. (2011). The shame of college sports. Retrieved from http://www.theatlantic.com/magazine/archive/2011/10/the-shame-of-college-sports/308643

Byers, W., & Hammer, C. (1997). *Unsportsmanlike conduct: Exploiting college athletes*. Ann Arbor: University of Michigan Press.

Clotfelter, C. T. (2011). *Big-time sports in American universities*. New York: Cambridge University Press.

Eitzen, D. S., & Sage, G. H. (1982). *The sociology of American sport*. Dubuque, IA: William C. Brown.

ESPN. (2009). Binghamton in the Big Time [Television series episode]. In *Outside the Lines*. Bristol, CT: ESPN.

Figler, S. K. (1981). *Sport and Play in American Life*. Philadelphia: Saunders College Publishing.

Hanford, G. H. (1978). Intercollegiate athletics today and tomorrow: The president's challenge. *Educational Record*, 57(4), 232–235.

Hanford, G. H. (1979). Controversies in college sports. *The Annals of the American Academy of Political and Social Science*, 445(1), 66–79.

Harper, S. R. (2006). *Black male students at public flagship universities in the U.S.: Status, trends and implications for policy and practice*. Washington, DC: Joint Center for Political and Economic Studies.

Harper, S. R., Williams, C. D., & Blackman, H. W. (2013). *Black male student-athletes and racial inequities in NCAA Division I college sports*. Philadelphia, PA: University of Pennsylvania, Center for the Study of Race and Equity in Education.

Kaye, J. (2010). *Report to the Board of Trustees of the State University of New York*. New York: Skadden, Arps, Slate, Meagher, & Flom, LLP.

Leonard, W.M. (1986). The sports experience of the black college athlete: Exploitation in the academy. *International Review for the Sociology of Sport*, 21(1), 35–49.

Lindo, J. M., Swensen, I. D., & Waddell, G. R. (2011). Are big-time sports a threat to student achievement? NBER Working Paper 17677, Cambridge, MA.

Moltz, D. (2010, February 12). Bad news Binghamton. Retrieved from www.insidehighered.com

O'Neil, D. (2010, January 20). Bearcats try to move on after turmoil. Retrieved from http://sports.espn.go.com

Pappano, L. (2012, January 20). How big-time sports ate college life. Retrieved from www.nytimes.com

Purdy, D. A., Eitzen, D. S., & Hufnagel, R. (1982). Are athletes also students? The educational attainment of college athletes. *Social Problems*, 29(4), 439–448.

Sander, L. (2010, February 11). Report faults Binghamton U. for weak oversight of athletics. Retrieved from http://chronicle.com

Savage, H. J., Bentley, H. W., McGovern, J. T., & Smiley, D. F. (1929). *American college athletics bulletin number twenty-three*. New York: The Carnegie Foundation for the Advancement of Teaching.

Smith, R. K. (2000). A brief history of the National Collegiate Athletic Association's role in regulating intercollegiate athletics. *Marquette Sports Law Review*, 11(1), 9–22.

Sylwester, M., & Witosky, T. (2004, February 18). Athletic spending grows as academic funds dry up. Retrieved from http://usatoday30.usatoday.com/sports/college/2004-02-18-athletic-spending-cover_x.htm

Thamel, P. (2009a, February 21). At Binghamton, Division I move brings recognition and regret. Retrieved from www.nytimes.com

Thamel, P. (2009b, March 8). In America east, a statement is made. Retrieved from http://thequad.blogs.nytimes.com

Thamel, P. (2009c, September 23). Binghamton player arrested on charges of selling cocaine. Retrieved from www.nytimes.com

Thamel, P. (2009d, September 24). Mayben kicked off Binghamton basketball team after arrest. Retrieved from www.nytimes.com

Thamel, P. (2009e, September 25). Binghamton cuts five more players as concerns grow. Retrieved from www.nytimes.com

Thamel, P. (2009f, October 2). SUNY board to oversee an audit of Binghamton. Retrieved from www.nytimes.com

Thamel, P. (2010a, February 11). Report faults Binghamton's leaders in scandal. Retrieved from www.nytimes.com

Thamel, P. (2010b, March 1). Binghamton skips conference tournament. Retrieved from www.nytimes.com

Thamel, P. (2010c, October 18). Binghamton avoids major sanctions. Retrieved from www.nytimes.com/2010/10/19/sports/ncaabasketball/19binghamton.html

Underwood, J. (1980, May 19). The writing is on the wall. Retrieved from www.si.com/vault/1980/05/19/824666/the-writing-is-on-the-wall-the-rash-of-phony-transcripts-and-academic-cheating-spells-out-the-fact-that-athletics-are-now-an-abomination-to-the-ideals-of-higher-education-victims-the-student-athletes-culprits-the-system-and-thos

8

COVERING UP MURDER

The Death of Patrick Dennehy at Baylor University

Karen Weaver

In 2012, Baylor University was on top of the world. The once quiet, academically focused Baptist campus in Waco, Texas, found it had hit the trifecta in college sports. Its quarterback, Robert Griffin III, had been named a Heisman Trophy winner. Brittany Griner, the 6'8" basketball start and 2012 Olympic team member, led the Lady Bears to an amazing 40–0 record and the second NCAA Championship in school history. Griner dominated women's basketball as no woman had since Diana Tarausi did for the University of Connecticut a decade before. The men's basketball team finished the year 30–8, losing to eventual national champion Kentucky in the Elite Eight (Bishop, 2012). Locals were giddy with excitement and their newfound accolades. Today, top athletes are flocking to West Texas for the opportunity to play for the Baylor Bears. Making a bowl game in football each year? A given. Now their sights are set much higher: former regent and prominent lobbyist Buddy Jones told the *New York Times*: "I told the athletic director at Texas, we want to grow up and be you guys."

Baylor University was a much different place prior to 2003. A classic bottom feeder in the perennially powerful Big 12 Conference since its entry in 1996, the University underwent a renaissance guided by an ambitious and visionary president, Robert Sloan. Athletic facilities were sprouting up all over campus; athletic director Tom Stanton hired highly successful women's basketball coach Kim Mulkey from Louisiana Tech to replace the legendary Sonja Hogg; Mulkey had made her name as an All American and head coach at Louisiana. He also hired Matt Knoll to lead the men's tennis program. Both would produce Baylor's first ever national championships not long after they were hired. Then Stanton hired Dave Bliss to revive a moribund men's basketball program relegated to the basement of the Big 12. At the time, Bliss was considered to be a "phenomenal hire," one that would lead Baylor men's basketball into the national spotlight. He did – just not in the way that anyone expected.

The Case

Bliss arrived on campus in 1999 and immediately made a positive impression. Bliss had built a reputation as a "reformer" over his 28 years of coaching. He was a coach willing to give athletes a "second chance" if they were kicked out of a program. He believed that the athlete had simply wandered away from the flock and if he received enough teaching and preaching, he might be able to be saved. In the coaching fraternity, he was connected – his first job came from Bob Knight at Indiana University. Including stops at Oklahoma, Southern Methodist (SMU), and New Mexico, Bliss had always remained employed despite the fact that he had left both the SMU and New Mexico programs in shambles (Dohrmann, 2003). He left behind at SMU a litany of NCAA violations, including a booster who had illegally paid former basketball players. While at New Mexico, two of his players were implicated in a theft that was ultimately covered up by campus police; only when the local media discovered that it had not been reported to the district attorney's office did Bliss respond – by suspending the players for one game. In 1998, another player, while entertaining a recruit, was detained by local police for firing a gun in the air while driving the recruit around town. Bliss commented to the local paper: "If every basketball player . . . that had a gun gave up their eligibility, we'd have fewer players." The die had been cast.

One year later, Baylor's athletic director, Tom Stanton, recruited Bliss. Baylor nearly doubled his annual salary to $600,000. He arrived to a program that had been 0–12 in the Big 12 and 6–24 overall; but the reformer had arrived to change Baylor's luck. True to form, he immediately went after junior college and four-year college transfers; in his first five years, he recruited 21 transfers (Dohrmann, 2003). Many who came to play also brought guns and a drug habit. Marijuana use was rampant on the team; athletic department personnel found out through drug testing who on the team had been using drugs, but Bliss did not follow department guidelines to discipline his players.

One of the transfers who arrived was Carlton Dotson; he came from Paris (TX) Junior College. Another transfer, from New Mexico, Patrick Dennehy, joined the team in 2002–2003. Dennehy was required to sit out his first year at Baylor, which meant he could not play. Dennehy had been kicked off of New Mexico's team the previous year despite being named to the All-Mountain West Conference team. The 6'10" forward dreamed of playing in the NBA and was looking for a fresh start. Over the next couple of months, Dennehy and Dotson became fast friends and occasional roommates.

At the end of his redshirt year, in June 2003, Dennehy, accompanied by Dotson, went to a gravel pit to shoot targets (USA Today, 2005a). They had bought guns because, according to Dotson, they had received phone calls threatening their safety. Despite a dozen or so reporters following this story, no one has been able to substantiate from whom these calls came. June became July, and suddenly no one had heard from Patrick. Dennehy's family became especially worried when he did not contact his dad on Father's Day. Family members began calling the Baylor coaching staff and players, asking if anyone knew where their son was. Weeks went by before a break came. Suddenly on July 20, Dotson called the state police from his home in Maryland and told them he "was hearing voices" and told them where they could find the body of Patrick Dennehy in Waco, Texas (Wiley, 2003). The police found Dennehy's SUV in Virginia, just over the Maryland state line, with the license plates removed and not far from Dotson's rural home town. The SUV had last been seen 1,200 miles west in Waco.

Maryland State Police contacted officials in Waco and told them where to look for Dennehy's body. What they found was stunning and gruesome – he had been decapitated and there were two gunshot wounds to the head (Wiley, 2003). Dotson was arrested and immediately jailed. Soon after, a Dallas Morning News intern maneuvered her way into the jailhouse to ask Dotson the question everyone wanted to know: "Why did you do it?" Ralph Wiley, a writer for *Sports Illustrated*, explained Dotson's reply this way: "Carlton Dotson told [the intern] that if somebody drew down on you with a piece, then pulled the trigger, and it didn't fire, or misfired, what would you do?"

Dotson had little in the way of a future in front of him. Wiley wrote:

> Carlton Dotson had no car, no money, no future at Baylor; his scholarship had been revoked; his wife cut short their brief union in part because Dotson was "hearing voices," according to his ex-mother-in-law, who reported this to Baylor coaches. In fact, Dotson had seen a psychiatrist.
>
> *(2003)*

Dotson's attorneys told the court that he was incompetent to stand trial (The State of Texas v. Dotson, 2003; USA Today, 2005a).

Meanwhile, back on Baylor's campus, strange things began to happen. An internal review committee had uncovered illegal tuition payments made to the accounts of two Baylor basketball players, one of whom was Dennehy. Investigators confronted Bliss to ask him what he knew. Bliss began to tell a bizarre tale – he told the investigators, his assistants, and several of his players to lie to NCAA and Baylor authorities about the source of the funds. Bliss told them to paint Dennehy as a drug dealer and that they had "seen him with a 'tray' containing a variety of drugs and $100 bills." One of Bliss's assistants, newly hired Director of Basketball Operations Abar Rouse, was extremely uncomfortable with what Bliss was doing. Deciding that no one would believe him if he revealed Bliss's plans, he met with the head coach and surreptitiously taped the conversation. When the tapes were made public a few days later, Kirk Watson, in-house counsel for Baylor, had this to say: "The tapes reveal a desperate man trying to figure out how to cover himself and to cover up" NCAA violations (Washington Times, 2003).

Bliss resigned on August 8, 2003, one day after attending Dennehy's funeral. Several newspapers contacted Bliss when this new narrative emerged. His comments were telling: "The bizarre circumstances painted me into a corner and I chose the wrong way to react. I have cooperated completely and will continue to do so because I have disappointed a lot of people" (Washington Times, 2003). Baylor's president, Robert Sloan, announced the resignations of Bliss and Athletic Director Tom Stanton on the same afternoon. He also announced the following: Baylor would self-impose a probation for no less than two years; the men's basketball team would not participate in the 2003–04 Big 12 or NCAA tournaments; remaining players on the team who wished to transfer would be immediately given their release; and an overhaul of the drug-testing system on campus, including who administered the tests and who was informed of the results, would take place immediately.

Two years after the shooting, in June 2005, Dotson was sentenced to 35 years in prison. Dennehy's mother has vowed to attend all future parole hearings to make sure "Dotson doesn't walk the streets again" (USA Today, 2005a; Moore, 2005). In August 2005, the NCAA put Baylor on five years' probation and pronounced a "show cause" order for former head coach Bliss and two former assistant coaches. A "show cause" order means that if any of these men were to seek employment as a coach at another NCAA institution they would be required, along with their new employer, to meet with the NCAA and demonstrate why they should be hired. The order was in place until 2015 for Bliss and his former assistants (USA Today, 2005b). Today, Bliss works as the athletics director and Dean of Students at Allen Academy in Bryan, Texas. Abar Rouse, the Baylor alumnus and assistant who secretly taped the conversation with Bliss, has been unable to find another coaching job.

Sociocultural Context

Too often, coaches are held up as the saviors and father figures for young men who are fatherless and have no male role models in their lives. James Duderstadt mentions this challenge in his book *Intercollegiate Athletics and the American University* (2003). Duderstadt calls this separation between the athletic department and the rest of the college campus a battle over "feudal kingdoms" (p. 204), which results in athletic directors and some coaches isolating the student-athlete's experience from typical student life. Some of this is a function of athletics as an auxiliary enterprise (read: self-financed), and some of it has to do with coaches wanting to maintain strict control over their charges. Duderstadt, a former president at the University of Michigan, writes: "Their time, their experiences, their friends, and even their studies are dominated by athletics, if not directly by their coaches" (p. 204).

Duderstadt addresses the issue of isolationism as a fundamental flaw in the kingdom of athletics, particularly among minority students. Rather than encouraging minority athletes to engage and interact with other students (White and other ethnicities), athletics discourages the broader interaction of multicultural students. In an era where colleges and universities are beginning to ask hard questions about the roles race and ethnicity play in the lives of students, faculty, staff, and academic programs, athletics perpetuates the segregation of minorities into narrow silos.

The larger questions surrounding the culture that Bliss and other coaches created include whether athletics at the Division I level can truly be called a holistic experience for a student-athlete. Some of the more recent literature on campus cultures and student development provides new streams of thought on the value of student-affairs personnel receiving training to learn how to approach a student on a variety of levels, not just as an athlete. Harper and Antonio (2008) state that "deep learning about power, privilege, and social injustice [is] unlikely to occur through fun exercises with short-lived opportunities for processing and trivial reflection" (p. 5). Athletic departments have relegated these kinds of activities to freshmen seminars and the NCAA-mandated Student Athlete Advisory Councils but rarely engage students on anything substantial (Duderstadt, 2003).

Griffin, Nichols, Peréz, and Tuttle (2008) explain this concept in more detail. Minorities attending primarily White institutions (PWI) need to be engaged in campus life from the moment that they arrive on campus for orientation. Leadership opportunities and student groups and activities all need to be presented as inclusive and welcoming (p. 126). Student-affairs personnel are encouraged to introduce the incoming students to minority leaders, building a peer-support system that can be valuable in the first few weeks of trying to "fit in." In revenue-generating programs, schools such as Baylor orient their student-athletes much differently; besides the usual introductions of "who's who" in the athletics department and NCAA compliance paperwork and drug-testing information, little, if any, time is spent talking about life outside the athletic department. It is as if the academic world were an entirely separate entity. Indeed, academic counselors employed by the athletic department are charged with monitoring a student-athlete's academic conflicts, not the racially challenging environment he or she may be navigating as a minority at a PWI.

Athletic departments also demonstrate precious little interest in engaging parents of student-athletes, other than to be sure they have tickets to the game and know where the team is staying. Helping the parents understand the challenging environment their sons and daughters are negotiating while providing education and information to them about how to be supportive would seem to be critical, yet few, if any, Division I athletics programs have created this type of information flow (Griffin et al., 2008).

Hill and Magolda (2008) write about the collegiate "subcultures" that exist on campuses, and you do not have to look far to see the divide. Members of political clubs rarely interact with the theater group; fraternities and sororities rarely hang out with athletic teams. If these subcultures engage each other in "superficial" ways, and without planned and structured exercises, they will rarely debate sensitive and personal topics. Within the athletics department, many different subcultures exist: male and female athletes, the sport culture itself, perhaps those groups who share a common locker room or weight-training facility, even those who are injured and in the athletic training room each day. But the lack of discourse among these groups reinforces the status quo – it simply is not safe to reach outside your group to discuss "hot topics" (p. 251).

To create an academic community that embraces differences and encourages discussions around power, privilege, and access would be risky. Encouraging socializing and deep discussions among athletic subcultures (or any other subculture) requires that student-athletes be given the direction, power, permission, and physical space to break down these old stereotypes. Conversations would need to be substantive and could include issues such as socioeconomic challenges, gender biases, equity, and a democratic sharing of ideas (p. 257). Contrast those concepts with Coach Bliss's idea of "saving souls"; if student-athletes were given the tools to start thinking about these larger issues, they may not need to have been saved. Athletics departments that are isolated from the rest of the college community do not have the human capital to address these concerns; the personnel are focused on winning and revenue generation.

Alternate Ending

Had Dave Bliss and the Baylor athletics program understood how difficult the transition to a new campus might be for student-athletes, and had programming been made available to them to help them integrate into a new culture as transfer students, perhaps Dotson, Dennehy, and other players would not have felt so alone. The culture of Division I sports promotes an isolationist mentality amongst the athletes and coaches – the belief is simple: the more time teammates spend together, the more cohesive they will be as a team. Players, then, are not encouraged to access an external support system to enable them to survive outside the team, which can be problematic if team dynamics disintegrate. Bliss was not "saving" his athletes by giving them a second chance; rather, he was dumping them into a program that had no structures in place to support them. Too often, coaches "run" players off teams and out of school instead of directing them to the support systems that exist across campus for typical students. These student-athletes who hop from program to program are labeled as "troublemakers" by coaches, necessitating someone to "rescue" them and give them a second chance.

Obviously, the availability of guns to Dotson and Dennehy enabled a tragedy to occur. One could easily argue that if it were harder to get a gun or if there were a lengthy waiting period, perhaps the shooting of Dennehy would not have occurred. The internal investigation that ensnared the head coach was a different story. Bliss chose to deliberately side step the NCAA rules that limit 1) how many players can be on scholarship and 2) who can pay the tuition bills on behalf of a student-athlete. These actions brought the NCAA down hard on Baylor's program. If Bliss had been given the latitude to build a program slowly (i.e. with freshmen who stay for four years and do not bring excess "baggage" along with them from other failed stops), the pressure of winning immediately may have been abated. Instead, the combination of being the doormat in the Big 12, the quick fixes in recruiting that had worked (for a time) along the way, and the president's ambitious plan to raise Baylor's profile justified, in Bliss's mind, the shortcuts he took in his recruiting.

Another obvious alternative ending to this scandal may have been written if the athletics department followed its own drug-testing procedures. It was clear early in Bliss's tenure that he was recruiting athletes who were using illegal drugs. The fact that these student-athletes were not held accountable for their behavior or entered into a rehabilitation program allowed the mentality of "anything goes as long as we win" to develop. That can be a dangerous message to send to young men or women who have already demonstrated poor decision-making skills.

Finally, Bliss's track record (beyond wins and losses) should have been examined much more closely prior to his hire. There was clear evidence of the behavioral patterns that some of his Baylor players were demonstrating at other schools (SMU and New Mexico). Combine that history with a religious-based university that is a PWI located in a rural area of Texas, and the situation had the potential to explode. The lack of internal support systems (not to mention following established protocols for drug testing) created a combustible powder keg ready to explode.

The tragedy that occurred at Baylor University in 2003 clearly does not define the college today. The athletic success that its high-profile teams have enjoyed in such near proximity to this devastating scandal is nothing short of remarkable. It is difficult to pinpoint exactly what turned around – it could be a change in personnel, or it could be time fades the memory. Like so many other scandals written about in this book, one thing is clear: given the right mix of people and cultures, anything can, and usually does, go wrong when there is pressure to win at any cost.

References

Bishop, G. (2012, February 26). Baylor's athletic program hits the big time. Retrieved from http://nyti.ms/2cNiXkF

Dohrmann, G. (2003, August 18). Bliss out: Baylor coach Dave Bliss's reliance on JUCO transfers and troubled castoffs helped cost him his job. Retrieved from www.si.com/vault/2003/08/18/348269/bliss-out-baylor-coach-dave-blisss-reliance-on-juco-transfers-and-troubled-castoffs-helped-cost-him-his-job

Duderstadt, J. J. (2003). *Intercollegiate athletics and the American university*. Ann Arbor: University of Michigan Press.

Griffin, K. A., Nichols, A. H., Peréz II, D., & Tuttle, K. D. (2008). Making campus activities and student organizations inclusive for racial/ethnic minority students. In S. R. Harper (Ed.), *Creating inclusive campus environments for cross cultural learning and student engagement* (pp. 121–138). Washington, DC: National Association of Student Personnel Administrators.

Harper, S. R., & Antonio, A. L. (2008). Not by accident: Intentionality in diversity, learning and engagement. In S. R. Harper (Ed.), *Creating inclusive campus environments for cross cultural learning and student engagement* (pp. 3–13). Washington, DC: National Association of Student Personnel Administrators.

Hill, D. C., & Magolda, P. (2008). Enacting multicultural and democratic ideals on campus: Challenges and possibilities. In S. R. Harper (Ed.), *Creating inclusive campus environments for cross cultural learning and student engagement* (pp. 235–258). Washington, DC: National Association of Student Personnel Administrators.

Moore, D. L. (2005, June 8). Murder, scandal forced changes at Baylor. Retrieved from http://usatoday30.usatoday.com/sports/college/mensbasketball/big12/2005-06-08-baylor-changes_x.htm

The State of Texas v. Carlton Eric Dotson. Primary Offense: Murder, (54th District Court, McLennan County, Texas 2003).

USA Today. (2005a, June 15). Dotson sentenced to 35 years for murder. Retrieved from www.usatoday.com

USA Today. (2005b, June 23). NCAA puts Baylor on 5 years of probation. Retrieved from http://usatoday30.usatoday.com/sports/college/mensbasketball/2005-06-23-baylor-ncaa_x.htm

Washington Times. (2003, August 16). Tapes reportedly catch Bliss telling players to lie. Retrieved from www.washingtontimes.com/news/2003/aug/17/20030817-123016- 8238r

Wiley, R. (2003). Two dreams die in Waco. Retrieved from http://sports.espn.go.com/espn/print?id=1588378&type=page2Story

Competition Schemes, Academics, and Unfair Advantages

the maximum wagering amount. But it was the suspicions that arose around the Las Vegas sports books that prompted an investigation from the NCAA.

In fall 2005, the MGM Mirage sports book, along with other sports gambling sites in Nevada, presented their concerns to the Nevada Gaming Control Board (Fish & Tanber, 2007), who then shared the information with the NCAA. Nearly a year later, in summer 2006, the NCAA began an investigation, only after numerous complaints and public discussions about the abnormally large amount of high-dollar bets placed on a then-upcoming UT and Kent State football game. UT school officials, according to Fish and Tanber (2007), were not aware of a possible scandal until an NCAA representative visited the campus on October 11, 2006, to explain that there had been some large, out of the ordinary, bets placed on Kent State and that Las Vegas officials were concerned. Less than a month after the visit, Mike O'Brien, the UT athletic director, received notice that the NCAA did not need to continue the investigation. It was not until the FBI contacted school officials on March 30, 2007, that UT school officials learned of the scandal on their campus.

The FBI had been investigating gambling activities in the Detroit area for more than two years before speaking with Toledo officials. According to White (2011b), investigators tapped Manni's telephone and subsequently, in December 2005, recorded conversations between Manni and Rockets' running back McDougle. In one conversation, the two talked about recruiting players to help gamblers win their bets on the GMAC Bowl game against the University of Texas El Paso later in that same month. McDougle also asked Manni to place a $2,000 bet on the game for him (Ashenfelter & Sipple, 2007). Around the same time, UT players were seen with Manni and Karam at an exclusive gambling club in Detroit. Also in December 2005, McDougle was interviewed for the first time; he complied with all FBI questioning. He told FBI agents that Manni had given him a car, a phone, and other expensive gifts (Fish & Tanber, 2007).

When the investigation turned from simply questioning into a legitimate criminal investigation, it was thought by federal authorities that Manni, McDougle, and possibly a few others were bribing UT basketball and football players to influence the final scores of games. However, in March 2006, McDougle was interviewed for a second time; this time he was significantly less cooperative with authorities than when he was initially interviewed. Set off by his lack of cooperation, and by mounting evidence against him, authorities arrested McDougle soon after the second interview (Fish & Tanber, 2007). McDougle and six other Toledo players (for a total of seven players), along with Manni and Karam, were charged with influencing or attempting to influence the final scores of UT games. McDougle, Adam Cuomo, Quinton Broussard, Keith Triplett, Anton Currie, Kashif Payne, Sammy Villegas, and Manni and Karam all were indicted by a grand jury, and each separate case was taken to federal court.

McDougle (the first person to be charged with conspiracy to commit sports bribery in a point-shaving scheme) had received more than $5,000 in food, money orders, and other gifts from Manni. While it was acknowledged that McDougle did not change his style of play as a result of Manni's influence, McDougle recruited other players to participate in the scheme. In 2007, the initial charge against McDougle was dropped due to a procedural error, and while McDougle had suffered no legal punishment up to this point, the accusation was enough for him to be suspended from UT football during what would have been his final season with the program. McDougle also failed to receive a degree from UT. In 2009, however, he was indicted again, and he pleaded guilty to conspiracy and bribery in the summer of 2011 (Blade staff, 2011).

Cuomo admitted to having started the point-shaving scheme with Manni by providing information on games, players, and statistics, as well as helping to place bets on the competitions (Fish, 2009). Cuomo also admitted to getting other players involved by introducing them to Manni solely for the purpose of having them participate in the scheme. Initially, in May 2009, Cuomo pleaded not guilty when he and Broussard were arraigned on charges of conspiring with Manni and Karam to influence the results of Toledo games. However, in 2011, Cuomo changed his plea to guilty, agreeing that he had, in fact, introduced players to Manni for the sole purpose of participating in the point-shaving scheme. Similarly, Broussard pleaded guilty to conspiracy in August 2011 and admitted to having received more than $2,000 during the time he worked with Manni. In fact, Broussard had been paid $500 to fumble the football in the GMAC Bowl game in 2005 (Sowinski, 2010). In agreeing to testify against the other codefendants, Broussard received a reduced sentence of up to six months.

Triplett, on the other hand, claimed that he knew Manni but that he never shaved points. In fact, Triplett entered a not guilty plea to the charges against him, despite evidence that he had been in communication with Manni and suspicions that he had altered his play. Currie and Payne, UT basketball players, pleaded not guilty as well, while their teammate, Villegas, on the other hand, admitted to altering his play during multiple games from 2004 to 2006. Villegas was charged with the felony "conspiracy to influence a sporting contest by bribery" by federal prosecutors and pleaded guilty in 2008 (White, 2011b). He had been in communication with Manni and had received gifts as payment for information, and he also admitted to having intentionally missed two free-throw shots in a game against Central Michigan University. The maximum punishment he faces is five years in prison and $250,000 in fines (Sowinski, 2010).

In a federal indictment filed in September 2009, it was approximated that Manni and Karam wagered more than $400,000 dollars on and against UT between November 2005 and December 2006 (Raghuveer, 2009). The entire scandal is assumed to have begun in fall 2003, continuing through December 2006. Throughout the entire investigation, Manni has maintained his innocence, insisting that he was simply friends with the athletes. Karam has pleaded not guilty to the charges of conspiracy.

Court hearings took place well over a year after a grand jury indicted the men on conspiracy charges. Because of the large number of people involved, their various plea arrangements, and court delays, none of the conspirators had received a sentence as of February 2014. The maximum punishment for their offenses is $250,000 in fines. Manni and Karam, however, could each face up to 20 years in prison in addition to a $250,000 fine for wire fraud. The players could each be fined $250,000 and face up to six months in jail (Raghuveer, 2009). The athletes who actually altered their play could receive harsher punishment.

Throughout the investigation, the UT community exhibited solidarity. In a letter released to the public, school officials indicated that they had faith in the honesty and integrity of the coaches in both sports and had no plans to question their actions. As a result of this scandal, beginning fall 2009, all incoming and current athletes were required to sign a form acknowledging their understanding of the consequences they would face if they were involved with illegal activities. It should be noted that UT and its officials did not suffer any repercussions from the NCAA for this alleged incident because they were unaware of the point-shaving scheme.

Sociocultural Context

To facilitate our understanding of the UT case, this chapter utilizes stakeholder theory as an analytical lens. The stakeholder perspective emerged from the seminal work of Freeman (1984) and allows one to discern management decisions by concentrating on individuals who can impact and are impacted by an organization's purpose and priorities. While stakeholder theory initially gained traction in the field of business, it has also been influential with scholars who examine the stakeholder context of intercollegiate athletics (Putler & Wolfe, 1999; Trail & Chelladurai, 2002; Wolfe & Putler, 2002).

Stakeholders may be either internally or externally involved in an organization. Specifically, they are defined as the "persons or group that have or claim ownership, rights, or interests in a corporation and its activities, past, present, future" (Clarkson, 1995, p. 106). In this sense, the stakeholder approach is a departure from traditional economic views, which suggest that organizations are primarily responsible for their shareholders or stockholders (Argandona, 1998). This theory thus allows for a more thorough identification of multiple types of stakeholders as well as their congruent and competing interests and priorities in a given organizational context (Donaldson & Preston, 1995; Friedman, Parent, & Mason, 2004).

The stakeholder-management literature recognizes three major steps in stakeholder analysis: (1) identifying the stakeholder groups (Starik, 1994); (2) determining the stakeholders' interests (Jones & Wicks, 1999); and (3) evaluating the type and magnitude of stakeholder power or salience (Donaldson & Preston, 1995; Etzioni, 1964; Freeman, 1984; Mitchell, Agle, & Wood, 1997). Power is an important factor in the application of stakeholder theory, and while several definitions exist in the literature, Etzioni (1964) classifies three main types: coercive, utilitarian, and normative. Coercive power refers to the application of physical force in response to noncompliance. Those who use utilitarian power promise material rewards, such as money, for compliance. And normative power utilizes and promotes shared values to control others.

The UT scandal primarily involved two stakeholder groups – community businessmen and college athletes – who had self-interests that undermined the traditional values and integrity of American higher education. This scandal revealed the business enterprise of intercollegiate athletics and that the commercialism of and overemphasis on the revenue-generating sports of football and men's basketball are quite widespread (Eitzen, 2009). According to the American Gambling Association (2011), it is estimated that more than $2.5 billion is illegally wagered on the NCAA Men's Division I basketball championship each year. In contrast, an estimated $80 million to $90 million is legally wagered on the championship each year. The unscrupulous gamblers and businessmen in this scandal, Manni and Karam, attempted to capitalize on the multibillion dollar enterprise through bribery of vulnerable UT athletes. And despite the undeniable potential for negative consequences related to gambling on college sports, billions of dollars continue to be wagered each year, bringing the NCAA more and more exposure and, in turn, increased revenue (Duderstadt, 2003).

The stakeholder power of both Manni and Karam is also relevant to this case (Mitchell et al., 1997). While the extent to which stakeholder groups are salient is situational and contingent upon the particular environment (Trail & Chelladurai, 2002), Manni and Karam bribed Cuomo and other UT athletes to carry out their directives. According to Etzioni (1964), if we were to classify the power used in the stakeholder relationships discussed here, we would see that the UT athletes were controlled through utilitarian power. That is, Manni and Karam provided material rewards to induce UT athletes to engage in a point-shaving scandal. This abuse of power, coupled with the greed and scandalous behaviors of Manni and Karam, certainly led to the undesirable yet predictable outcome described in this chapter.

Although Manni and Karam initiated the improper activities, the UT athletes are not exempt from criticism; their actions were a clear violation of the NCAA's rules governing intercollegiate athletics. Violations such as these highlight both the unfair financial constraints that perhaps make some athletes vulnerable to illegal activities (e.g. point-shaving or taking money from agents) and the exploitative nature of college sports. Many scholars argue that athletes, particularly in the revenue-generating sports of football and men's basketball, are not receiving fair market value for their strong contributions to the business of college athletics (McCormick & McCormick, 2008; Staurowsky, 2004; Zimbalist, 2001). For example, the NCAA signed a deal with CBS Sports and Turner Sports, selling the rights to the NCAA tournament for the next 14 years for $10.8 billion in 2010. While student basketball players receive athletic scholarships as a form of compensation for their play, they do not benefit from television revenue, which averages more than $700 million a year. Moreover, colleges and universities are free to sell athletes' images (through, for example, jerseys and video games), and yet the profiled athletes do not receive a share of the profits from their status. In this sense, the current system is exploitative and hypocritical and benefits selected stakeholders while neglecting other stakeholders – the athletes who actually create the product and render the services (Byers, 1997; Sack & Staurowsky, 1998; Zimbalist, 2001).

The UT scandal brought to light the "big business" of college athletics and, more precisely, the unscrupulous stakeholders in college athletics who have self-interests that are inconsistent with the core values and mission of American higher education (Bowen & Levin, 2003; Gerdy, 2006; Sack, 2001). This scandal brought with it elements that, to some degree, reflect society at large – greed, exploitation of the most vulnerable, and abuse of power – which raises important questions about athletes and the business of college athletics. The UT point-shaving episode is one of a few serious and high-profile cases in the history of college sports. Other noteworthy gambling cases include, but are not limited to, Kentucky in 1952, Seton Hall in 1983, Boston College in 1995, and Northwestern in 1997.

Alternate Ending

Illegal gambling, such as what took place at UT, is an increasing concern in inter-collegiate athletics. In 1996, the NCAA amended Rule 10.3 to prohibit sports wagering among athletes; Rule 10.4 authorizes severe consequences for college athletes who violate this rule. The NCAA has also raised awareness about gambling in college sports through various educational initiatives. Despite these efforts, however, effective strategies and initiatives designed to curb gambling in college sports have been conspicuously absent.

There is a serious need for fresh ideas to address the current challenges that gambling poses for internal and external stakeholders of athletics. It is unlikely that gambling on college sports will ever be eliminated; therefore, it is prudent to identify creative ways to deter athletes from participating in illegal schemes. To this end, college administrators need to consider strategies that both better compensate athletes and lessen constraints on their potential commercial opportunities. For instance, the UT athletes involved in the scandal received as little as $500 for their improper activities. And yet, Fish and Tanber (2007) reported McDougle often did not have enough money to buy food. As such, the NCAA should consider increasing current stipends for athletes because such measures could reduce the seduction to gamble or engage in illegal acts. In an encouraging move, the NCAA has allowed conferences to increase offered athletic scholarships (NCAA, 2011).

Critics of the NCAA amateur model tend to believe that the most highly pub-licized athletes in the revenue-generating sports of football and men's basketball, who are disproportionately African American, are denied a significant amount of their fair market value (Branch, 2011; Donnor, 2005; Hawkins, 2010). Huma and Staurowsky (2011) recommend that colleges and universities: (1) increase scholar-ships to fully cover the cost of attendance; (2) implement the Olympic amateur model, so that all college athletes have commercial opportunities and can be paid as amateurs; and (3) allow athletes in revenue-generating sports to receive television revenue that can be placed in an educational lockbox and can be accessed by them either during college for degree-completion purposes or at the time of graduation.

The aforementioned recommendations would go a long way toward alleviating the vulnerability and desperation of athletes. This approach offers an alternative that is less likely to compromise athletes' academic or athletic futures. Indeed, perhaps the UT athletes, if they had been given this alternative, together with ongoing education about the consequences of point-shaving, would have been less inclined to participate in these illegal activities.

Unfortunately, the NCAA has been reluctant to adopt an alternative model that allows athletes to be compensated for their athletic talents. They have used varying definitions of "amateurism" to protect themselves and to justify athletic scholarships as sufficient compensation for the services of athletes (McCormick & McCormick, 2008). Until the NCAA redefines "amateurism" and more fully includes athletes in the business model of college athletics, the temptation to participate in illegal acts will persist. The NCAA must find a plausible resolution that will not compromise the well-being of athletes or the integrity of college sports.

References

American Gambling Association. (2011). Sports wagering. Retrieved from www.america ngaming.org

Argandona, A. (1998). The stakeholder theory and the common good. *Journal of Business Ethics*, 17(9), 1093–1102.

Ashenfelter, D., & Sipple, G. (2007). Toledo games were fixed, FBI says. Retrieved from http://bpp.wharton.upenn.edu

Blade staff. (2011, July 8). Former University of Toledo running back Harvey "Scooter" McDougle pleads guilty to conspiracy to influence sporting events by bribery. Retrieved from www.toledoblade.com

Bowen, W. G., & Levin, S. A. (2003). *Reclaiming the game: College sports and educational values*. Princeton, NJ: Princeton University Press.

Branch, T. (2011). The shame of college sports. *The Atlantic Monthly*, 308(3), 80–110. Retrieved from www.theatlantic.com/magazine/archive/2011/10/the-shame-of- colle ge-sports/308643/

Byers, W. (1997). *Unsportsmanlike conduct: Exploiting college athletes*. Ann Arbor, MI: University of Michigan Press.

Clarkson, M. B. (1995). A stakeholder framework for analyzing and evaluating corporate social performance. *Academy of Management Review*, 20(1), 92–117.

Donaldson, Y., & Preston, L. E. (1995). The stakeholder theory of the corporation: Concepts, evidence, and implications. *Academy of Management Review*, 20(1), 65–91.

Donnor, J. K. (2005). Towards an interest-convergence in the education of African American football student-athletes in major college sports. *Race, Ethnicity and Education*, 8(1), 45–67.

Duderstadt, J. J. (2003). *Intercollegiate athletics and the American University*. Ann Arbor, MI: University of Michigan Press.

Eitzen, D. S. (2009). *Fair and foul: Beyond the myths and paradoxes of sport*. New York: Rowman & Littlefield.

Etzioni, A. (1964). *Modern organizations*. Englewood Cliffs, NJ: Prentice Hall.

Fish, M. (2009, April 24). Cuomo admits point-shaving role. Retrieved from http://sports. espn.go.com/espn/news/story

Fish, M., & Tanber, G. (2007, August 29). As summer ends, heat is on in Toledo point-shaving case. Retrieved from http://sports.espn.go.com/espn/news/story

Freeman, R. E. (1984). *Strategic management: A stakeholder approach*. Boston, MA: Pitman/ Ballinger.

Friedman, M. T., Parent, M. M., & Mason, D. S. (2004). Building a framework for issues management in sport through stakeholder theory. *European Sport Management Quarterly*, 4(3), 170–190.

Gerdy, J. (2006). *Air ball: American education's failed experiment with elite athletics*. Jackson: University Press of Mississippi.

Hawkins, B. (2010). *The new plantation: Black athletes, college sport, and predominantly white institutions*. New York: St. Martin's Press.

Huma, R., & Staurowsky, E. J. (2011). *The price of poverty in big-time college sport*. Norco, CA: National College Players Associations.

Jones, T., & Wicks, A. (1999). Convergent stakeholder theory. *Academy of Management Review*, 24(2), 206–221.

McCormick, A. C., & McCormick, R. A. (2008). The emperor's new clothes: Lifting the veil of amateurism. *San Diego Law Review*, 45(2), 6–17.

Mitchell, R. K., Agle, B. R., & Wood, D. J. (1997). Toward a theory of stakeholder identification and salience: Defining the principle of who and what really counts. *Academic Management Review*, 22(4), 853–886.

NCAA. (2011). DI Board adopts package of proposals. Retrieved from www.ncaa.com/news/ncaa/article/2011-10-27/di-board-adopts-package-proposals

Putler, D., & Wolfe, R. (1999). Perceptions of intercollegiate athletic programs: Priorities and tradeoffs. *Sociology of Sport Journal*, 16(4), 301–325.

Raghuveer, A. (2009). Six former UT athletes face federal bribery charges. Retrieved from www.northwestohio.com

Sack, A. (2001). Big-time athletics vs. academic values: It's a rout. *The Chronicle of Higher Education*, 59(1), 2–21.

Sack, A. L., & Staurowsky, E. J. (1998). *College athletes for hire: The evolution and legacy of the NCAA's amateur myth*. Westport, CT: Praeger Publishers.

Sowinski, G. (2010, February 24). Sentencing set for Villegas in point-shaving scandal. Retrieved from www.limaohio.com

Starik, M. (1994). The Toronto conference: Reflections on stakeholder theory. *Business and Society*, 33(1), 89–95.

Staurowsky, E. J. (2004). Piercing the veil of amateurism: Commercialisation, corruption, and U.S. college sport. In T. Slack (Ed.), *The commericalisation of sport*, pp. 143–163. New York: Routledge.

Trail, G., & Chelladurai, P. (2002). Perceptions of intercollegiate athletic goals and processes: The influence of personal values. *Journal of Sport Management*, 16(4), 289–310.

White, E. (2011a, January 20). Cuomo guilty in point-shaving scheme. Retrieved from www.foxtoledo.com

White, E. (2011b, July 18). McDougle pleads guilty in bribery probe. Retrieved from www.foxtoledo.com

Wolfe, R., & Putler, D. (2002). How tight are the ties that bind stakeholder groups? *Organization Science*, 13(1), 64–80.

Zimbalist, A. (2001). *Unpaid professionals: Commercialism and conflict in big-time college sports*. Princeton, NJ: Princeton University Press.

10

ACADEMIC MISCONDUCT AT FLORIDA STATE UNIVERSITY

Joy Gaston Gayles and Christopher Faison

Academic scandals and student-athlete misconduct have plagued college sports for centuries. However, it was not until the 1980s when academic standards were first put into place as an attempt to curb abuses in college sports and bridge the growing divide between intercollegiate athletics and higher education. Over the last three decades, academic scandals have not gone away, and, in some ways, they have become worse than in years past. Year after year the media is inundated with academic and social misconduct scandals involving student-athletes at Division I institutions, including one at Florida State University.

The Case

In September 2007, Florida State University's president, Thomas Kent "T.K." Wetherell, a former Seminoles football player in the mid-1960s, sent a letter to the NCAA reporting the initial details of an academic scandal within the university's athletics department. During the spring 2007 semester, the FSU Office of Audit Services learned about one student-athlete who had taken an online quiz for another athlete and then shared the answers to the quiz with athletes before they were scheduled to take the same quiz. University officials interviewed 75 individuals about the incident. Thirty-nine of the 75 students interviewed about academic misconduct admitted that they received inappropriate help from the academic learning specialist, academic advisor, and tutor for an online music class at FSU (Dinich, 2009). Penalties were tough and affected over 500 student-athletes, some of which had nothing to do with the incidents of academic misconduct. Further, it appears that student-athletes who were cooperative were penalized more so than student-athletes who were uncooperative (Roberts, 2009).

The final report from the university stated that the academic scandal involved approximately 61 athletes across ten different athletic teams at the university

(Thomas & Belson, 2009). The ten athletic programs included football, baseball, men's track and field, women's track and field, men's swimming, women's swimming, men's basketball, women's basketball, softball, and men's golf. In the report that was submitted to the NCAA, the university president indicated that a tutor and course instructor distributed the answers to exam questions and wrote papers for student-athletes (Sports Illustrated, 2009; Thomas & Belson, 2009), which is a clear violation of the code of student conduct and NCAA rules. In addition, an academic learning specialist at Florida State University was named in the report as providing inappropriate academic assistance to student-athletes in the form of writing, editing, and typing student-athletes' papers.

When the academic misconduct scandal was initially reported to the NCAA, news organizations filed a lawsuit to make the records public. As a result, a circuit judge ruled in favor of making the files available to the media (Sports Illustrated, 2009). The public was very critical about the extent to which the university tried to keep the records of academic misconduct private and the resources and time dedicated to protecting the scandal from public disclosure. In a time of economic crisis and dwindling state funding for higher education, critics such as Murray Sperber questioned if protecting records of academic misconduct should be a top priority for a university president. Murray Sperber, Professor Emeritus at Indiana University, also made the point that cheating takes on a new meaning when institutional representatives are involved in the misconduct. More specifically, Sperber stated that, when academic cheating involves students receiving inappropriate assistance from the institutional agents, it erodes the confidence in any efforts to align college sports with the academic mission of higher education institutions. Institutional agents such as faculty, administrators, and staff are held to a higher standard for upholding the academic integrity of the institution. When institutional agents participate in academic misconduct, the public becomes increasingly skeptical of the role of intercollegiate athletes on college campuses; instead of building community, intercollegiate athletics becomes a source of tension and embarrassment for college campuses.

Although the FSU president reported the incident to the NCAA before the NCAA found out about it from another source, the penalties that the NCAA enacted were not softened. In fact, according to Mark Jones, a former enforcement employee at the NCAA, the NCAA is not as forgiving for self-reporting academic misconduct as one would think. Nevertheless, the NCAA expects institutions to fully cooperate with investigations of academic misconduct. President Wetherell contended that the students did not intend to cheat; they were simply given inappropriate assistance (Roberts, 2009).

The NCAA stated that the academic misconduct case involved "impermissible benefits, unethical conduct by three former academic support services staff members, and a failure to monitor by the university" (Dinich, 2009). In response to the charges of academic misconduct, the NCAA put FSU on probation, reduced athletic scholarships, and stripped the university of all wins during the timeframe in which the 61 student-athletes were involved in the academic scandal. More specifically,

36 FSU football players were suspended from the Gaylord Hotels Music City Bowl against Kentucky in December 2007. In addition, ten players were suspended for the first three games of the 2008 football season. The penalty also included having wins stripped from Coach Bowden's record. FSU appealed the decision to strip 12 wins from the 2006–2007 season from Coach Bowden's record but was not successful (ESPN College Sports, 2010). Having wins stripped from Coach Bowden's record was controversial in part because of the duel between the late Joe Paterno and Bobby Bowden for the most victories in major college football. The appeal will challenge the nature, number, scope, and seriousness of the violations in relation to the penalties imposed on the institution.

Sociocultural Context

Abuses in college sports, such as academic misconduct among student–athletes, are not new (Bok, 2003). Abuses in college sports have led many to question the appropriateness of intercollegiate athletics within higher education institutions, as the goals and functions of each do not always align (Duderstadt, 2003; Flowers, 2007; Shulman & Bowen, 2002). However, the reality is that intercollegiate athletics play a major role on most Division I campuses across the country – a role that is not well understood or studied (Clotfelter, 2011). Therefore, it is important to examine the historical context of intercollegiate athletics and how college sports has evolved over time as we continue to deal with the challenge of reforming intercollegiate athletics.

Potential Benefits of College Sport Participation

Despite the mismatch between the values of higher education and the goals of intercollegiate athletic programs, scholars such as Shulman and Bowen (2002) argue that there are indirect links between the two. The first of four indirect links discussed here is that participation in sports provides the opportunity for a balanced life. This need for balance played a huge role in the birth of intercollegiate athletics on college campuses. College students during the colonial period needed something to do outside of the classroom to offset the rigor of the classroom experience (Rudolph, 1962). Early forms of competition were between upperclassmen and lowerclassmen, and it was not long until the first regatta match between institutions (Harvard and Yale) took place (Smith, 1988).

The second link involves leadership development, which is more directly tied to the mission of most higher education institutions. Participation in college sports fosters teamwork, competitiveness, sportsmanship, discipline, self-control, and other qualities that are characteristic of good leaders. Third, intercollegiate athletics is deeply ingrained in the campus culture and over time has become a unique community-building activity. Game days, homecoming, and other special athletic events have become ritualistic. It is one of the few times that faculty, students, staff, alumni, and the community come together for a common interest. The downside, however, is that cheating and other unethical behaviors can destroy the sense of community and the reputation of the institution. The final link is the revenue-generating capacity of intercollegiate athletic programs. High-profile programs such as Division I football and men's basketball typically generate enough money to support a host of non-revenue generating sports, providing opportunities for more students to participate in college sports. Further, one of the ways in which alumni stay connected to the institution is through athletics; that alumni stay connected to the institution through athletics has been found to be the cause, at least in part, of alumni giving to other areas/programs of the institution.

From Amateurism to Commercialism

It is safe to say that the closest that intercollegiate athletics has come to aligning itself with the mission of higher education institutions is when it was first established as a student-organized activity during the colonial period. This is one period in history when athletic events were truly amateur in nature. The first college football game was played between Rutgers and Princeton in 1869. Although other college sports competitions had taken place between institutions, there was something about football games that excited and unified the campus community in ways that no other sport had been able to do previously. By the 1870s, college administrators began to capitalize on the excitement and growing interest around college sports (Thelin, 1996; Duderstadt, 2003), which stimulated its evolution from sportsmanship to gamesmanship (Duderstadt, 2003). Also, during the post-Civil War period, intercollegiate athletic clubs were established and other attempts to professionalize and commercialize college sports were initiated.

Not all institutions were happy about the shift in college sport, as many were concerned about the increased commercialism and inappropriate behaviors associated with athletic events on college campuses (Rudolph, 1962). In 1905, President Roosevelt called a meeting of university presidents to discuss and reform intercollegiate athletic programs. The NCAA was born out of this meeting and was officially established in 1906. The role of the NCAA at that time was to act as a governing body, by establishing rules and regulations for fair play. By 1929, the Carnegie Foundation (Sperber, 1998) produced a report outlining major issues with football, such as unethical behaviors of coaches, fans, and students, as well as their concern about the commercialization of college sports. Further, in 1946, the president of the University of Chicago was successful in encouraging the institution to disassociate with the Big Ten conference for reasons outlined in the Carnegie Foundation report.

As college sports continued to shift from extracurricular activity to a competitive enterprise, abuses in college sports increased in frequency (Thelin, 1996; Smith, 1988). The win-at-all-costs attitude that most athletic programs developed at this time brought with it unethical practices and behaviors that were thought to help programs win games. In response to continued abuses in college sports, the NCAA created the Sanity Code in the 1950s (Smith, 1993). Institutions found guilty of engaging in unethical behaviors would be penalized by loss of bowl game participation, spring training, and scholarships. The reform effort did not pass with a majority vote, however, but the Ivy League institutions did decide to adopt the code.

College sports on today's Division I campuses are considered by many to be highly commercialized events that both generate and cost large sums of money. Over time, intercollegiate athletics has moved from student-organized competitive events to a form of public entertainment with coaches and high-profile players who are local celebrities. The problem with commercialism and college sports is that it takes money to make money.

What is more, high-profile coaches are paid enormous salaries to win games and championships. Athletic directors are also paid large salaries to fill the stands, attract national attention to the athletic program, and generate enough revenue from football and men's basketball to support non-revenue generating teams. Admissions offices are burdened with admitting student-athletes who fall well below the average in terms of academic preparation and aptitude. Student-athletes must balance the demands of the classroom with the demands of the field or court. Given the nature of these competing interests and the tension that they create, it is not surprising to see abuses occurring in college sports. Unfortunately, the pressure that builds from these competing interests appears to become more intense over time. In the 1980s, more than half of the NCAA Division I institutions were either sanctioned, on probation, or in violation of NCAA rules (Putler & Wolfe, 1999). Moreover, it is the pressure from these competing interests that leads to unethical behaviors that ultimately call into question the role of college sports on college campuses.

Alternate Ending

Nothing besides avoiding the cheating itself likely would have changed the outcomes of this case. The NCAA still would have enacted the same penalties. Notwithstanding, the perception of the university's attempt to minimize the severity of this situation could have been avoided had FSU officials preemptively released documents that journalists and others were demanding. When President Wetherell sent a letter to the NCAA in September 2007 reporting the initial details of academic misconduct in the university's athletics department, he and others should have pledged to make publicly and swiftly available the full details of the scandal on a website. This seems especially important given that the state of Florida has one of the most stringent open-records laws in the country. Vacating 14 wins plus four years' probation and a reduction in scholarships over three years were major penalties for the FSU football team. Public scrutiny, especially from the media, concerning the university's lack of transparency and cooperation, unnecessarily exacerbated this case. Wasting institutional resources on litigation and having a circuit judge eventually force FSU to comply with requests for documents made the university's leaders, not just those in the athletics department, appear even more complicit in covering up this scandal.

References

Bok, D. (2003). *Universities in the marketplace: The commercialization of higher education.* Princeton, NJ: Princeton University Press.

Clotfelter, C. T. (2011). *Big-time sports in American universities.* New York: Cambridge University Press.

Dinich, H. (2009, March 7). NCAA penalties extend to 10 FSU sports. Retrieved from http://sports.espn.go.com/ncf/news/story?id=3958292

Duderstadt, J. J. (2003). *Intercollegiate athletics and the American university.* Ann Arbor: University of Michigan Press.

ESPN College Sports. (2010, February 8). FSU loses 12 football wins, '07 track title. Retrieved from http://sports.espn.go.com/ncaa/news/story?id=4895204&campaign=rss&source=ESPNUHeadlines

Flowers, R. D. (2007). Win one for the gipper: Organizational foundations of intercollegiate athletics. *Journal for the Study of Sports and Athletes in Education,* 1(2), 121–140.

Putler, D. S., & Wolfe, R. A. (1999). Perceptions of intercollegiate athletic programs: Priorities and tradeoffs. *Sociology of Sport Journal,* 16(4), 301–325.

Roberts, S. (2009, March 24). Learn a lesson, lose the wins. Retrieved from http://sportsillustrated.cnn.com/2009/writers/selena_roberts/03/24/florida-state/index.html

Rudolph, F. (1962). *The American College and University: A History.* New York: Knopf.

Shulman, J. L., & Bowen, W. G. (2002). *The game of life: College sports and educational values.* Princeton, NJ: Princeton University Press.

Smith, R. A. (1988). *Sports and freedom.* New York: Oxford University Press.

Smith, R. A. (1993). History of amateurism in men's intercollegiate athletics: The continuance of a 19th-century anachronism in America. *Quest,* 45(4), 430–447.

Sperber, M. (1998). *Onward to victory: The crises that shaped college sports.* New York: H. Holt.

Sports Illustrated. (2009, August 28). Judge: NCAA must FSU notes. Retrieved from http://sportsillustrated.cnn.com/2009/football/ncaa/08/28/florida.state.cheating/index.html

Thelin, J. R. (1996). *Games colleges play: Scandal and reform in intercollegiate athletics.* Baltimore, MD: Johns Hopkins University Press.

Thomas, K., & Belson, K. (2009, October 14). Documents in fraud cause made public by Florida State. Retrieved from www.nytimes.com/2009/10/15/sports/15ncaa.html

11

FAKE "PAPER CLASSES" AT UNC CHAPEL HILL

Timothy Zimmer and Shaun R. Harper

The University of North Carolina at Chapel Hill is one of the most storied and highly regarded postsecondary institutions in the United States. *U.S. News & World Report* consistently ranks it among the top five public universities. It is best known for its selective admissions, its groundbreaking research, its Carolina Covenant (a financial-aid initiative that allows low-income students to graduate debt-free), and its Southern architectural charm. The university is also famous for its powerhouse men's basketball program, which has made 19 Final Four appearances and won 47 Atlantic Coast Conference championships and five NCAA men's basketball championships. Michael Jordan is incontestably the most celebrated former Tar Heel student-athlete. Coach Dean Smith, a Basketball Hall of Fame inductee and recipient of the Presidential Medal of Freedom from U.S. President Barack Obama, spent 29 years at the helm of this powerhouse basketball program before his retirement in 1997. UNC has amassed for itself a reputation of being one of the most academically *and* athletically exceptional universities in the nation. But unfortunately, an academic scandal involving a long-standing partnership between athletics and the Department of African, African American, and Diaspora Studies tarnished UNC's sterling image.

The Case

In 1979, Deborah "Debby" Crowder began working as a student services manager in what, at the time, was called African and Afro-American Studies. A UNC graduate herself, Crowder was an ardent supporter of the university's athletics programs, caring so much for the program that she was sometimes "unable to come to work for a day or two after the Tar Heels lost a basketball game" (Wainstein, Jay, & Kukowski, 2014, p. 14). She was also seriously committed to assisting struggling students, a passion that would eventually lead to one of the biggest academic fraud scandals in intercollegiate athletics. Unbeknownst to many at the university, a number of students (the majority of whom were student-athletes) were enrolling in fake "paper classes" to earn high grades. In many instances, these grades either kept or pushed students' grade point averages beyond the threshold needed to maintain eligibility or graduate (Ganim & Sayers, 2014). Between 1993 and 2011, over 3,100 students received fake grades for one or more courses they took with Crowder and Dr. Julius Nyang'oro, chair of African and Afro-American Studies (New, 2014; Wainstein et al., 2014).

Nyang'oro first arrived at Chapel Hill in 1984 as a visiting assistant professor in a program that would later become the Department of African, African American, and Diaspora Studies (AFAM). He had earned his law degree from Duke University in 1990 and was granted tenure by UNC in 1992, just two years after being asked to join AFAM's permanent faculty. He eventually became department chair, a position in which he served for nearly 20 years (Wainstein et al., 2014). Unlike his predecessors, Nyang'oro had a "hands-off" approach to department management and paid little attention to curriculum. Some described the department as "balkanized," asserting that Nyang'oro "was an inattentive administrator who was often out of the country, even when he was supposed to be teaching" (Lyall, 2013). Many saw his continual reappointment as department chair a demonstration of UNC's indifference or disregard for AFAM. Crowder took advantage of Nyang'oro's more lenient management style by offering watered-down courses in an attempt to assist struggling students.

According to Kenneth Wainstein, a former U.S. Department of Justice official who investigated and later released his accounts of the fraud in October 2014, Crowder began to cut corners by "designing and offering independent study classes that awarded high grades with little to no regard for the quality of the student's work in the course" (Wainstein et al., 2014, p. 16). The independent study courses effectively eliminated the professorial role and directed all student resources toward Crowder, who was not a faculty member. Crowder tailored AFAM coursework for students, listing Nyang'oro as the instructor of record and registering struggling students (a majority of whom were athletes) in her courses. She would then send independent study topics to students, receive and grade their papers with little concern for quality, and sign the grading sheet with Nyang'oro's signature. If a student submitted a paper after the end of the semester, Crowder would waive the tardiness and change the "incomplete" paper to a letter grade, almost entirely A's and B's (Lyall, 2014; New, 2014).

Because of a four-class limit on independent studies, Crowder would offer the same paper classes under the guise of traditional lectures (Stancill, 2014). Despite the dates, times, and classroom assignments posted in the course catalogue, these classes would continue to operate in the same fashion: students would receive a paper topic, turn it in, and receive a grade from Crowder without much (oftentimes no) interaction with AFAM faculty. A few offered courses included AFAM Bioethics, Southern Africa, Contemporary Africa, Black Nationalism, and Arts as an Aesthetic (Wainstein et al., 2014).

Grades earned in Crowder's classes were notably higher than others in the department. Despite the average grade of a 3.28 in regular AFAM courses, students in Crowder's paper classes earned a 3.62 (Wainstein et al., 2014). The discrepancy was even wider among student-athletes, who averaged a 3.55 in the paper classes compared to a 2.84 in regular AFAM courses. According to the Wainstein report, Crowder's inflated grading system was so significant that each paper grade Crowder assigned increased a student's GPA by an average of 0.03 grade points. Over time, these classes became so popular among student-athletes (especially those on the football and men's basketball teams) that, of the 154 students who enrolled in five or more AFAM lecture classes, 70 percent were student-athletes (Kane, 2015). Counselors in the Academic Support Program for Student-Athletes (ASPSA) directed their athletes toward Crowder's classes in efforts to maintain NCAA and UNC academic eligibility. Seen as "GPA boosters," at least two counselors, one in football, went so far as to suggest to Crowder what grades their athletes needed in order to remain eligible (Wainstein et al., 2014). As a result, student-athlete enrollments – especially among those in football and basketball – skyrocketed in Crowder's paper classes.

As part of their independent investigation, Wainstein and his colleagues were able to analyze 150 final papers that students submitted. They determined that 41 percent of those papers were at least one-quarter plagiarized, and 17 percent were at least half plagiarized. In all, it is estimated that, of the 3,933 total enrollments in AFAM paper classes between 1999 and 2011, approximately 48 percent of those were student-athletes, a majority of whom were members of the football and men's basketball programs (New, 2014). To compare, approximately 4 percent of students attending UNC Chapel Hill are student-athletes at any given time. As student-athletes continued to excel in the paper classes, ASPSA grew evermore dependent on AFAM. Knowing full well that "Crowder did not grade paper-class papers with a discriminating eye and that a student could receive a high grade for turning in a paper of any quality," some ASPSA tutors went so far as to write portions of an assignment for their student-athletes to submit (Wainstein et al., 2014, p. 4). The Wainstein report reveals a connection between Crowder's relationship with ASPSA Associate Director Cynthia Reynolds (football), academic counselor Wayne Walden (men's basketball), and academic counselor and tutor Jan Boxill (women's basketball), which accounted for 6 percent of student-athlete enrollments in the paper classes. UNC head football coach Butch Davis had 181 enrollments in paper classes during his tenure. Similarly, UNC men's head basketball coach Roy Williams had 167 of his players enrolled in paper classes before their eventual discovery. Both claimed to have played no part in the scheme (Ganim & Sayers, 2014).

News of Crowder's impending retirement in 2008 sent shockwaves through the UNC athletics department. Much to the dismay of ASPSA counselors, this meant that AFAM paper classes – or classes graded by Crowder, at least – would cease to exist the following year. Among the more worried were ASPSA football counselors, who had relied on Crowder's grading to keep their players eligible. In an effort to make players more aware of this development, counselors urged players to submit their papers in time to be graded by Crowder (Wainstein et al., 2014). Upon her departure in 2009, the football team's GPA dropped to 2.10 (its lowest in a decade) and 48 players earned less than a 2.0 that fall semester (Giglio, 2014). Nyang'oro was quick to pick up where Crowder had left off, but a fateful meeting with Senior Associate Dean Jonathan Hartlyn in 2011 put a decisive end to the scheme. A grand jury indicted Nyang'oro for fraud in December 2013; those charges were subsequently dropped (Associated Press, 2014). UNC reports the following on its website: "The University estimates spending approximately $7,565,940 to date for services provided by three law firms and one public relations agency that were directly related to the academic irregularities" (UNC, 2015).

Sociocultural Context

Two important questions help place this scandal in a larger sociocultural context: (1) Why did this happen in African American Studies, as opposed to physics or economics, and (2) why did it take so long for academic officials to discover that fake paper classes were being offered semester after semester at UNC?

Disciplinary Stratification in Higher Education

Certain disciplines and academic programs – namely science, technology, engineering, and mathematics (STEM) – tend to be viewed as more prestigious than majors like sociology, education, and ethnic studies. The latter are thought to be easier and less demanding. They are not usually majors that weed out students in the first year; undergraduates mostly switch to these majors instead of depart them to pursue degrees in STEM fields. Furthermore, ethnic studies courses are usually far more writing intensive, with students being graded on written papers as opposed to examinations and lab work. One other contrast is that STEM fields and majors offered in most business schools tend to be less diverse by race and gender, with significantly higher numbers of White male faculty. Hence, an academic scandal of this sort was far likelier to happen in a perceivably lower-status field like African American Studies than in UNC's highly regarded Kenan-Flagler Business School. To be sure, we are not suggesting that one is any more or less rigorous than the other. But undeniably, certain majors are privileged by their perceived rigor in comparison to others. For this reason, a field like chemistry is a lot less likely than is African American Studies to be targeted by an athletics department for academic misconduct partnerships. Coaches and athletics department staff rarely funnel academically low-performing student-athletes into classes and majors that are mostly White, male, and perceivably more prestigious.

Declining Faculty Oversight

Colleges and universities are complex, highly decentralized places. Faculty members in English departments, for example, usually know very little about what their colleagues are doing in political science and the law school. In fact, professors within the same department sometimes know too little about what is happening outside of their respective programs. Unless there are student complaints or suspicions of academic misconduct, faculty members usually stay out of each other's affairs, which is a privilege that academic freedom affords them. Likewise, at many institutions, deans, provosts, and other academic administrators afford programs, departments, and academic schools the luxury of largely governing themselves and overseeing their own processes for matters like independent studies. The increasing presence of adjunct, part-time, and contingent faculty exacerbate these problems. In comparison to prior periods in U.S. higher education, there are fewer full-time, tenured, and tenure-track faculty to maintain oversight over academic programs and departments (Kezar & Sam, 2013). Shifts in faculty composition increase institutional susceptibility for academic misconduct.

Alternate Ending

Although many UNC employees have been fired or disciplined in connection with the scheme, there was much that university officials could have done to prevent such an occurrence. Wainstein et al. (2014) discovered the following: "One administrator became aware in 2005 or 2006 that Nyang'oro was routinely listed as the instructor-of-record for a number of independent studies – approximately 300 per year" (p. 5). No faculty member can responsibly direct that many independent studies. Had the university had clearer policies and stronger oversight, Crowder, Nyang'oro, and their co-conspirators would not have gotten away with committing so much academic fraud for so many years. Furthermore, if the athletics department, along with a faculty oversight committee, had kept closer watch on student-athletes' course enrollment patterns, they would have noticed much earlier that several were enrolled in AFAM courses in which they were earning mostly A's and B's. Lyall (2014) notes that the department was essentially offering a "shadow curriculum" from which the athletics department largely benefitted. Light would have been shed on this much earlier had UNC created stronger, more serious academic accountability systems.

References

Associated Press. (2014, July 3). Fraud charge dropped against ex-UNC professor Julius Nyang'oro. Retrieved from www.foxsports.com/college-football/story/fraud-charge- dropp ed-against-ex-north-carolina-professor-070314

Ganim, S., & Sayers, D. (2014, October 23). UNC report finds 18 years of academic fraud to keep athletes playing. Retrieved from www.cnn.com/2014/10/22/us/unc-report-aca demic-fraud

Giglio, J. (2014, October 22). UNC academic counselors told football coaches that players needed the paper classes. Retrieved from www.newsobserver.com/sports/college/ acc/ unc/article10104221.html

Kane, D. (2015, June 13). Findings provide clues to UNC's fate. Retrieved from www.cha rlotteobserver.com/news/local/article24026728.html

Kezar, A., & Sam, C. (2013). Institutionalizing equitable policies and practices for contingent faculty. *The Journal of Higher Education,* 84(1), 56–87.

Lyall, S. (2013, December 31). A's for athletes, but charges of fraud at North Carolina. Retrieved from http://nyti.ms/JteK6F

Lyall, S. (2014, October 22). U.N.C. investigation reveals athletes took fake classes. Retrieved from http://nyti.ms/1rgqkRz

New, J. (2014). Two decades of 'paper classes'. Retrieved from http://ihenow.com/2gayHzx.

Stancill, J. (2014, October 24). Woeful lack of oversight at UNC enabled Professor Debby's deception. Retrieved from www.newsobserver.com/news/local/education/unc-scandal/a rticle10107065.html

University of North Carolina at Chapel Hill. (2015). University responds to public records requests for legal, communications firm expenses. Retrieved from http://carolinacommitment.unc.edu/university-responds-to-public-records-requests-for-legal-communications-firm-expenses.

Wainstein, K. L., Jay III, A. J., & Kukowski, C. D. (2014). Investigation of irregular classes in the Department of African and Afro-American Studies at the University of North Carolina at Chapel Hill. Retrieved from http://3qh929iorux3fdpl532k03kg.wpengine.netdna-cdn.com/wp-content/uploads/2014/10/UNC-FINAL-REPORT.pdf

12

THE NCAA ON DRUGS

Players, Performance-Enhancing Drugs, and the Need for Tougher Testing Policies and Practices

Ross D. Aikins, Marc E. Christian, and Shaun R. Harper

Barry Bonds, Lance Armstrong, and Marion Jones are among the more prominent names on the ever-growing roster of high-profile athletes linked to performance-enhancing drug (PED) use. For most athletes, the motives to use PEDs are seemingly as transparent as the illegality of their use in competition. Armstrong accumulated an estimated $218 million in career earnings before being stripped of his seven Tour de France titles by the United States Anti-Doping Agency (USADA) for doping throughout his historically successful and lucrative cycling career (Levinson & Novy-Williams, 2013). Jones was similarly forced to relinquish her five Olympic medals and was incarcerated for lying to a grand jury for her role in the same PED scandal that implicated Bonds (Fainaru-Wada & Williams, 2006), who is fourth on the list of career earnings in major league baseball (MLB) at $188 million. At the top of that list, however, is Alex Rodriguez, who has earned over $350 million over the course of his career (baseballreference.com, 2014) and who was a central figure in the 2012 Biogenesis scandal involving 12 other MLB players, including former National League MVP Ryan Braun and the University of Miami baseball program (Schmidt & Eder, 2013).

Pending ongoing sanctions from the MLB and the U.S. Department of Justice, the Biogenesis laboratory investigation may be the single biggest PED controversy in professional sports history in terms of the number of players involved and total games suspended; unpaid NCAA student-athletes are a part of this scandal. Concurrently, as Biogenesis broke, a 2012 Associated Press report detailed a culture of widespread PED use in intercollegiate athletics, specifically within NCAA Division I football programs (Associated Press [AP], 2012). Whether for the glory of gameday heroics or the promise of future paychecks, the confluence of this report and recent events suggests that PED use may be no less pervasive in some college locker rooms than in the pros. But what evidence is there to suggest a problematic culture of PED use among student-athletes, and what policies are in place to discourage and prevent it?

This chapter uses several recent drug scandals in college sports to introduce and discuss many complex issues related to doping, testing, enforcement, health, ethics, and the future of PED use within college athletics.

An Emerging Scandal in College Sports

Before the Biogenesis Labs investigation of 2012, there was the Bay Area Laboratory Co-Op (or "BALCO") investigation that began in 2003, which linked Barry Bonds, Marion Jones, Jason Giambi, and other prominent athletes to PED use (Fainaru-Wada & Williams, 2006; Mitchell, 2007). The BALCO scandal marked the beginning of the very public PED crisis in professional baseball that prompted the U.S. Congress to get involved. Senator George Mitchell's 2007 report of an independent investigation into the use of illegal steroids and other performance-enhancing substances (known as *The Mitchell Report*) not only named 89 MLB players either known or alleged to have used steroids or PEDs (Mitchell, 2007), but also catalyzed changing public assumptions about the sanctity of professional sports, assumptions that are only beginning to carry over into intercollegiate athletics.

The details and scope of most high-profile professional doping scandals vary throughout the past decade, but are all woven with the same threads of cutting-edge sports medicine and the meritocratic pressure to succeed in fiercely competitive, high-stakes sports environments. They also generally share a surprising absence of positive (failed) tests. Problematically, these threads all tie into the current state of intercollegiate PED use. Unlike many of the college sports scandals in this book, PED use in intercollegiate athletes is an ongoing and remarkably well-hidden crisis. In December 2012, the Associated Press compiled data from 61,000 players from all 120 NCAA Football Bowl Subdivision teams which, along with interviews from players, dealers, testers, and experts, all pointed to an underreported PED problem (AP, 2012). The report found both testing and enforcement to be inconsistent across schools and athletics conferences. Said the report, "by comparison, in Kentucky and Maryland, racehorses face tougher testing and sanctions than football players at Louisville or the University of Maryland" (AP, 2012). The AP report critiqued the testing establishment and NCAA for focusing on marijuana and other street drugs (e.g. cocaine and ecstasy) over PEDs. Additionally, players are routinely given advance notice of testing, and producing occasional positive tests for non-PEDs of abuse creates the perception of a rigorous "drug-testing" program regardless of the drug itself and, importantly, whether it is a PED (Pilon, 2013).

But the bulk of the evidence in the 2012 AP report hinged on physiologically unfeasible amounts of weight being gained by a statistically anomalous proportion of college football players. After accounting for height, body type, and comparable weight gains made by fellow athletes, the AP analysis suggested that single-year weight gains of 20, 40, and even 80 pounds were extreme outliers, even for growing young men in a sport that self-selects quantifiably extreme body types (AP, 2012). Furthermore, 11 of these cases went on to fail drug tests in the NFL. Still, inordinate weight gain and correlations do not constitute the same kind of evidence as a trend of failed tests. Noting these limitations can make the case for pervasive doping at the college level seem as slippery as pro dopers themselves.

Anabolic steroids comprised of a large and growing class of natural or synthetic versions of testosterone are arguably the best-known athletic PEDs because of how they foster muscle growth and limit catabolism (breakdown of muscular protein). College students typically use steroids to enhance physical appearance and athletic performance (Berning, Adams, Stamford, & Finewman, 2004; Pope, 1988), but there are clear adverse health consequences related to nonmedical steroid use, including damage to the liver, musculoskeletal, reproductive, and cardiovascular systems (Bahrke & Yesalis, 2004; Pope & Brower, 2005), and psychiatric effects such as depression, violence, and suicidal ideation (Kanayama, Pope, Cohane, & Hudson, 2003; Pope, Kouri, & Hudson, 2000).

According to the NCAA's own survey of over 20,000 student-athletes across all divisions in 2009, 0.4 percent of student-athletes self-reported anabolic steroid use within the past 12 months (NCAA, 2012), which is approximately on par with the 0.7 percent reported among all U.S. college students in 2009 (Johnston, O'Malley, Bachman, & Schulenberg, 2012). However, a study based on a nationally representative sample of colleges between 1993 and 2001 revealed that student-athletes are nearly twice as likely to use steroids than non-athletes and that men are approximately seven times more likely to use steroids than women, estimating past-year nonmedical steroid use prevalence at 1.5 percent among male student-athletes (McCabe, Brower, West, Nelson, & Wechsler, 2007). The NCAA and other professional sports organizations also ban the use of amphetamines (e.g. Adderall and methamphetamine). Despite this, 6.4 percent of student-athletes report nonmedical Ritalin or Adderall use within the past year (NCAA, 2012).

New data suggest that rapidly increasing rates of PED use at the prep level may foreshadow a future problem for college athletes. In 2013, the number of high school students who reported using HGH within the past year more than doubled from 5 percent to 11 percent, and steroid use increased from 5 percent to 7 percent, with more precipitous increases occurring among African American and Hispanic teens (Partnership Attitude Tracking Survey, Teens & Parents [PATS], 2013). These "dramatic" increases coincided with a far greater awareness of the marketing and promotion of PEDs, principally online (PATS, 2013), which raises questions about the habits of students who enter and compete in higher education. In 2008, quarterback prospect Jared Foster was kicked off the University of Mississippi football team and arrested by local authorities for dealing the banned steroid nandrolone. "Everybody around me was doing it," said Foster, who told the AP that he used steroids in high school to gain 25 pounds of lean muscle mass and impress college recruiters (AP, 2012). Foster was one of several former players cited in the AP report who attested to a broader culture of PED use than reported in NCAA data.

Controlled substances of abuse also do not differ greatly from PEDs in their corrosive ability to affect lives and ruin intercollegiate sports programs, as was the case with the synthetic marijuana ("spice") scandal involving the 2010–11 NCAA Division I football champion Auburn University. Between 2009 and 2011, Auburn football had a major problem with spice, but it went unreported in the midst of both a championship run and a separate recruiting scandal involving star quarterback Cam Newton. Nonetheless, it was the emergence of the new, synthetic, then-undetectable drug, spice, that hastened the dismissal of a head coach, decimated two recruiting classes, and left four players charged with armed robbery. Not unlike the herbicide-saturated roots of the hallowed oak trees that proudly stood in Toomer's Corner, the spice affliction of Auburn football was a slow poisoning from within.

To be clear, spice is not a PED but, in 2009, it and other synthetic drugs were increasingly favored among frequently drug-tested populations such as active-duty military soldiers, parolees, and college student-athletes, largely because no screening had yet been developed to detect its use (Wells & Ott, 2011; Piggee, 2009). More than 11 percent of high school students in America were using spice in 2011, making it the most-used illicit drug other than marijuana itself (Johnston et al., 2012).

According to an ESPN investigation, spice became a problem in Auburn's football program in 2009, just as the drug was emerging nationally (Assael, 2013). Auburn may have had an opportunity to supply and implement drug screenings from a California lab in 2010 that could detect spice but instead opted to use its own drug-testing vendor, who, coincidentally or not, developed a spice test two weeks *after* the 2010–11 championship. In the six months following their championship, at least a dozen Auburn football players failed drug screenings for spice, sometimes repeatedly, without sanctions (Assael, 2013). Part of the problem with enforcement was that spice was a brand new drug, and there were no policies specifically governing synthetic marijuana, despite a clause that would have enabled Auburn to include it (Assael, 2013). Doing so would have allowed for parental notification, suspensions, and mandatory counseling for players who tested positive. BCS Championship MVP running back Michael Dyer was one such player.

Dyer failed synthetic marijuana tests six times between February and June of 2011, before it was banned and sanctioned, but unfortunately not before a handgun belonging to Dyer was used by four teammates under the influence of spice to commit a robbery at a local trailer park community in March 2011. Dyer was ultimately released from Auburn for testing positive for marijuana (not spice) for a third time in November 2011. Coach Gene Chizik was fired in 2012, and though many attribute his departure to a disappointing win/loss record following the 2010–11 championship season, there is little doubt that both the drugs and the related player arrests contributed. As of April 2013, 43 percent of the 2009 and 2010 football recruiting classes had left Auburn (Assael, 2013).

Though not a PED scandal itself, the Auburn spice controversy exemplifies how drug testing will probably always be a step behind the chemists and manufacturers who synthesize new drugs, including PEDs. The confluence of winning and a more-sensational recruiting controversy also masked the spice epidemic at Auburn football until too late. The DEA took emergency action in March 2011 to ban synthetic cannabinoids as "a group" (Office of National Drug Control Policy [ONDCP], 2014) but Auburn could not afford to wait.

Sociocultural Context

Not only are anabolic steroids, HGH, amphetamines, and other purported PEDs illegal in competition by the NCAA, but they are also federally controlled substances, and their nonmedical possession, distribution, and use are felonies by law. Since 1986 the NCAA has instituted a drug-testing program to monitor both PED and recreational drug use. The program originally tested student-athletes at championship events but expanded to a year-round program in 1991, testing a selection of student-athletes from each Division I and II institution. In addition to the NCAA's own testing, 90 percent of D-I, 65 percent of D-II, and 21 percent of D-III schools conduct their own drug-testing programs (NCAA, 2014). As of 2014, the NCAA annually invests $4.5 million to collect and analyze an estimated 13,500 urine samples – approximately 16 percent of the total D-I and D-II student-athlete population – and an additional $1.5 million for educational programs for its member institutions (NCAA, 2014). Protocols and procedures are backed by the World Anti-Doping Agency to ensure that independent and certified collection agencies are used when processing drug tests.

On the surface, these measures appear to be significant, but the enforcement of banned substances has been highly criticized. Experts argue that the current state of testing is woefully deficient: drug testing lacks uniform testing standards, there is a high variation between penalties handed down by athletic programs for identical positive tests, and there is no mandatory reporting of positive tests by institutions to the NCAA (AP, 2012). These three factors (testing, penalties, and reporting) diminish the concept of enforcement to where institutions can selectively choose to police themselves at the expense of student-athlete health and safety. But why, other than ethical bankruptcy and skewed priorities, would institutions do this?

Part of the answer, again, relates to money. Despite the obligation for institutions to have drug-testing programs in place, there is currently little incentive to have rigorous (and expensive) programs. According to a 2009 NCAA survey of 491 athletic directors, only 59 percent of institutions surveyed test for anabolic steroids, compared to 99 percent that test for marijuana, 98 percent for amphetamines, and 97 percent for cocaine (NCAA, 2011). Next to alcohol (26 percent), anabolic steroids were the least-tested banned substance, according to the NCAA AD survey. Colleges and universities are reluctant to pour resources into drug testing for steroids, "when cheaper ones for drugs like marijuana allow them to say they're doing everything they can to keep drugs out of football" (AP, 2012). Drug tests that detect steroids or HGH can cost "$100 to $200, while a simple test for street drugs might cost as little as $25" (AP, 2012). Ultimately, it costs more to put procedures in place that have the potential to cause more institutional embarrassment (i.e. a PED scandal) than cheaper options that are relatively innocuous and currently status quo. Others have expressed philosophical reasons against testing. For example, former Georgetown University President Timothy Healey said, "testing would involve the assumption of guilt without cause and athletes shouldn't be singled out simply because they are involved in athletics" (Snider, 2005).

In addition to testing variations, the NCAA allows each institution to determine its own penalties for positive tests, thus creating a highly deregulated system, and, ultimately, a questionably level playing field. Colleges and universities are not required to follow the NCAA policy of immediate one-year suspension for first-time offenders and a permanent ban for second offenses (Snider, 2005; AP, 2012). According to the AP report, coaches have "wide discretion" at the University of Alabama, and "Notre Dame's student handbook says a player who fails a test can return to the field once the steroids are out of his [or her] system" (AP, 2012). These enforcement inconsistencies have the potential to lead to where, "on any given game day, a team with a strict no-steroid policy can face a team whose players have repeatedly tested positive" (AP, 2012).

On top of these criticisms of testing and enforcement, the absence of a defined reporting structure for test results has not made the efforts of the NCAA or its member institutions to eliminate banned substances seem any more evident. Put simply, institutions are not required to report testing in any specific way, neither internally at the school nor to the NCAA (Farrey, 2000; Snider, 2005). The result is diminished transparency as a system. Travis Tygart, President of USADA, stated, "there also needs to be a level of transparency to the testing program to ensure accountability for who is being tested, what they are being tested for and how often testing is occurring" (Pilon, 2013).

The NCAA and member institutions do not deserve all the blame for policy inconsistencies that may enable drug use, as many athletes themselves are willfully cheating a system that has loopholes. Therapeutic use exemptions (TUE), for example, allow some athletes to use otherwise banned substances. TUEs are intentioned to promote fairness for individuals with legitimate medical conditions, but evidence suggests that many professional athletes may exploit TUE clauses. In the MLB, for example, 28 out of 35 TUEs were filed for ADHD medications prior to the amphetamine ban of 2006. In 2007, 111 TUEs were filed, 103 of which were for ADHD medications (Blum, 2008). This type of medical exemption gamesmanship likely occurs at the collegiate level, despite a lack of direct evidence. Approximately 25–48 percent of college students self-referred for ADHD examinations were found to "malinger" or feign symptoms to procure medications (Sullivan, May, & Galbally, 2007). College students are at increased risk for the nonmedical use of ADHD medications (Johnston et al. 2012; Substance Abuse and Mental Health Services Administration, 2009), for which past-year prevalence estimates range from 11.1 percent nationally (Johnston et al., 2012) to as high as 35.5 percent on some campuses (Low & Gendaszek, 2002). Though the primarily academic motives driving collegiate nonmedical prescription stimulant use differ from those of PED users in pro sports (Teter et al., 2005; Rabiner et al., 2009), student-athletes are exposed to multiple motivational risk factors. Team doctors should thus be wary of coercion to medicate.

As seen with spice and new synthetic drugs of abuse, many banned PEDs begin as legal supplements, and drug policies, like the testing landscape, are routinely behind emerging drug trends. The steroid precursor androstenedione was legal in

1998 when Mark McGuire used it to help set a new home run record but was then banned federally by congress in 2004 (Saletan, 2005; Mitchell, 2007). GHB was similarly prized as a legal and widely available bodybuilding and sleep supplement with steroid-like properties, but its euphoric effects led to recreational misuse and earned it the reputation as a date-rape drug, subsequently becoming federally controlled in 2000 (Saum, Mott, & Dietz, 2004). Most recently, now-retired NFL pro-bowler Ray Lewis sparked controversy for his alleged use of a tonic spray that concentrated the active ingredients in the velveteen moss that grows on the antlers of deer, purported to aid recovery, similar to HGH. In addition to Lewis and pro golfer Vijay Singh, the unregulated supplement known as "deer antler spray" was reportedly hawked to members of the 2012 NCAA Championship University of Alabama football team (Epstein & Dohrmann, 2013). At the time, there were no federal or NCAA regulations for this substance.

The Dietary Supplement Health and Education Act of 1994 created a new class of consumer products that could be purchased by individuals of any age and were exempt from FDA regulations, which helped U.S. sales of dietary supplements grow from \$8.8 billion in 1994 to \$20.8 billion in 2004 (Nichter & Thompson, 2006). It is an industry that has become entrenched in intercollegiate athletics. According to 2011 NCAA data, 22 percent of Division I Football Bowl Subdivision institutions accepted either products or financial incentives from nutritional supplement companies (NCAA, 2011). Legal supplements are also expensive, which may prompt some questions of equity in addition to health considerations.

Drug specificity and athletic context matter tremendously when examining PED use among student-athletes. In other words, different drugs have different applications for athletes in different sports or even different player positions. Anabolic steroids may be a likely PED of choice for the offensive lineman looking to gain mass, whereas the now-banned dietary supplement ephedra (also an amphetamine) may be more applicable for the rower or wrestler looking to lose weight (Powers, 2001), and endurance athletes such as Armstrong benefited from oxygenating blood trough doping (replacement) and erythropoietin (Siebert, 2013).

In broader contexts, student-athletes serve as just one part of the larger conversation of enhancement drug use in society. Performance musicians, thespians, and public speakers use anxiolytic medications to quell stage fright and bolster professional success (Elliott, 2003; Wesner, Noyes, & Davis, 1990; Bourgeois, 1991; Chatterjee, 2006). And the use of amphetamines in the military dates as far back as World War II; more recently, amphetamines were administered to U.S. soldiers in the Iraq and Afghanistan conflicts (Iversen, 2006). Juxtaposing varying PED applications brings attention to ethical questions: is it less tenable for a student-athlete to use a PED than the soldier who does so in combat as literally a matter of life and death?

When weighing the ethics of PED use, researchers and bioethicists often invoke two meaningful distinctions. The first concerns whether intercollegiate athletics is a "zero-sum" or "non-zero-sum" activity (Goodman, 2010). For example, individual success in a zero-sum activity necessarily occurs at the expense of another's failure, which would seem to apply to intercollegiate athletics where there is a finite quantity of champions crowned or places on the podium. The second parameter regards whether the value of college sports is found more in the process (e.g. training, hard work, and lessons learned through the process of a season) or the outcome (i.e. winning). Subconsciously or not, a student-athlete who uses PEDs is thus more likely to view her or his athletic participation as an "outcome good" rather than "process good" (Goodman, 2010). Though it may be idealistic in the climate of big-time college sports, stakeholders concerned with the sanctity of intercollegiate athletics may consider appropriating these principles to dissuade PED use as an unethical choice that cheats oneself out of the process.

Problematizing the future of drug use and enforcement in intercollegiate athletics are questions about the permanence of the NCAA itself amid conference realignments and the possible succession of elite college football programs. A shifting national drug-policy landscape complicates matters further, as seen with the growing legalization and acceptance of marijuana. While voters in many states are increasingly deciding which drugs they want the right to use and professional athletes are generously compensated to take risks about what they put in their bodies, student-athletes must contend with the confluence of recreational choices afforded to all developing young adults along with powerful coercive pressures to succeed in competition. In this current era of player safety, coaches, institutions, and policies must function to protect the health and safety of college student-athletes.

Alternate Ending

The International Olympic Committee (IOC), MLB, NFL, NBA, and other professional sports organizations have adopted and enforced more uniform drug-testing methods than has the NCAA. Steroids and PEDs, not just marijuana and street drugs, are included in these screenings. Testing for the Philadelphia 76ers, for example, is the same as it is for every other NBA team. And the Miami Heat is not allowed to determine on its own what sanctions to impose on players who test positive for PEDs and other drugs. The uniformity of these practices is not new within other multi-team organizations. The burgeoning scandal of PED use in intercollegiate athletics could be curtailed if the NCAA adopts and enforces more rigorous screenings just as professional sports leagues have done in recent years. But why have they not done so?

Testing college student-athletes would be significantly more costly because the NCAA has more member institutions than does any other amateur or professional sports organization. In D-I alone, there are more than 170,000 student-athletes who play on over 6,000 sports teams. By comparison, the NFL has only 32 teams and nearly 1,700 total players. Implementing and regulating sophisticated drug-testing practices that are consistent with smaller athletics associations would be logistically tougher for the NCAA with its 450,000 student-athletes in 23 sports across three divisions. But NCAA member institutions somehow manage to check transcripts at the end of every semester to determine academic eligibility, transport every player to and from one sports competition to the next, and facilitate fitness and practice sessions for students and their teammates. Likewise, statistics on the performance of individual players are meticulously documented at every contest. Each of these activities demands logistical coordination and some level of standardization. Hence, enforcing an equitable testing and enforcement system that includes PEDs is something the NCAA could surely implement responsibly, especially when other sports associations have responded more swiftly and uniformly in this era of elevated PED scrutiny.

As noted previously, tests that detect steroids or HGH use can cost $100 to $200 per player (AP, 2012). Further noted in the AP report, "for a school to test all 85 scholarship football players for steroids twice a season would cost up to $34,000 . . . that's about 0.2 percent of the average big-time school football budget." It is possible that the per-player costs for jerseys, helmets, cleats, jock straps, mouth guards, and pads for student-athletes on a football team exceeds the cost of higher-end, more routine drug testing. Moreover, the University of Alabama paid Nick Saban nearly $5.4 million to coach its football team during the 2012–13 academic school year (USA Today, 2014). Surely, it could have afforded $34,000 (or so) to test all of its scholarship football players twice that year. But why would it? An increased number of players failing sophisticated drug tests is not in an institution's best interest, right? Being required to report such findings to the NCAA and athletic conference compliance offices would likely result in suspensions and other penalties for players, as well as considerable media attention. What coach, athletics director, or university president wants that? A more important question is what coach, athletics director, or university president wants student-athletes to risk their health and safety to win games? Care for student-athlete health should prompt institutions to do more than what is minimally required in current drug-screening practices.

As with concerns over concussions and most other scandals written about in this book, the longer the NCAA and its member institutions neglect to preemptively act, the worse the problem is likely to get. Given the performance pressures student-athletes face (some of which are self-imposed), it would be foolish of the NCAA and conferences to believe that PED use is minimal or nonexistent. To be fair, MLB and the IOC were forced to act more aggressively because of threats to their credibility. The NCAA may not yet have a credibility problem (at least not one pertaining to PED use). Unlike scandals covered in other chapters, this one has not yet reached the level of public exposure, widespread media attention, tragedy, and institutional embarrassment. Hence, it is not yet too late for the NCAA to actualize the alternate ending imagined in this chapter.

References

Assael, S. (2013, April 4). Coming Down. Retrieved from http://es.pn/2a0etWB

Associated Press. (2012). Steroids loom large over programs. Retrieved on March 3, 2014 from http://espn.go.com/college-football/story/_/id/8765531/steroids-loom-major-college-football-report-says

Bahrke, M.S., & Yesalis, C.E., (2004). Abuse of anabolic androgenic steroids and related substances in sport and exercise. *Current Opinion in Pharmacology*, 4(6), 614–620.

BaseballReference.com. (2014). Retrieved on March 7, 2014 from www.baseball-reference. com/leaders/leaders_salaries.shtml

Berning, J. M., Adams, K. J. F., Stamford, B. A. F., & Finewman, I. M. (2004). Prevalence and perceived prevalence of anabolic steroid use among college-aged students. *Medicine & Science in Sports & Exercise*, 36(5), S350.

Blum, R. (2008, January 16). Use of ADD drugs soars in MLB as amphetamines are banned. Retrieved on September 15, 2010 from http://usatoday30.usatoday.com/sports/baseball/ 2008-01-15-3097108221_x.htm

Bourgeois, J. A. (1991). The Management of Performance Anxiety with Beta-Adrenergic Blocking Agents. *Jefferson Journal of Psychiatry*, 9(2), 13–28.

Chatterjee, A. (2006). The promise and predicament of cosmetic neurology. *Journal of Medical Ethics*, 32(2), 110–113.

Elliott, C. (2003). *Better Than Well: American medicine meets the American dream*. New York: W.W. Norton & Co.

Epstein, D., & Dohrmann, G. (2013, February 14). The zany story of two self ordained sports science entrepreneurs. Retrieved from www.si.com/nfl/2013/01/28/strange-la b-lured-numerous-athletes

Fainaru-Wada, M., & Williams, L. (2006). *Game of Shadows: Barry Bonds, BALCO, and the steroids scandal that rocked professional sports*. New York: Gotham Books.

Farrey, T. (2000, December 20). Mouse beats cat in NCAA testing. "Crossing the Line, The Failed War on Steroids. Retrieved from http://espn.go.com/gen/s/2000/1207/929862. html

Goodman, R. (2010). Cognitive Enhancement, Cheating, and Accomplishment. *Kennedy Institute of Ethics Journal*, 20(2), 145–160.

Iversen, L. (2006). *Speed, Ecstasy, Ritalin: The Science of Amphetamines*. New York: Oxford University Press.

Johnston, L. D., O'Malley, P. M., Bachman, J. G., & Schulenberg, J. E. (2012). *Monitoring the Future national survey results on drug use, 1975–2011*. Ann Arbor: University of Michigan Institute for Social Research.

Kanayama, G., Pope, H. G., Cohane, G., & Hudson, J. I. (2003). Risk factors for anabolic–androgenic steroid use among weightlifters: a case–control study. *Drug Alcohol Depend*, 71(1), 77–86.

Levinson, M., & Novy-Williams, E. (2013, February 21). Armstrong's cheating won record riches of more than $218 million. Retrieved on March 7, 2014 from www.bloomberg. com/news/2013-02-20/armstrong-s-cheating-won-record-riches-of-more-than-218-   mil lion.html

Low, K. G., and A. E. Gendaszek. (2002). Illicit use of pschostimulants among college students: a preliminary study. *Psychology, Health & Medicine*, 7(3), 283–287.

McCabe, S. E., Brower, K. J., West, B. T., Nelson, T. F., & Wechsler, H. (2007). Trends in non-medical use of anabolic steroids by US college students: results from four national surveys. *Drug and alcohol dependence*, 90(2), 243–251.

Mitchell, G. J. (2007). *Report to the commissioner of baseball of an independent investigation into the illegal use of steroids and other performance enhancing substances by players in Major League Baseball*. New York: Major League Baseball, Office of the Commissioner.

National Collegiate Athletic Association (NCAA). (2011). Drug Education/Drug Testing Survey: Preliminary Results. Retrieved on July 22, 2014 from www.ncaa.org/sites/default/ files/15.%20INstitutional%20Drug%20Education%20and%20Testing%20Survey%202011. pdf

National Collegiate Athletic Association (NCAA). (2012). National Study of Substance Use Trends Among NCAA College Student-Athletes. Indianapolis, IN: Author.

National Collegiate Athletic Association (NCAA). (2014). Understanding the NCAA's drug testing policies. Retrieved on March 26, 2014 from www.ncaa.org/health-and-safety/p olicy/drug-testing

Nichter, M., & Thompson, J. J. (2006). For my wellness, not just my illness: North Americans' use of dietary supplements. *Cult Med Psychiatry*, 30(2), 175–222.

Office of National Drug Control Policy (ONDCP). (2014). Synthetic Drugs. Retrieved on March 19, 2014 from www.whitehouse.gov/ondcp/ondcp-fact-sheets/synthetic-drugs-k2-spice-bath-salts

Partnership Attitude Tracking Survey, Teens & Parents (PATS). (2013). The MetLife Foundation: Partnership for Drug-Free Kids. Accessed on July 25, 2014 from www.drug free.org/wp-content/uploads/2014/07/PATS-2013-FULL-REPORT.pdf

Piggee, C. (2009) Investigating a not-so-natural high. *Anal Chem.*, 81, 3205–3207. DOI:10.1002/jms.1558

Pilon, M. (2013, January 6). Drug-testing company tied to NCAA stirs criticism. Retrieved from www.nytimes.com/2013/01/06/sports/drug-testing-company-tied-to-ncaa- dra ws-criticism.html?_r=0

Pope, H. G., (1988). Anabolic-androgenic steroid use among 1,010 college men. *Physician and Sportsmedicine*, 16(7), 75.

Pope, H. G., & Brower, K. J.. (2005). Anabolic–androgenic steroid abuse. In Sadcock, B. J. & Sadock, V. A. (Eds.), *Kaplan and Sadock's Comprehensive Textbook of Psychiatry*, vol. I, eighth ed (pp. 1318–1328).Philadelphia: Lippincott Williams and Wilkins.

Pope, H. G., Kouri, E. M., & Hudson, J. I.. (2000). Effects of supraphysiologic doses of testosterone on mood and aggression in normal men: a randomized controlled trial. *Archives of General Psychiatry*, 57(2), 133–140.

Powers, M. E. (2001). Ephedra and its application to sport performance: Another concern for the athletic trainer? *Journal of Athletic Training*, 36(4), 420–424.

Rabiner, D. L., Anastopoulos, A. D., Costello, E. J., Hoyle, R. H., McCabe, S. E., & Swartzwelder, H. S. (2009). Motives and perceived consequences of nonmedical ADHD medication use by college students: are students treating themselves for attention problems? *Journal of Attention Disorders*, 13(3), 259–270.

Saletan, W. (2005). The beam in your eye. Retrieved on March 20, 2014 from www.slate. com/articles/health_and_science/human_nature/2005/04/the_beam_in_your_eye.single. html

Saum, C. A., Mott, N. L., & Dietz, E. F. (2004). Rohypnol, GHB, and Ketamine: New Trends in Date-Rape Drugs. In J. A. Inciardi & K. McElrath (Eds.), *The American Drug Scene* (4th ed., pp. 302–318). Los Angeles: Roxbury Publishing Company.

Schmidt, M. S., & Eder, S. (2013, February 6). Drug Inquiry Focuses on Athletes' Ties to Team at University of Miami. Retrieved on March 7, 2014 from www.nytimes.com/2013/02/ 07/sports/major-league-baseball-sees-university-of-miami-as-a-hub-for-performance-enhancing-drugs.html?_r=2&

Siebert, D. (2013, January 16). Lance Armstrong confesses to PEDs: What is erythropoietin (EPO) blood doping? Retrieved on March 18, 2014 from http://bleacherreport.com/ articles/1471562-lance-armstrong-confesses-to-peds-what-is-erythropoietin-epo-blood-doping

Snider, R. (2005, January 25). Colleges vary on drug-use penalties. Retrieved from www. washingtontimes.com/news/2005/jan/25/20050125-120427-8183r/?page=all

Substance Abuse and Mental Health Services Administration. (2009). *The NSDUH Report: Nonmedical Use of Adderall® among Full-Time College Students*. Rockville, MD: Author.

Sullivan, B. K., May, K., & Galbally, L. (2007). Symptom exaggeration by college adults in attention-deficit hyperactivity disorder and learning disorder assessments. *Applied Neuropsychology*, 14(3), 189–207.

Teter, C. J., McCabe, S. E., Cranford, J. A., Boyd, C. J., & Guthrie, S. K. (2005). Prevalence and motives for illicit use of prescription stimulants in an undergraduate student sample. *Journal of American College Health*, 53(6), 253–262.

USA Today. (2014). NCAAF coaches salaries, 2013. Retrieved on July 29, 2014 from www.usatoday.com/sports/college/salaries

Wells, D. L., & Ott, C. A. (2011). The "New" Marijuana. *Annals of Pharmacotherapy*, 45(3), 414–417.

Wesner, R. B., Noyes, R. N., & Davis, T. L. (1990). The occurrence of performance anxiety among musicians. *Journal of Affective Disorders*, 18(3), 177–185.

THIRD QUARTER

Abuse and Harm to Student-Athletes

13

THE BOBBY KNIGHT PLAYER-ABUSE SCANDALS AT INDIANA UNIVERSITY

James Soto Antony, Jennifer Lee Hoffman, and Jacob Houston

Bobby Knight becomes furious over two turnovers in a competition between Indiana University and the University of Michigan. He proceeds to grab his sophomore player Jim Wisman by the jersey and jerks him into his seat.

A 19-year-old college freshman, Kent Harvey, greeted Bobby Knight with, "Hey, what's up, Knight?" Knight fiercely grabbed Harvey by the arm, hard enough that his nails dug into Harvey's skin, and responded, "Son, my name is not Knight to you. It's Coach Knight or it's Mr. Knight."

These two incidents demonstrate what Bobby Knight was most criticized for in his career: an inability to control his temper. He lashed out at players, the press, and the public. Often these outbursts were verbal tirades. On occasion, there were physical threats, or even physical contact. This lack of emotional control eventually led to him being fired as a basketball coach. However, his being fired took time, with many incidents passing without much consequence. The tale of Bobby Knight is an egregious, and cautionary, one, considering that the two examples given above occurred across a span of almost 30 years, at different institutions. In short, these two incidents might serve as bookends of numerous instances of Bobby Knight's uncontrolled temper and emotional outbursts.

The questions that this case raises are: How does someone who demonstrates such behavior across multiple institutions and toward different constituents remain a coach for more than 30 years (even getting hired by one institution after being fired by another)? What are the implications for higher education when it not only tolerates, but protects and continues to retain, individuals who exhibit such behavior?

Bobby Knight is undeniably a legendary coach. He is considered, by most in the sports world, to be one of the greatest coaches in history (ESPN, 2012). Yet his emotional outbursts spanned several decades. His career and associated antics are well documented (e.g. a Google search of "Bobby Knight" yields about 13,900,000 results).

The attention Bobby Knight received is largely attributable to the length of his career as a coach, during which he enjoyed great success on the court. This lengthy tenure afforded the press and other authors ample time to write about him. But because he had a somewhat complicated (some might say contentious) relationship with the media, a level of additional attention was placed on his behavior.

For the purposes of this chapter, then, we do not exhaustively describe any one single incident representing Bobby Knight's explosive temper. There are literally dozens (all the details of which are readily available within thousands of publicly available documents), making it near impossible for one incident to adequately capture the complexity and richness of a case such as Bobby Knight's. As such, we briefly outline four illustrative examples that depict the diversity of Bobby Knight's temperamental behavior across 30 years. These incidents are certainly interesting and potentially illustrative, each in their own right. But, collectively, they provide a fuller and more nuanced composite of Bobby Knight's temper than any one single, isolated event can, and they help to answer the two core questions we pose above.

The Cases

Physical Altercation with Puerto Rican Police Officer

During the Pan American Games in 1979 in Puerto Rico, Knight was involved in a physical altercation with a Puerto Rican police officer. Knight and his U.S. team were just finishing up a practice, when the Brazilian women's basketball team entered the gym, in a loud manner, 15 minutes prior to when they were supposed to enter.

Knight proceeded to exclaim to the Brazilian team, "Hey, we have the gym until eleven. If you're not gonna be quiet, you've got to get the hell out of here." Jose D. Silva, a police officer who was guarding the entrance to the gym, responded: "I say that they stay." Knight and Silva then engaged in a heated argument.

Silva shook a finger in Knight's face; Knight punched Silva in the eye. The police officer responded by arresting Knight and took him to the police station. Knight was immediately placed in a jail cell. However, he was released after ten minutes. When asked about the event later, Knight stated, "F 'em, f 'em all. I'll tell you what, their [Puerto Ricans] basketball is a hell of a lot easier to beat than their court system. The only thing they know how to do is grow bananas" (Papanek, 1979).

Verbal Abuse of Daryl Thomas

On November 24, 1985, Bobby Knight had what is now an infamous verbal outburst during the final week of practice before the official start of the basketball season at Indiana University. During a team scrimmage, Knight observed what he deemed many flaws in the playing and felt that the team was in no way performing to his standards. One player on the team, Daryl Thomas, was, according to Knight, underperforming during the practice, infuriating Knight. The team stopped their scrimmage and began to watch the film of their current practice.

As Feinstein (1986) described in his award-winning look at Knight, Knight ordered that the film be stopped. He exclaimed:

> Daryl, look at that. You don't even run back down the floor hard. That's all I need to know about you, Daryl. All you want to be out there is comfortable. You don't work, you don't sprint back. Look at that! You never push yourself. You know what you are Daryl? You are the worst fucking pussy I've ever seen play basketball at this school. The absolute worst pussy ever. You have more goddamn ability than 95 percent of the players we've had here but you are a pussy from the top of your head to the bottom of your feet. An absolute fucking pussy. That's my assessment of you after three years.
>
> (Feinstein, 1986, p. 5)

Knight then exploded at the rest of his team and called them names. He told his assistants to "get them [the basketball team] the fuck out" (Feinstein, 1986, p. 7).

Knight became infamous for his extreme cursing and name-calling of players. For the most part, his players became accustomed to his verbal attacks. In fact, one of Knight's graduate assistant coaches, Dan Dakich, informed freshman Ricky Calloway that, "When he's [Knight] calling you an asshole, don't listen. But when he starts telling you why you're an asshole, listen. That way you'll get better" (Feinstein, 1986, p. 4).

The above example is illustrative of numerous documented incidents in which Knight employed a coaching style characterized by taunts, abusive language, and verbal attacks. The second example, and perhaps the most widely known incident, tells the story of one of Knight's physical outbursts.

The Chair Toss

On February 23, 1985, during a game against Purdue, Indiana's biggest rival, a foul was called against Indiana after a scramble over a loose ball. What occurred next is best described in the words of ESPN reporter Rick Weinburg (2012):

> The Boilermakers seize a quick lead that rapidly balloons to an 11–2 embarrassment for the Hoosiers on their own floor. It's only four minutes into the contest, and Knight, whose temper tantrums and vile antics have earned him as much attention as his many victories, was seething. You can sense something bad is going to transpire, especially when Knight flies off the bench when a foul is called on Hoosiers guard Steve Alford with 15:59 left in the half.
>
> Fifty-eight seconds later, when a foul is called against Indiana's Marty Simmons, Knight vehemently protests again as he stalks the sidelines – yelling, pointing, fuming. Then, as Purdue inbounds the ball, another foul is called on Indiana,

this time on Daryl Thomas. Knight goes absolutely ballistic, cussing and shrieking at the officials. He is finally hit with a technical by referee Fred Jaspers. Enraged over his team's lackadaisical start and the officials' calls, Knight loses it. He turns toward the Hoosiers' bench, fuming, wanting to take out his rage on someone, something, anything. Instinctively, he picks up a folding chair from the Hoosiers' bench, and just when you think he's going to slam it into the floor, he hurls it across the court, to the utter shock and disbelief of everyone watching.

The chair is heading right toward the wheelchair section of the arena, sliding, twisting and turning across the court, a site so outlandish and so unusual that it's like a mirage. Everyone in Assembly Hall, other than Knight, is incredulous. Knight's own players and staff have seen his uncontrollable rage before – usually at closed practices. But this is an actual game, being played in front of thousands of people in the stands and many more on TV.

Knight walked into the coaches' locker room and broke into tears. The athletic director of Indiana, Ralph Floyd, and Indiana president, John Ryan, met Knight in the room. Knight immediately apologized to President Ryan. Knight was suspended for one game. According to his players, Knight had a reputation for throwing chairs. One day during practice, he became exceptionally angry; out of a stack of 20 chairs, he threw 13 of them (Feinstein, 1986). Though he did not physically hurt anyone during this incident, Knight has been accused of physically abusing players.

Choking Neil Reed

Neil Reed, a junior who had started 72 games for Indiana University, claimed, in a televised CNN/*Sports Illustrated* report, that Bobby Knight grabbed his neck and choked him over a disagreement they had had in 1997. Reed stated:

At that point coach thrust right at me, just came right at me. [He] wasn't far away enough to where I couldn't see something coming, was close enough to come at me and reach and put his hand around my throat, he came at me with two hands but grabbed me with one hand.

Even though the incident was caught on camera, Bobby Knight claimed he did not remember it. In fact, Knight stated, "Maybe I grabbed Neil Reed by the shoulder. Maybe I took him by the back of the neck. I don't know. I don't remember everything that I have ever done in practice" (Abbott, 2000). In addition to allegations that Knight physically abused his players, there were instances in which Bobby Knight physically abused other people who were not on his team.

These are just four of numerous examples of Knight's inability to control his temper both on and off the basketball court. In the next section, we discuss the sociocultural implications of the Knight case.

Sociocultural Context

Despite his antics and behaviors, Bobby Knight ran a tight basketball program. The overwhelming majority of his players graduated – they were not in trouble with the law or at the center of broad media coverage for anything other than their success on the court. The Indiana men's basketball program was free of NCAA violations during his tenure as coach. Knight was never in the crosshairs of the NCAA for serious recruiting or any other major rule violations. He won national championships and league championships and coached an Olympic gold medal-winning team. Moreover, the successful coaches who coached with, or played for, Bobby Knight, constitutes an impressive roster. Most of his former players have been his staunchest supporters.

Without doubt, there is a lot of gray area between the controversial behavior of Bobby Knight and what the NCAA, for example, would formally consider right or wrong. Yet it is this gray area that creates so much trouble for higher education leaders, coaches, athletic administrators, the media, and fans. Within this gray area is a broad array of effective coaching styles, no two of which are completely alike. And, among the legendary coaches such as Bobby Knight (and numerous other coaches in every single sport), this gray area simultaneously contains coaching genius and behavior that, to an outsider, appears outrageous. What is right or wrong when it comes to motivating elite athletes to perform at levels that exceed all expectations? Because the gray area is a contested space, it is difficult to come to a consensus about whether vulgar language, threats, or even downright belittling and bullying can be accepted ways to coach in some circumstances.

As a society that is infatuated with athletics, we cannot solve all problems within athletics by specifically defining what, within this gray area, is formally right or wrong. The NCAA rulebook is already the size of a telephone directory. Coaches, players, and fans, will (at best) behave according to the strict letter of the rules. As such, if the rule does not say that something cannot be done, then in the minds of coaches, players, and fans, it is functionally legal to do.

The Bobby Knight case, if nothing else, teaches us that there will never be enough rules or laws to protect (with absolute certainty) against every potential controversy. The case of Bobby Knight illustrates that, when all is said and done, NCAA rules alone are no substitute for clearly articulated expectations, norms of ethical behavior, and institutional values. These expectations, norms, and values constitute the threshold beyond which a coach's behavior is deemed unacceptable. As a whole, the reason Bobby Knight was ultimately fired from Indiana University is because he violated the expectations, norms of ethical behavior, and institutional values his (relatively new) boss, President Miles Brand (who, not surprisingly, went on to become the NCAA president) clearly articulated to Knight. Perhaps the presidents who preceded Miles Brand had also articulated their expectations, norms, and values to Bobby Knight. But President Brand was the first president at Indiana to hold Bobby Knight accountable.

The case of Bobby Knight stimulates us to think about the classic tension that big-time college athletics programs present for the university. Rules alone cannot provide institutions the security that a winning, clean athletics program will not also present terribly challenging situations with which to deal. But we must remind ourselves that everything a college or university does (including athletics) deserves to be guided by clear expectations, norms of ethical behavior, and strongly held institutional values.

Perhaps higher education has difficulty dealing with the tensions and controversies raised by big-time athletics because, in general, higher education is not very good at dealing with, and appropriately shaping, the behavior of challenging individuals. After all, athletics programs do not enjoy hegemony over controversial larger-than-life personalities. Any high-caliber academic department often contains at least one, if not many, successful professors who might be at the cutting edge of scholarship while also being eccentric or, in some cases, downright unpleasant to be around. Colleges and universities do not deal well with moderating the behavior of these individuals either. Institutions of higher education are places that attract genius while fiercely protecting individuals' independence and autonomy. Genius is often challenging to harness with rules because an overly regulatory environment can stifle the very creativity, innovation, and performance that genius provides and that an institution of higher education most cherishes.

What made Bobby Knight unique was his visibility. There is a high probability that at least one prominent academic at Indiana University was, during the Bobby Knight years, also abrasive to his or her students, overly demanding, difficult to be around, and temperamental, yet wildly successful. But people pay attention to athletics.

The idea that even faculty can be as challenging and controversial as some coaches is offered not to normalize abusive, erratic, and eccentric behavior, but to suggest that the problem is not specific to athletics. Alas, there are more coaches and professors who do not raise controversy than those who do. That is the good news. The not-so-good news is that higher education does an average job of developing and articulating clear expectations, norms of ethical behavior, and strongly held institutional values. The downright bad news is that, even with the articulation of expectations, norms, and values, higher education leaders rarely hold others accountable, thereby tolerating, if not enabling, difficult individuals and their behavior.

As we indicated above, the only reason Bobby Knight persisted across a span of 30 years was because those around him tolerated him and enabled him. Eventually, someone at Indiana held him accountable. Of course, Texas Tech University was more than happy to give Bobby Knight another shot. And Bobby Knight continued to deliver, in all senses of the word, as the second example at the beginning of this chapter (which occurred at Texas Tech) illustrates.

The implications for higher education are clear. Setting, and even articulating, expectations, norms for ethical behavior, and institutional values are good places to start, but they are not enough. Leaders need to develop systems of evaluation that hold everyone accountable for behavior that is inconsistent with those expectations, norms, and values. Leaders need to be consistent in their application of these systems of evaluation and cannot be afraid to act in ways that uphold these expectations, norms, and values. This takes time. And if an institution has not consistently evaluated and held individuals accountable, the first instances of doing so can be trying (as we demonstrate in the next section). But, over time – and with vigor and ongoing diligence – the expectations, norms, and values will define an institution's culture and, as such, few will tolerate and enable inappropriate behavior.

Alternate Ending

February 1985, when Bobby Knight threw a folding chair across the court, was a watershed moment. With 17,000 in the arena and millions more watching on television, this was the most public and remarkable of his outbursts. More should have been done. Decades of persistent abuse could have been avoided had Indiana University President John Ryan held a press conference a day or two after the notorious chair-tossing incident and read a statement like the following:

> It is with great regret that I announce the termination of Head Coach Bobby Knight from Indiana University. Bobby Knight is a gifted coach and teacher, but his recent actions defy sportsmanship and are not consistent with the values of the Indiana University community. A high-caliber basketball program is a key feature of the IU community, one that has always exemplified competitive play at the highest level.
>
> We expect sportsmanship at the highest level and cannot condone these actions. If a professor or university administrator were to behave this way toward a colleague or student, no matter his talents or stature, this would not be tolerated. Abusive, even boorish, behavior is not condoned by our institution.
>
> The actions of the head basketball coach at IU and the national stature that this position commands have brought significant and negative national attention over the actions of our most visible and prominent ambassador. If the coach can throw a chair, then what is to stop someone in the crowd from throwing objects in the intense moments of a close game? The actions of Bobby Knight create a dangerous environment that is unsafe for players, coaches and fans.
>
> My sincere apologies to the Purdue basketball team, Purdue University, and the Big 10 Conference. A new interim coach has been named for the remainder of the season.

Ryan did not do this, presumably because of the friendships, allies, winning seasons, championships, and power that Bobby Knight had amassed over the course of his first 14 years in Bloomington. The famed Hoosiers men's basketball coach stayed for a total of 29 years, some of which included other moments at which his temper embarrassed Indiana University.

References

Abbott, R. (2000, September 9). The Knight tape: Video captures encounter between IU coach, ex-player. Retrieved from http://sportsillustrated.cnn.com/thenetwork/news/2000/04/11/knight_cnnsi/

ESPN. (2012). ESPN25: The 25 best coaches. Retrieved from http://sports.espn.go.com/espn/espn25/story?page=listranker/25bestcoaches

Feinstein, J. (1986). *A season on the brink: A year with Bobby Knight and the Indiana Hoosiers.* New York, NY: Macmillan.

Papanek, J. (1979, July 23). Triumph and turmoil in the Pan-Am Games. SI Vault. Retrieved from http://sportsillustrated.cnn.com/vault/article/magazine/MAG1095174/index.htm

Weinburg, R. (2012). 85: Bobby Knight looses cool, tosses chair. Retrieved from http://sports.espn.go.com/espn/espn25/story?page=moments/85

14

PRAYING TO PLAY

A Coach's Control of Players' Spiritual Lives at Oakland University

Demetri L. Morgan, Horatio W. Blackman, and Shaun R. Harper

On June 12, 2013, Oakland University (OU) President Dr. Gary Russi announced his retirement after nearly 20 years at the helm of the mid-sized university located outside of Detroit, Michigan (Murray, 2013). With a distinguished record, the announcement came as a surprise to many and led to widespread speculation about his departure (Semarez, Kampe, & Dulberg 2013). A few hours before Russi's announcement, the OU athletics department released a statement that the women's head basketball coach, Beckie Francis, who had led the team for 13 years, had been "relieved of her duties . . . effective immediately" (Oakland University [OU], 2013). Gary Russi and Beckie Francis were known as OU's "power couple" because of their marriage to each other in 1999 and subsequent visibility and notoriety on campus (Graham, 2013). Their simultaneous resignations sparked a media frenzy to find out the underlying cause of the departure of two of the University's most well-known employees. A group of Francis' former players began to speak to the media about their experiences with her. It was then that the shocking details of Francis' misconduct began to emerge.

The Case

Francis began her collegiate women's basketball coaching career in 1990 as an assistant coach at the University of Buffalo. She had responsibilities for player recruiting and academic counseling on top of her basketball-related activities. While at Buffalo, Francis gained the invaluable experience of being involved with the team's transition from Division II to Division I. This experience allowed her to secure the next coaching job, this time as head coach at Stony Brook University. Stony Brook was preparing to transition from Division III to Division II, and Francis took over to head up that process. Francis did not have much success on the court while at Stony Brook, with a 30–48 record during her three-year stint. After the 1997 season, Francis was hired by Oakland University to help the Golden Grizzlies transition from Division II to Division I. In her first year as head coach, Francis' team was 20–7. In her third year at OU, her team won their first regular season championship and, in her fifth year as head coach, the Golden Grizzlies made it to the NCAA tournament; this was the first time in Francis' career that a team she coached advanced to the tournament (OU, 2013).

After the 2002 season, Francis took a three-year sabbatical for health reasons and was rehired in 2005 (Kampe, 2013a). From 2005 to 2013, Francis' success was inconsistent; her team made it to the Women's National Invitation Tournament (WNIT) twice but also suffered through three losing seasons during that time span. Despite Francis' mixed record on the basketball court, during her annual evaluations she was praised, especially for her efforts off the court (McCabe & Snyder, 2013). For example, according to the NCAA's academic progress rates, "a team-based metric that accounts for the eligibility and retention of each student-athlete," Francis' teams performed in the top twentieth percentile of all Division I women's basketball programs, even achieving a perfect rating of 1,000 during the 2009–2010 season (NCAA, 2013).

Furthermore, in October 2012, Francis made national headlines when she revealed in an interview with the Associated Press that her father had sexually abused her as a child (Blitchok, 2012). Francis used her story to press Michigan legislators to pass "Erin's Law," a policy that would create changes in grade school curricula to help students understand and talk about sexual abuse (Lage, 2012). For her efforts and bravery, in February 2013, Francis was recognized and awarded the prestigious U.S. Basketball Writers Association (USBWA) Most Courageous award, named in honor of the highly regarded former University of Tennessee head women's basketball coach, Pat Summitt (USBWA, 2013). Annual evaluations of Francis also reveal that her focus on the off-the-court issues cascaded down to her team's image with OU's athletics director noting that the "program is service oriented and represents the university very well" (McCabe, 2013). Francis was seemingly excited about and committed to her future at OU, as evidenced by the coaching changes she made just as the Golden Grizzlies were preparing to switch into the more prestigious and competitive Horizon Athletic League (Kampe, 2013b).

At the conclusion of the 2012 basketball season, a women's basketball player requested a transfer from OU. The university granted the request, and upon the player's departure, interview administrators cited "non-secular conduct and behavior on the part of the women's basketball head coach" (Wolchek, 2013). This prompted an internal review by the athletics department at the behest of the university's general counsel that ended in "corrective action being taken" according to a statement released by the university (McCabe & Snyder, 2013). While the university's policies prohibit the discussion of student, personnel, or interview matters, in the wake of Francis' termination, former players began to share stories with media outlets.

Former OU player Jenna Bachrouche shared with a reporter that she transferred from OU because Coach Francis had on numerous occasions made her feel uncomfortable about her religion and her weight. Bachrouche identified as a Muslim and, when she first arrived at OU, older players warned her that she should follow the team's unofficial motto of "praying to play" if she wanted to make it at OU (Wolchek, 2013). Francis also policed her player's sexual activities, warning them not to hang out with men, including players on the men's basketball team (Ryan, 2013). Francis also referred to the women's team as a "Christian basketball team" and shared with players her personal testimony before one season during a film review session (Wolchek, 2013). Bachrouche said she had been afraid to speak up because Francis was married to President Russi, and she did not think people in the athletics department would take her seriously.

Other former players also spoke out about the treatment that they received from Francis. Stacey Farrell, a point guard for Francis who enrolled in 2007, described how Francis had an irrational fixation on players' weights (McCabe & Snyder, 2013). There were times when Francis instructed players to take photos of themselves in only their sport bras and spandex to chart body changes. Francis even went so far at times as to stop practice, approach players, and demand to "feel their six-pack" (Gloria Ryan, 2013). Bachrouche detailed how she had to have friends sneak her snacks because Francis and other players told her that she was eating too much at meal times. This focus on weight and food led to a culture where at least four players developed eating disorders (McCabe & Snyder, 2013). Karli Harris, a player who transferred from OU in 2010, recalled that Francis' player treatment bordered on harassment and that much of her energy was focused on "stupid, trivial things" (McCabe & Snyder, 2013). Players used terms such as "emotional and mental abuse" when describing Francis' behavior, but they noted feeling powerless to do anything about it because of the relationship between Francis and Russi.

Francis' dual emphasis on practicing Christianity and players' weights affected more than just the players' off-the-court lives. A former player, who did not want to be identified in her interview with reporters, discussed how it became quite apparent that players who were not skinny received less playing time. Coach Francis would assume that players were not taking care of their bodies and as a punishment would not give heavier players as much playing time as their thinner counterparts. Older players told younger players that, if they wanted to receive playing time, they needed to tell the following to anyone who asked: "You are a virgin. You are Christian. You do not drink. You do not smoke. You do not talk to guys. You sit in your dorm room and study" (McCabe & Snyder, 2013). Francis was involved with the campus organization the Fellowship of Christian Athletes and would encourage players to attend their meetings. Although this was presented as "optional," women's basketball team members knew that if they wanted to play, they had to follow along, Harris said. In the last two years of Francis' time there, seven players left OU. This is a staggering number considering the team carries only 15 players each year. It is evidence, however, of the hostile culture that was created under Francis.

Uncertainty remains about the exact details of Francis' termination, but the university did release a statement indicating that she was fired "with cause" (Kampe, 2013b). Neither Francis nor Russi have commented publicly on either of their departures, although Francis released a statement shortly after the announcement of her termination saying that she was "staying positive" and "looking forward to the future" (Kampe, 2013a). The athletics department hired assistant men's basketball coach Jeff Tungate to take over the women's program in the interim. The fallout of the scandal has led to national discussions about the pressure coaches put on players, the connection between sports and eating disorders, and religious freedom (Hamilton, 2013; Kampe, 2013c).

Sociocultural Context

The firing of Beckie Francis gave the nation yet another look into the systemic culture of abuse in intercollegiate athletics. Allowed to go unchecked for a number of years, and in fact praised for her on- and off-court accomplishments, Francis terrorized young women who she was responsible for developing. Her actions, the lack of voice that her student-athletes felt they had, and the time that it took for Francis to be removed from her position reflect the university's inability to adequately monitor its staff. While Francis was eventually terminated with cause for conduct deemed to "adversely affect the order or efficient operation of the women's basketball program," she had already caused damage to the young women who played on her team (Kampe, 2013b).

Mass Media and Women's Body Image

Research consistently shows that media and pop culture are extremely powerful factors when women are judging their beauty (Levine & Smolak, 2006). This fact led those who study women, mental health, and perceptions of beauty to coin the term "normative discontent" to describe the internalized imperfection that a majority of women feel about their own bodies (Cheng, 2006). The culture of thinness that dictates perceptions of beauty have led to severe health problems for many young women. For women student-athletes, psychosocial issues concerning weight and judgments about physique are exacerbated. Female athletes already contend with the culture of thinness impressed upon them by mainstream media but have added pressure associated with maintaining a certain physique to optimize athletic performance. In a study that Kato, Jevas, and Culpepper (2010) conducted, 49.2 percent and 40.2 percent of female Division I and Division III college athletes, respectively, were found to exhibit eating disorder attitudes and behaviors.

Christian Dominance

Not only did Francis harm OU women's basketball team members through her obsession with their bodies, her use of religion represented another overreach of power and violation of students' rights. Too often, Christianity is dominant on college campuses in the U.S., and other religious faiths and traditions are ignored and otherwise disrespected (Ahmadi & Cole, 2015). While debates over religious freedom and expression occur on many campuses, it is nonetheless astounding that a coach would impress upon players her own religious beliefs and, in effect, infringe on their religious freedoms. Francis was cited with repeated attempts to convert a former player, Jenna Bachrouche, to Christianity, and frequently inserted herself into players' off-court romantic relationships (Kampe, 2013b). Her actions ultimately led to Bachrouche transferring to another university (McCabe & Snyder, 2013).

Workplace Nepotism

What is perhaps most disturbing about this case is not that these claims of abuse allegedly took place for several years, but that, during Francis' tenure, student-athletes did not feel as if they had an avenue for recourse. Francis came to OU in 1997 and soon after began dating President Russi; they eventually married. The president's and head women's basketball coach's status as the power couple on campus undoubtedly placed student-athletes in a position in which they felt powerless to defend their rights. Indeed, any attempt to challenge Francis may have been fruitless given Francis' support from the university's administration (including her spouse) throughout her tenure. She consistently received positive reviews for her performance (both on and off court), which had to pass through her husband for final evaluation. Despite these positive evaluations – which were accompanied by significant pay raises that led to a salary increase from $50,000 to $136,000 in her 13 years at the university – there were warning flags that the administration overlooked. During her 13-year tenure, 36 of her 170 players left the program early. That amounts to one-fifth, or 20 percent, of women's basketball players at OU. Seven members of the team left in her last two seasons alone. It was not until Bachrouche asked for a transfer to retain immediate eligibility and cited religious oppression as her cause for leaving that the university chose to take action.

Alternate Ending

It is possible that women's basketball team members at Oakland University would have suffered less abuse from their coach if they had access to a variety of reporting resources. Being able to anonymously report their experiences with Coach Francis to the university, the intercollegiate athletics conference in which Oakland held membership, and the NCAA likely would have made the women feel less powerless. Student-athletes must be made aware of their right to report *problematic* behaviors they see or experience that involve their coaches and athletics administrators. There must be reporting options that exist beyond the boundaries of the athletics department, as insularity, departmental culture and politics, and a desire to win or protect a coach's reputation may compel some athletics administrators to ignore what student-athletes say about the toughness of their coaches.

Some may also believe that students are merely complaining because their coaches are pushing them too hard or not giving them sufficient playing time. External persons could help determine if particular coaching strategies and behaviors are abusive.

Had student-athletes been aware of ways to report Coach Francis' actions to authorities beyond the athletics department or outside of the university, perhaps feedback and certain directives could have been given to the coach well before her abuse drove so many women away from the OU basketball team. Maybe Beckie Francis could have been somehow sanctioned earlier, before the situation there resulted in termination. Reporting systems may be available at all three levels (institution, conference, and NCAA), but student-athletes might not always know they exist. Hence, effectively promoting these resources is important. If students are presented lists that include examples of what constitutes abuse from their coaches, along with phone numbers they can call and external advocates they can contact, scandals such as the one that occurred at Oakland could be avoided.

References

Ahmadi, S., & Cole, D. (2015). Engaging religious minority students. In S. J. Quaye & S. R. Harper (Eds.), *Student engagement in higher education: Theoretical perspectives and practical appoaches for diverse populations* (2nd ed., pp. 171–185). New York: Routledge.

Blitchok, D. (2012, October 19). Germantown native and Oakland University women's basketball coach Beckie Francis reveals childhood sexual abuse. Retrieved from www.dailyfreeman.com

Cheng, H. S. (2006). Body image dissatisfaction of college women: Potential risk and protective factors (Doctoral dissertation, University of Missouri-Columbia, MO). Retrieved from https://mospace.umsystem.edu

Graham, K. (2013, August 5). Rise and fall of OU's power couple. Retrieved from www.oaklandpostonline.com

Hamilton, C. (2013, July 24). Coaches, athletes and eating disorders: What we can learn from Oakland University. Retrieved from www.nationaleatingdisorders.org

Kampe, P. (2013a, September 3). Former Oakland University women's basketball coach Beckie Francis' award may have come during investigation of her conduct. Retrieved from www.theoaklandpress.com

Kampe, P. (2013b, September 9). Oakland University says women's basketball coach Beckie Francis fired with cause. Retrieved from www.theoaklandpress.com

Kampe, P. (2013c, September 3). Power can't be used to pressure, officials say after former Oakland University player accuses coach of religious intimidation. Retrieved from www.theoaklandpress.com

Kato, K., Jevas, S., & Culpepper, D. (2010). Body image disturbances in NCAA Division I and III female athletes. *Journal of Sport Science and Medicine*, 14(1), 1–2.

Lage, L. (2012, October 12). Beckie Francis, Oakland University Basketball Coach, Breaks Silence About Sexual Abuse. Retrieved from www.huffingtonpost.com

Levine, M., & Smolak, L.. (2006). *The prevention of eating problems and eating disorders: Theory, research and practice.* New York: Routledge.

McCabe, M. (2013, June 1). Oakland says Beckie Francis fired with cause. Retrieved from www.usatoday.com

McCabe, M., & Snyder, M. (2013, July 21). Players' shocking allegations against former NCAA women's basketball coach. Retrieved from www.usatoday.com

Murray, D. (2013, June 13). OU President Gary Russi announces retirement; women's basketball coach Beckie Francis relieved of her position. Retrieved from www.daily tribune.com

NCAA. (2013, June 21). Academic Progress Rate (APR). Retrieved from www.ncaa.org

Oakland University. (2013, June 12). Beckie Francis relieved as women's basketball coach. Retrieved from www.ougrizzlies.com

Ryan, E. G. (2013, July 22). Nightmare NCAA basketball coach fired over 'no fat sluts' rule. Retrieved from http://jezebel.com

Semarez, M., Kampe, P., & Dulberg, D. (2013, August 1). Oakland University's Gary Russi leaves legacy of expansion. Retrieved from www.theoaklandpress.com

USBWA. (2013, Feburary 21). Francis, Kelly to receive USBWA's Most Couregous Awards. Retrieved from http://sportswriters.net

Wolchek, S. (2013, August 12). Ex-Grizzly roars back at Oakland coach. Retrieved from www.oaklandpostonline.com

15

NO DRINKING, NO DRUGS, NO LESBIANS

Coach Rene Portland and the Culture of Homophobia in Women's Basketball at Penn State

Edward J. Smith

The Pennsylvania State University Lady Lions were considered a powerhouse in NCAA women's basketball during the 2004–2005 season. Fans and commentators alike attributed the team's success to the leadership and discipline of head coach Rene Portland, a woman who had gained national acclaim over the course of her stellar 25-year career at Penn State. Portland had been a pillar of women's basketball for nearly four decades. A native of Broomall, Pennsylvania, she was a three-year starter for the famed Immaculata College women's basketball team, where she and her team won three consecutive national championships in the early 1970s (The Chronicle of Higher Education, 2007a; Mosbacher & Yacker, 2009). After brief coaching stints with St. Joseph's University and the University of Colorado, Portland was hired in 1980 by the then–Penn State football coach, the late Joe Paterno, during his tenure as the athletic director. Paterno believed Portland would someday make women's basketball at Penn State "something special" (Longman, 1991; Mosbacher & Yacker, 2009), commenting that the hiring of Portland was one of the best decisions he had ever made as an athletics director (Greenberg, 2007; Longman, 1991).

Portland amassed a strong résumé of dominance, which included 21 NCAA tournament appearances and five Big Ten Conference championships. Much of her success rested on her long-held expectation of recruiting and retaining strong *student-athletes* who competed at the highest level, both on the court and in the classroom. To many of her peers, Portland was a champion of women's rights, advocating for gender equity with regard to training facilities, funding, and administrative support (The Chronicle of Higher Education, 1989; Longman, 1991). Notwithstanding, her attitude toward lesbians generally and lesbian athletes in particular was also well known by the intercollegiate athletics community. Portland's anti-gay stance had received moderate media coverage since the beginning of her coaching career and, in 1986, she publicly admitted to the *Chicago Sun-Times* that she would not allow lesbians on her basketball team, saying:

I will not have it in my program. I bring it up and the kids are so relieved. The parents are so relieved, but they would probably go without asking the question otherwise, which is really dumb. I have training rules. And I will never have to say what my training rules are.

(Figel, 1986)

This stance eventually matured into a national scandal after Jennifer Harris, one of the team's best players, filed a lawsuit against the veteran coach, alleging that she was removed from the team because she had been perceived to be a lesbian (Mosbacher & Yacker, 2009). The allegation prompted backlash within the Penn State community and ultimately led to Portland's resignation in 2007.

The Case

In spring 1991, the *Philadelphia Inquirer* featured a professional profile on Portland, which included reports from unnamed former Lady Lions, exposing detailed accounts of Portland's views and behavior regarding sexual orientation (Longman, 1991). The public reaction to the article was deeply critical of Portland and the Penn State administration, sparking several weeks' worth of large, highly publicized student protests on Penn State's campus (Griffin, 2007; Lederman, 1991). Several former players came forward to reflect and discuss the painful memories and emotions surrounding Portland's "no lesbian" policy (Lederman, 1991; Longman, 1991). It reopened the public conversation about Portland's homophobic remarks from just half a decade earlier and pinned the burden of accountability squarely on the shoulders of the Penn State administration. By this point, Portland was publicly hinged to an anti-lesbian policy, in both recruiting and management, and was widely known for a throng of "training rules" that included no drinking, no drugs, and no lesbians (Greenberg, 2007; Griffin, 2007; Longman, 1991; Mosbacher, 2009; Mosbacher & Yacker, 2009; Osborne, 2007; Yanity, 2011). While the controversy brought on a firestorm of formal complaints and campus-wide demonstrations, Penn State remained steadfast in their support of Portland and, as a reprimand, asked her to participate in a diversity and inclusion workshop facilitated by University of Massachusetts professor and noted scholar of homophobia in sports, Pat Griffin. At the same time, the university amended its nondiscrimination policy to include sexual orientation as a protected class (Mosbacher & Yacker, 2009; Lederman, 1991; Osborne, 2007; Yanity, 2011).

Despite her widely known discriminatory policies and practices, Portland received numerous individual accolades from the intercollegiate athletics community, including two National Coach of the Year awards from the Women's Basketball Coaches Association, two Big Ten Coach of the Year awards, and induction into the Pennsylvania Sports Hall of Fame (Mosbacher & Yacker, 2009; Osborne, 2007; Yanity, 2011). In fact, Portland is one of only nine NCAA women's basketball coaches to reach over 600 career wins (Yanity, 2011). However, she never won an NCAA National Title and had only one NCAA tournament Final Four appearance. Portland's greatest criticism came in fall 2005, when one of the Lady Lions' leading scorers filed a legal complaint that centered on Portland's homophobic practices and management policies.

Situating Jennifer Harris

Jennifer Harris was a talented All-American athlete from Central Dauphin High School in Harrisburg, Pennsylvania. Her athletic performance garnered recognition from *Parade Magazine*, Gatorade, and Nike (Osborne, 2007). As a National Honor Society member, Harris entered her senior year of high school heavily recruited by a host of strong collegiate basketball programs from academically strong institutions. With opportunities abound, Harris chose to attend Penn State University, primarily on the promise that coach Rene Portland would be her "mom away from home" (Lieber, 2006). This assertion supported Harris's notion that she belonged at Penn State and would thrive under the supportive guidance of her future head coach.

Harris arrived at Penn State in fall 2003; she was soon barraged with accusations from Portland that she (Harris) and her teammate were dating. Although Harris denied the accusations, Portland's probe persisted for the duration of her first season. Without any evidence, Portland concluded that the teammate in question was gay, suggested that she was encouraging similar "deviant" behavior, and dismissed Harris's teammate at the end of the 2003–2004 season (Osborne, 2007). For fear of retribution by her powerful coach, Harris never reported Portland's accusations to Penn State officials. Harris also feared further harassment by the coach, a loss of playing time, or, worse, termination from the basketball team, which would also result in Harris losing her scholarship. While deeply hurt by the removal of her teammate, Harris decided to finish her first year at Penn State, with hopes that her issues with her coach would soon be resolved (Greenberg, 2007; Mosbacher & Yacker, 2009).

Harris made a significant contribution to Penn State's success during her sophomore season, persisting through the pain she suffered during her time under Portland. Although Harris maintained that she was not a lesbian, Portland's aggressive probes continued during Harris's second season; Portland questioned Harris's sexual identity – in private or publicly – close to ten times (Greenberg, 2007; Harris v. Portland et al., 2005). While Harris continued to turn in strong performances on the basketball court, the premedicine major soon struggled to sleep, eat, and perform in the classroom (Mosbacher & Yacker, 2009). Portland's string of biased comments and behaviors came to a head on March 20, 2005, when Portland dismissed Harris and two other teammates after an upset loss to Liberty University and prohibited them from interacting with former teammates, attending team functions, or using university athletic facilities (Harris v. Portland et al., 2005; Mosbacher & Yacker, 2009).

With legal counsel from the National Center for Lesbian Rights (NCLR), Harris filed a federal lawsuit on December 21, 2005, against Portland, athletics director Timothy Curley, and Penn State University at large (Harris v. Portland et al.,

2005). The lawsuit focused on the claim of sexual orientation discrimination, asserting that Portland wrongly believed that Harris was a lesbian and, as a result, dismissed her from the team (Harris v. Portland et al., 2005; Osborne, 2007). Portland repudiated the claims, saying she removed Harris from the team due to her performance, attitude, and lack of commitment (The Chronicle of Higher Education, 2007a, 2007b; Harris v. Portland et al., 2006a; Lieber, 2006; Newhall & Buzuvis, 2008).

After filing a motion to dismiss the suit (Harris v. Portland et al., 2006a), Penn State conducted an internal review and found that Portland had created a "hostile, intimidating, and offensive environment" (Lieber, 2006; The Chronicle of Higher Education, 2006, 2007a; Greenberg, 2007; Yanity, 2011) for Harris based on Harris's perceived sexual orientation. Portland was found to be in violation of the university's antidiscrimination policy, which prompted Penn State to levy a fine of $10,000 against the coach and further required Portland to participate in another Pat Griffin–led diversity and inclusiveness training (Greenberg, 2007; The Chronicle of Higher Education, 2006). The university also assured the campus community that Portland would be terminated if she again violated the school's antidiscrimination policy (Greenberg, 2007). In a formal statement, Portland claimed the university's investigation was "flawed," asserting that she would remain the coach of the Lady Lions throughout the duration of her contract (The Chronicle of Higher Education, 2006). Yet, in March 2007, the institution reached a confidential financial settlement with Harris, and two months later, Rene Portland resigned as head coach of Penn State women's basketball team.

Sociocultural Context

Jennifer Harris's lawsuit against her former basketball coach and university drew an unprecedented amount of media coverage and public concern about sexual orientation discrimination in intercollegiate athletics – the case became a lens through which to view the issue of homophobia and related discrimination in women's sports. Needless to say, this case exposes the lack of support for student-athletes at large due to an institutional power structure and fear of retaliation. Even more disturbing was Penn State's attempt to either ignore or conceal Portland's long-standing discrimination which, as many are now aware, was a part of a larger institutional history of suppressing administrative maleficence.

The Pervasive Culture of Homophobia in Women's Basketball

Researchers have examined the highly homophobic institution of organized sports (Griffin, 1998a, 1998b; Kauer & Krane, 2006; Krane, 1998; Messner, 1992; Pronger, 1990; Wolf Wendel, Toma, & Morphew, 2001), and have argued that inter-collegiate athletics rests outside the reach of most mechanisms that address problems of discrimination and hate (Baird, 2002; Gregory, 2004; Griffin, 1998a, 2007; Krane, 1998; Mosbacher & Yacker, 2009; Wolf Wendel et al., 2001). Homophobia and sexual-orientation discrimination impede inclusiveness within sports and maintain the establishment of masculinity and hyperheterosexuality (Griffin, 1998b; Pronger, 1990; Wolf Wendel et al., 2001). As in most cases, the discrimination starts long before the player arrives on campus and manifests itself early during the recruiting process. Harris alleged that Portland outlined her anti-lesbian policy well before her arrival (Mosbacher & Yacker, 2009; Osborne, 2007), demonstrating an entrenched culture that oppressed and suppressed the identity development of women basketball players at Penn State.

In 1994, former University of Maryland at College Park field hockey star, Vicki Yost, sued the school's head coach and senior associate athletics director, claiming she had been forced to conceal her sexual identity during her time on the team (Blum, 1994; Hensley, 1994). The NCLR also negotiated a practical and financial settlement with the University of Florida on behalf of Andrea Zimbardi, who experienced discrimination and prohibition from softball team practices and events in 1999 based on her sexual orientation (Osborne, 2007).

Many coaches claim that any lesbian stigma can deter potential players from attending their programs. In turn, they have been known to engage in negative recruiting, whereby coaches insinuate that other teams – usually competing for the same player – are rife with lesbian activity, and compel potential recruits, and their families, to avoid the teams altogether (Griffin, 1998a). Portland was widely known for her biased recruiting, offering a "lesbian-free program," reassuring parents, guardians, and players that they could feel safe and secure from the cloak of "Lesbianism" (Mosbacher & Yacker, 2009). Simply put, there was a sense that Portland thrived in that type of discriminatory environment and, if anyone did not like it, they could go somewhere else – which, unfortunately, is what many women did.

Racial Discrimination and Cultural Stereotypes in Women's Basketball

Women of color face significant and additional challenges in overcoming the cultural stereotypes that participation in sports offers (Women's Sports Foundation, 2007). Depending on the sport, Black female athletes, in particular, are moderately or severely underrepresented in intercollegiate athletics (Women's Sports Foundation, 2003) and absorb the lion's share of racial discrimination and cultural stereotyping. Newhall and Buzuvis (2008) observe that Harris's claim of discrimination on the basis of sexual orientation received significant ethical and intellectual attention, but the public discussion often ignored the allegations of racial discrimination. Portland's instructions that Harris, a Black woman, dress in a more "traditional" feminine style of clothing, wear make-up, and stop wearing her hair in cornrows, as the braids looked too masculine, highlight the complexity of intersectional identity. One can easily take these directives, under the context of Don Imus's characterization of the Rutgers University women's basketball team as "nappy-headed hoes" in 2007, as a requirement that Harris not only refine her gender identity and presentation, but that she cover up her blackness.

Some troubling statistics emerged when the NCLR filed the Harris suit (2005), namely that Portland recruited a majority White team (60 percent) between 1997 and 2005, and that, during that same period, Black women comprised more than 60 percent of the players who were terminated – including the player Portland alleged to be gay during Harris's first season – or who quit. This took place at the same time that Black players constituted a majority of players in women's intercollegiate basketball at large (Harris v. Portland et al., 2006b; Newhall & Buzuvis, 2008), which speaks to the racial undertones of Portland's ugly package of discriminatory policies, practices, and behavior. Even in responding to the suit, Portland was unrelenting in her cultural bias, claiming that Harris was lazy and undedicated, playing into long-held stereotypes of Black athletes (Newhall & Buzuvis, 2008; Osborne, 2007; Williams, 2007).

The Institutional Culture of Cover-Up

Penn State's administration during Graham Spanier's 16-year tenure as president has faced fierce criticism and scrutiny for its history of ignoring, dismissing, or concealing any threat of embarrassment to the university (Perez-Pena, 2011; Yanity, 2011). Penn State's athletics department administration failed to meaningfully respond to the detailed accounts of Portland's discrimination. Further, it denied Harris and her family the opportunity to discuss her termination with athletic department officials and even filed a motion to dismiss the case after receiving the suit from the NCLR (Harris v. Portland et al., 2006a). This tells the Penn State community – and makes a statement to the public – that preserving institutional prestige is prioritized over sexual orientation and racial equity. The scandal involving former Penn State football coach Jerry Sandusky and the sexual abuse of young boys over a 15-year period exposes yet another institutional effort to hide instances of human exploitation from authorities and the public.

Another, less nationally publicized example of Penn State's culture of cover-up occurred when death threats were sent to Black football players during April 2001. When concerned students met with then–head football coach Joe Paterno, he claimed that "he was only a football coach" and that there was nothing more he could do to protect his students or investigate the threats (Hoecker, 2002; Mock, 2012). The threats horrified the community surrounding Penn State as the threats turned into reality when a Black man's body was found by police near the campus. Administrators claimed the death was completely unrelated and refused to investigate the threats. Even more disturbing, Paterno, Spanier, and former Senior Vice President for Finance and Business Gary Schultz were all at Penn State during these three scandals (Mock, 2012).

Alternate Ending

It is unlikely that homophobia and sexual orientation discrimination in women's basketball is going to end or even be mitigated through small or piecemeal efforts such as ascribing diversity workshops (as was required of Rene Portland). Effective crisis management would have entailed Penn State administrators taking meaningful action long before Jennifer Harris's lawsuit in 2005; they had multiple opportunities to terminate Portland's coaching contract and remove her from her leadership position, if not in 1986 then certainly by 1991. The termination could have been a viable and symbolic step toward creating a supportive campus climate for all students, specifically Lesbian, Gay, Bisexual and Transgender (LGBT) student-athletes. Yet Penn State chose to maintain its prestige over nurturing social justice. Allowing Portland to remain in leadership proved to be more costly, as Penn State paid dearly in the settlement and resolution of this case.

In addition to terminating Portland, Penn State could have increased efforts to diversify athletics administration – from leadership to coaches – and facilitate a unit-wide mandatory training on effective approaches to working with LGBT athletes. It would have behooved Penn State to include the voices of nonathletic staff in this training, inviting internal and external experts to facilitate a sustained dialogue about hate, oppression, and discrimination.

In basketball, defenders are encouraged to "take a charge" by moving quickly to arrive in the offensive player's path, with their feet firmly planted, squarely facing the offensive player with the ball. The defender steps into the offensive player's lane, plants her/his feet with a wide stance and braces for contact. At times, this could be a very painful decision, as the offensive player might collide into the defensive player. Ultimately, the defensive player is sacrificing her/his body by making a solid play that will turn the ball over, while inducing a foul call on the offensive player. Harris said she could not have lived with herself if she did not speak up after being terminated from the Lady Lions (Lieber, 2006). She had to "take a charge" for those young women who would come after her, knowing they would meet a similar fate. Harris never set out to be a civil- or gay-rights activist, but she did have the courage to advocate for herself and for her teammates, past and future.

Often, in instances of abuse, hate, and oppression in which the offense is reported, the alleged victim has to confront her/his assailant. Many victims fear the consequence of being face-to-face with their attacker. Harris did not know if the formal complaint would close educational doors for her, or if it would close doors on her future professional basketball pursuits. Yet it was important to her that this not happen to anybody else, and she absorbed a painful burden by engaging in a legal battle with a large institution. Perhaps Harris's complaints could have been part of a formal grievance system or hate-response protocol, specifically for student-athletes and intercollegiate athletic department staff, that does not require a student or staff member to register a complaint with a coach or immediate supervisor and that protects her confidentiality (Harris v. Portland et al., 2005). Penn State had the opportunity to institute such a procedure in 1991 after the backlash following the *Chicago Sun-Times* article. Yet they did not; this led to countless women being oppressed and suppressed due to Portland's discrimination.

References

Baird, J. A. (2002). Playing it straight: An analysis of current legal protections to combat homophobia and sexual orientation discrimination in intercollegiate athletics. *Berkeley Women's Law Journal*, 17(1), 31–67.

Blum, D. E. (1994). College sports' L-Word. Retrieved from http://chronicle.com

The Chronicle of Higher Education. (1989). Sports: Women as competitors. Retrieved from http://chronicle.com

The Chronicle of Higher Education. (2006). Penn State fines a coach for antigay bias. Retrieved from http://chronicle.com

The Chronicle of Higher Education. (2007a). Former player on women's basketball team settles bias lawsuit against Penn State. Retrieved from http://chronicle.com

The Chronicle of Higher Education. (2007b). Veteran coach at Penn State quits after disputes over treatment of lesbian players. Retrieved from http://chronicle.com

Figel, B. (1986). Lesbians in world of athletics. Retrieved from www.clubs.psu.edu/up/psup ride/articles/Chicago%20Sun%20Times%2006161986.pdf

Greenberg, M. (2007). Portland ponders leaving Penn St., sources say. Retrieved from http://articles.philly.com

Gregory, A. (2004). Rethinking homophobia in sports: Legal protections for gay and lesbian athletes and coaches. *Journal of Sports Law & Contemporary Problems*, 2(2), 264–293.

Griffin, P. (1998a). *Strong women, deep closets: Lesbians and homophobia in sport*. Champaign, IL: Human Kinetics.

Griffin, P. (1998b). Homophobia in sport: Addressing the needs of lesbian and gay high school athletes. In G. Unks (Ed.), *The Gay Teen*. New York: Routledge.

Griffin, P. (2007). Settling can mean victory: Reflections on the Rene Portland – Jen Harris lawsuit settlement. Retrieved from www.outsports.com

Harris v. Portland et al., Case No. 1:05-CV-2648, Complaint. (2005, December 21). Filed in the United States District Court for the Middle District of Pennsylvania.

Harris v. Portland et al., Case No. 1:05-CV-2648, Motion to Dismiss. (2006a, January 26). Filed in the United States District Court for the Middle District of Pennsylvania.

Harris v. Portland et al., Case No. 1:05-CV-2648, Amended Complaint. (2006b, May 26). Filed in the United States District Court for the Middle District of Pennsylvania.

Hensley, J. (1994). Terrapins are sued by ex-player. Retrieved from http://articles.baltim oresun.com

Hoecker, R. (2002). *The black and white behind the blue and white: A history of black protests at Penn State*. University Park, PA: The Pennsylvania State University Schreyer Honors College.

Kauer, K. J., & Krane, V. (2006). "Scary dykes" and "feminine queens": Stereotypes and female collegiate athletes. *Women in Sport and Physical Activity Journal*, 15(1), 42–55.

Krane, V. (1998). Lesbians in sport: Toward acknowledgement, understanding and theory. *Journal of Sport and Exercise Psychology*, 20(3), 237–246.

Lederman, D. (1991). Penn State coach's comments about lesbian athletes may be used to test university's new policy on bias. Retrieved from http://chronicle.com

Lieber, J. (2006). Harris stands tall in painful battle with Penn State coach. Retrieved from www.usatoday.com

Longman, J. (1991). Lions women's basketball coach is used to fighting and winning: Rene Portland has strong views on women's rights, lesbian players and large margins of victory. Retrieved from http://articles.philly.com

Messner, M. (1992). *Power at play: Sports and the problem of masculinity*. Boston, MA: Beacon Press.

Mock, B. (2012). The other Penn State cover-up: Death threats against black students. Retrieved from http://loop21.com

Mosbacher, D. (2009). No drinking, no drugs, no lesbians: How homophobia still rules in sports. Retrieved from www.huffingtonpost.com

Mosbacher, D., & Yacker, F. (Directors). (2009). *Training rules* [Motion picture]. San Francisco, CA: WomanVision.

Newhall, K. E., & Buzuvis, E. R. (2008). (e)Racing Jennifer Harris: Sexuality and race, law and discourse in Harris v. Portland. *Journal of Sport and Social Issues*, 32(4), 345–368.

Osborne, B. (2007). "No drinking, no drugs, no lesbians" – Sexual orientation discrimination in intercollegiate athletics. *Marquette Sports Law Review*, 17(2), 481–502.

Perez-Pena, R. (2011). Rich in success, rooted in secrecy. Retrieved from www.nytimes.com

Pronger, B. (1990). *The arena of masculinity: Sports, homosexuality, and the meaning of sex.* New York: St. Martin's.

Williams, C. (2007). Sexual orientation harassment and discrimination: Legal protection for student-athletes. *Journal of Legal Aspects of Sport*, 17(2), 253–283.

Wolf Wendel, L., Toma, J. D., & Morphew, C. (2001). How much difference is too much difference? Perceptions of gay men and lesbians in intercollegiate athletics. *Journal of College Student Development*, 42(5), 465–479.

Women's Sports Foundation. (2003). *Title IX and race in intercollegiate sport.* East Meadow, NY: Women's Sport Foundation.

Women's Sports Foundation. (2007). *Race and sport.* New York: Women's Sports Foundation.

Yanity, M. (2011). The stench from Penn State permeates big-time college sports. Retrieved from http://chronicle.com

16

HAZING ON WOMEN'S SPORT TEAMS AT THREE COLLEGES AND UNIVERSITIES

Marc E. Christian

Hazing humiliates and degrades student-athletes under the pretense that a shared experience instills feelings of belonging; this practice has persisted in higher education for decades (Hoover, 1999). Hazing dates back more than one hundred years in the Greek fraternal system (Rosner & Crow, 2003). Fraternities harbored hazing as a traditional rite of passage for "pledges to earn membership by displaying submission" to ensure that the fraternal system retained group stability and "high status on campus" (Nuwer, 1999). Hazing in fraternities led to deaths, dating as far back as 1873, and, as fraternities grew in popularity on campuses, so did these tragic incidents. These events empowered the news media to define fraternities through the lens of hazing. Fraternities are still considered strongholds for hazing, and the public continues to perceive these institutions as "virtual icons of depravity" (Nuwer, 1999). While hazing has defined fraternities for more than a century, hazing is now also a problem for other populations within higher education, including collegiate sports.

In 2011, 26-year-old Florida A&M marching band student Robert Champion was killed when the Florida A&M marching band beat him during a hazing ritual (Hightower, 2013). This tragic death not only highlights the continued belief that hazing is crucial for inclusion but also the extent to which hazing is now a practice outside of fraternities. Furthermore, hazing characterized the "relationship between male gender socialization and a host of beliefs and attitudes that lead to destructive behaviors" (Harper & Harris, 2010). A desire to assert "male aggressiveness" is reinforced by social interactions (hazing), as conforming to these ritualistic behaviors becomes a "strategy to protect oneself from teasing or subordination" (Harper & Harris, 2010). More importantly, this behavior highlighted that the groupthink, which men internalize to become "one of the boys," is not unique to one particular organization or group of individuals (Harper &

Harris, 2010). Rather, hazing is a preferred ritualistic ceremony for many populations in higher education.

While hazing has its roots in the Greek system, the high-profile nature of college sports shifted the focus from fraternities to the hazing scandals plaguing collegiate teams. The rise in hazing incidents in college athletics was confirmed in a 1998 report conducted by Alfred University in partnership with the NCAA. This seminal study found that more than a quarter million student-athletes were hazed when joining a collegiate athletic team, and more than half of all participants were required to partake in drinking contests or alcohol-related hazing (Hoover, 1999).

More significantly, one in five people hazed was subjected to conditions that were "unacceptable" and potentially illegal (Hoover, 1999). Such incidents included student-athletes engaging in or simulating sexual acts, being kidnapped and transported, or destroying property – 68,041 student-athletes, or 21 percent, who were hazed were subjected to this type of debasing activity. These statistics present a strong case that hazing is common practice on collegiate teams, but to appreciate the full impact of these statistics, they must be disaggregated by sex.

The long-standing narrative on hazing within higher education has focused on fraternities and male athletics, but a changing athletic culture has revealed that hazing among women's collegiate sports has also become rampant. The notion that men within higher education perpetrate hazing led to a bias, among coaches, athletic administrators, and other higher education officials, which effectively led these individuals to erroneously conclude that hazing was not as problematic in women's sports as it is in men's. The Alfred University survey proved otherwise. The study concluded that, of the more than a quarter million student-athletes who were hazed, 96,000 were women (Hoover, 1999). This is a significant number, and the Alfred University report paints a startling picture of women student-athletes regularly hazing as part of their athletic culture.

Delineating the line between malicious behavior that degrades student-athletes and the positive aspects of team-bonding activities is important to do when discussing hazing in women's sports. However, it is difficult to do, as the line is continually blurred. For instance, many "younger athletes seem to be notably desensitized to hazing . . . and the majority often do not acknowledge they were hazed" (Hoover, 1999, p. 8). Often, student-athletes are unaware that they were involved in hazing or rationalize hazing as a positive behavior and hence continually assert that hazing "[is] a non-issue" because it is "part of team chemistry . . . or a tradition" (Hoover, 1999). The existing culture within collegiate sports has condoned hazing as essential to establishing team identity, yet the process of hazing often fractures individuals and teams rather than uniting them. The line between team bonding and overt sexual, physical, and mental harassment is often confused by teams as they strive to develop their identities. As the following trio of case studies demonstrates, college sports hazing scandals always begin with good intentions but often leave individuals feeling abused and degraded, and teams divided.

The Cases

University of Oklahoma Women's Soccer

In 1997, Kathleen Peay enrolled at the University of Oklahoma as a freshman and member of the women's varsity soccer team. Having dreamt of "playing big time soccer," to Kathleen, the University of Oklahoma represented an incredible opportunity to realize her dreams. She was awarded a four-year scholarship to play soccer there (Garber, 2002). Despite the exceptional opportunity, Peay's soccer career ended prematurely. In October 1997, Peay was subjected to hazing during an away game against New Mexico. The hazing was intended to foster a sense of belonging, but it only left her feeling degraded and humiliated (Hoover, 1999).

The incident occurred at the behest and supervision of then–head coach Bettina Fletcher (Evans, 1999). Coach Fletcher, along with her two assistants, rented vans to transport the soccer team to an elementary school playground after competing against New Mexico. Peay had some idea of what was about to occur; the previous night she heard talk of an initiation (Garber, 2002). When the team arrived at the elementary school, Peay refused to exit the van and locked herself in the vehicle. In this moment, the coaching staff accosted Peay:

> Fletcher screamed at her with profane language to get out. Peay refused. Eventually, an assistant coach unlocked the door and Peay was forced to participate in the ceremony.
>
> *(Garber, 2002)*

Under the "full authorization" of the coaching staff, Peay and her fellow freshmen were "degraded in disgusting ways" (Evans, 1999). The freshmen were forced to wear adult diapers and blindfolds and "perform simulated sex acts on dill pickles and bananas and required to perform other bizarre sexually oriented acts" (Evans, 1999, p. 1). When a banana was forced into Peay's mouth, she spit out the fruit, but another banana quickly took its place. Aggravating the situation further, whipped cream, honey, and syrup "were sprayed on her hair and in her face, simulating ejaculation" (Garber, 2002). This incident left Peay feeling "embarrassed, belittled and humiliated" (Garber, 2002). Peay returned to school but did not report the incident despite the trauma she experienced.

Despite the devastating ordeal of that night and the life-long psychological impact, Peay stood to lose even more if she left Oklahoma. Peay had a four-year scholarship and soccer remained an important part of her life (Garber, 2002). However, a year after the hazing, pictures taken during the incident surfaced, and the University of Oklahoma took action; Peay was asked to make a statement regarding the incident, and with the support of one of her teammates' father, she found the strength to finally report the incident to the university (Garber, 2002). Shortly after the pictures surfaced, Coach Fletcher resigned – after three seasons and a 11–36 record – citing "personal and family reasons" (Garber, 2002).

While the resignation of Coach Fletcher brought some relief to Peay, she was battling feelings of "depression, guilt, anxiety and hopelessness" (Garber, 2002). Subsequently, Peay's doctor diagnosed her as suffering from post-traumatic stress disorder. In a debilitated mental state, Peay developed "fears about leaving her home and her family" (Garber, 2002). Peay decided not to return to Oklahoma for her junior year, as the hazing she suffered compromised her ability to function as a healthy and normal college student.

In October 1999, Kathleen Peay filed a federal lawsuit against the University of Oklahoma Board of Regents, former–head coach Bettina Fletcher, and her former assistant coaches (Evans, 1999). The suit sought damages in excess of $75,000 for the "physical, emotional and sexual" exploitation that Peay suffered during the hazing in New Mexico (The Oklahoman, 1999). In response to the lawsuit, OU athletic director Joe Castiglione stated:

> OU's athletic department is strongly committed to creating a positive environment and wholesome environment for all student-athletes . . . aggressively addressing all concerns brought to our attention which affect our student-athletes.
>
> *(Evans, 1999)*

Following this statement, Oklahoma filed a motion to dismiss the lawsuit in November 1999; the lawsuit was ultimately dropped in April 2000 (The Oklahoman, 2000). The culmination of this incident and lawsuit weighed heavily on Peay; she never returned to OU as a student or soccer player, and the emotional and physical burden left her without the desire to play the sport she once loved (Garber, 2002).

Northwestern University Women's Soccer

At the turn of the century, Northwestern University's women's soccer team held high hopes for the program, as new head coach, Jenny Haigh, took over the program. While the university anticipated that the new coach would bring the team and the university success, a hazing incident in 2006 ended up shaping their reputation and the experience of the team. The Internet eliminated any hopes of anonymity in the hazing case. While the team's lackluster record of 59–66–8 overall and 18–38–3 in the Big Ten from 2001 to 2005 never earned it national recognition, pictures posted to the Internet detailing the hazing incident would earn the team the national spotlight.

The Northwestern women's soccer team was one of the first college programs to experience the unwanted exposure of the Internet. In spring 2006, the website badjocks.com published photos of the soccer team hazing its players. The photos depicted the players giving lap dances, with captions indicating that they were a punishment for the female soccer players and for the Northwestern men's soccer team's enjoyment. Additional photos captured scenes of women blindfolded with their hands bound behind their backs, while others showcased two girls kissing

(Bannon, 2006a). In addition, the players were covered in marker and "appeared to be drinking beer" (Sprow, 2006). While none of the pictures explicitly labeled any of the players' names, it became clear what team it was when head coach Haigh's name was "scrawled in capital letters on one woman's thigh" (Bannon, 2006a). It was obvious that the women's soccer team was hazing its members and believed that it was doing so under the pretense of privacy and team bonding. This, as it turned out, was a false sense of privacy.

At the center of this scandal was Bob Reno, the owner of the website badjocks.com, who made the deliberate decision to post the pictures of the soccer players at Northwestern. Reno published his website to feature pictures of student-athletes acting in ways that would bring negative exposure to individuals and teams. Reno claimed that he found the pictures of the Northwestern team on a "student file-sharing network while searching for photographs about the Duke (lacrosse) case" (Sprow, 2006). Reno believed that he was doing the right thing when he posted the pictures of the soccer team on his site. Reno thought "if I can heighten the discussion by showing the pictures, then I'll feel like I did something right" (Sprow, 2006). Reno more than began a discussion, he ushered in a new era where no collegiate team is shielded behind a false sense of privacy and nothing is too sacred to post on the Internet.

In response to the pictures posted on badjocks.com, Northwestern's athletic director, Mark Murphy, suspended the women's team indefinitely, pending an investigation by the Division of Student Affairs (Morrison, 2006). The women's soccer team issued a letter of apology to the Northwestern community on May 15, 2006:

> We, the Northwestern women's soccer team, apologize for the negative attention, press, and controversy our alleged hazing incident has caused the University. We never foresaw that what began as a well-intentioned night of team unity and celebration would have such severe consequences, and we are embarrassed that our actions have become the source of such harsh criticism.
>
> *(Morrison, 2006)*

While the athletic department had no official comment on the statement released by the women's team, the athletic department reinstated the team after the investigation that student affairs conducted was concluded (Morrison, 2006). As a condition of being reinstated, several Northwestern players were suspended from the 2006–2007 regular season games (Bannon, 2006b). The Division of Student Affairs investigation concluded that the party in question included "underage drinking and additional inappropriate behavior that violated the university's anti-hazing policy" (Bannon, 2006b). Murphy further required the team to participate in community service and educational sessions on hazing.

Following the investigation, Jenny Haigh decided to resign as head coach. While there was "no official reason for the resignation, the announcement came 11 days after the conclusion . . . [of investigating] the hazing scandal" (Sullivan, 2006).

Even though, in 2004, Haigh had led the women's soccer team to their first winning season since 1998, the scandal that ripped her team apart and placed it on the national level for all to pass judgment might have been too much for her to bear.

Franklin and Marshall Women's Lacrosse

The women's lacrosse team at Franklin and Marshall College (F&M) has been, historically, a Division III national-level contender since 1987. The success that the team achieved was, in part, due to the leadership of head coach Lauren Paul. Paul was a 2003 graduate of F&M, and a two-time All-American player during her tenure on the lacrosse team there (Matuszewski, 2012). In 2008, Paul was hired to coach; during her first year as head coach, she led F&M to the 2009 NCAA Division III national championship, where they took the title. For her leadership on the field, Paul was named the 2009 Intercollegiate Women's Lacrosse Coaches Association coach of the year. Yet the success and momentum that Paul was able to generate at F&M came to a grinding halt in April 2012.

On April 12, 2012, the F&M lacrosse team and coaching staff discovered the team was under investigation for a hazing episode that "occurred more than a year earlier at an event known as Freshmen Fun Night" (Berman, 2012). F&M began a formal investigation into the hazing incident after the administration received information about an "unsanctioned student-organized event" from the Lancaster Police Department.

Five days after the coaches and team discovered they were being investigated, Paul was fired, and the team's juniors and all but one of its seniors were suspended due to the allegations. F&M's dean, Kent Trachte, said in a statement:

> F&M takes any allegation of hazing very seriously and has strong and clear policies against any form of hazing as part of our deep commitment to safeguarding student health, safety and well-being.
>
> (Matuszewski, 2012)

F&M's investigation revealed that hazing was present at the student-organized event and set off a chain of decisions by F&M's administration.

During Freshmen Fun Night, the freshmen on the team were allegedly subjected to activities that were consistent with hazing. A lawyer for then-freshman Paige Burns described the hazing as including the "forced consumption of excessive amounts of alcohol and events of a sexual nature, including being blindfolded and having semen sprayed at them" (Berman, 2012). Despite Burns's allegations, eight other players who were present, including two freshmen, denied that this occurred at the Freshman Fun Night. Other players on the team described the Freshmen Fun Night as including an egg race and other activities similar to a grade-school party – nothing that would include the spraying of semen on teammates (Berman, 2012).

Burns's former teammates believed that she made such accusations because she was cut from the lacrosse team before the season began. Burns and her lawyer had a very different perspective – it seemed to them that Burns was cut "in retaliation for complaining about hazing," which Burns brought to Paul's attention in November 2011 (Berman, 2012). Coach Paul denied that Burns was cut from the team due to complaining about hazing, but rather that she was cut due to "her performance on the field" (Berman, 2012).

Regardless of the competing versions of what happened that night, the F&M administration decided to fire the coaching staff and suspend a majority of the team's upperclassmen. Despite that the coaching staff had no direct involvement in the hazing, F&M determined that the incident warranted the removal of the coaches. The coaching staff seemed stunned, as Paul stated: "Honestly, I have no idea why I was fired . . . . They never told me the findings of the investigation. Ever" (Berman, 2012). F&M's administration clearly thought otherwise when Dean Trachte stated:

> We believe that all coaches are responsible for fostering a team culture that is consistent with the educational goals of the institution, and for being effective educators about matters such as hazing. . . . . We feel strongly that students must face consequences for violating college policies and engaging in activities that have no place on any college campus. At F&M, there is no greater priority than the well-being and safety of students.
>
> *(Lochary, 2012)*

The Vice President of Communications, Cass Cliatt, reaffirmed the college's stance: "Coaches at F&M are educators . . . responsible for maintaining a supportive environment and an atmosphere of trust consistent with the education goals of the institution" (AP, 2012).

But even as the coaching staff was being fired and the team was being disciplined, the school was developing a plan for how to reinstate the team. The administration offered to restore suspended players to the team, but under stipulations that included sharing predetermined playing time. The suspended players declined to return under these conditions because, as senior Erin Dunne stated, "What they gave us back, with the restrictions, was absolutely ridiculous. . . . . It wouldn't be our team. It would be the administration's team" (Berman, 2012). The stipulations from F&M's administration puzzled the student-athletes, as the requirements to return to play did not appear connected to the hazing incident, but rather it seemed to be a method to control the players in competition. Lauren Paul's lawyer, John Gallagher, viewed F&M's disciplinary actions with the students as inconsistent with the disciplinary action taken against his client. Gallagher believed that offering reinstatement to players implied a lack of evidence that hazing took place (Goldberg & Goldberg, 2012). Gallagher stated:

> The decision to reinstate the suspended players, coupled with the absence of any meaningful student discipline being pursued or carried out, particularly when viewed through the prism of F&M's stated principles where student

well-being is concerned, clearly suggest that whatever occurred in March 2011 did not constitute "hazing."

(Goldberg & Goldberg, 2012)

Regardless of whether hazing occurred in March 2011, the F&M women's lacrosse team was significantly handicapped by the allegations and investigation – players refused to return to the team, its successful coaching staff was terminated, and a once-exemplary program was blemished, hindering future recruiting efforts. Even though the team had a proud history of success at the Division III level, this incident has left the "Franklin and Marshall women's lacrosse team in a precarious position," as the future of its program is unknown (Berman, 2012).

Sociocultural Context

The exposure that the women's teams at OU, Northwestern, and F&M received from the media and throughout higher education was not only based on concerns about hazing but was also about the prevalence of sexual harassment and outlandish rituals in these hazing practices. Inextricably linked to these cases was how higher education administrators exposed the hazing, investigated it, and determined punishment for those involved in the hazing scandal. In the case of Northwestern, the role of social media and the Internet challenged conventional notions of what was private behavior and how student-athletes represent institutions.

Sexual Harassment

The hazing that Kathleen Peay and Paige Burns suffered exposed the sexual harassment that women frequently endure when participating in team-bonding ceremonies. Few students in higher education experience the exclusivity of participating on a college sports team, and student-athletes regularly defend this elite status through hazing. Student-athletes thrive in the aura that surrounds collegiate sports; membership in these sports implies to outsiders a certain status and athleticism, among other advantages. Hazing offers a way for the current members to defend their status, and it represents a rite of passage for new members to legitimize their exclusive membership. Furthermore, for those who haze the new members, it "satisfies some sort of primitive psychic need to symbolically take revenge for the hazing they themselves once endured" (Nuwer, 1999, pp. 37–38).

For Peay and Burns to attain full team-member status, they were required to participate in hazing rituals that modeled "traditionally masculine values, including strength, power and domination" (Waldron & Kowalski, 2009, p. 292). Known as the power and performance model of sport, women have increasingly participated in this behavior, as "opportunities at higher levels of competition have increased" (Waldron & Kowalski, 2009, p. 292). Women's college sports have historically existed in the shadow of men's sports – men's are aired most frequently on TV and garner the most money. Yet women's sports have consistently gained more coverage and funding in higher education (Crowley, 2000). As the opportunities for competition have increased, women's teams want student-athletes who evoke "traditionally masculine values" in the hopes that these qualities will lead to success. Hazing has become the platform to instill these qualities in women's athletics, as upperclassmen believe it is their responsibility to mold new student-athletes in the likeness of their team.

Upperclassmen student-athletes believe it is their responsibility to defend the standards of their team and they "justify actions that are outside the range of normal human behavior" to uphold these standards. Furthermore, hazers, who uphold these standards by "teaching newcomers precedence and getting weaklings to 'toughen-up' or quit, are rewarded a higher status within their team" (Nuwer, 1999, p. 38). As these values are upheld, "power and status" is conferred on these individuals who are "perceived [as] making the group better" (Nuwer, 1999, p. 38).

The cases of Kathleen Peay and Paige Burns tell the story of two women whose views about being part of a team conflicted with this idea that new members must participate in a ceremonial rite of passage. Peay, for example, viewed her recruitment and scholarship to play soccer at OU as legitimizing her membership on the team. Peay believed she did not need to participate in a hazing ritual to be conferred equal status with other newcomers to the team. Despite her recruitment and scholarship, Peay was not fully embraced by the team because she had not completed her hazing "socialization" with the team (Waldron & Kowalski, 2009). Burns was subjected to similar treatment. Knowing that Burns desired to belong to an elite Division III team, her elder teammates used their power and authority over her to allegedly degrade Burns. Blindfolding and spraying her with semen – an act that is completely unrelated to the sport of lacrosse – represented, to those who hazed her, a path for her to gain admission into and acceptance from her team.

At OU, it was the coaches who introduced hazing as a way to invoke a sense of privilege and demonstrate a commitment to the team and the desire to be a "worthy" teammate. Not only was the behavior inappropriate, in part because it took the form of sexual harassment, but Coach Fletcher also abused her status and power as head coach. Fletcher determined playing time and scholarships, among other things related to the team – things she could use in her favor to influence the behavior of her players (Hogshead-Makar & Steinbach, 2003).

What was concerning in the OU case was the willingness of a coach, specifically, to jeopardize the safety and well-being of her players, not to mention jeopardizing the integrity of the team. In college athletics, coaches are the first-line educators who players look to for appropriate behavior and conduct. Coaches must know how to educate their teams about hazing and its potential effects on individual players and their teams as a whole. The athletic departments that drive the priorities and values that coaches uphold are essential to achieving this. The current cultures in athletic departments fail to address the pervasiveness of hazing; some administrators believe in and defend the utility of hazing in college athletics, but others are simply ignorant to its existence on their campus (Nuwer, 1999; Hoover, 1999).

What was interesting in both the OU and F&M episodes was that the reporting of the alleged hazing was delayed – unfortunately, however, this is not unique to these schools or hazing episodes in general. Several studies have found that a reluctance to report hazing occurs because of a "fear of retribution" from fellow student-athletes and coaches (Waldron & Kowalski, 2009). The alleged sexual harassment that Peay and Burns suffered and their decision to not report the incidents was most likely motivated by a fear of retribution: these two women had everything to lose if they reported their hazing. Peay and Burns rationalized that, by acknowledging their sexual harassment to school officials when the incidents occurred, they risked being ostracized from their team and school, not to mention the emotional pressure they would have had to endure as an investigation was conducted.

Peay's and Burns's decisions to not immediately report the hazing they suffered was no surprise, as their unwillingness to report sexual harassment is indicative of the culture in higher education. Throughout higher education, "approximately two thirds of all college students experience some form of sexual harassment; yet fewer than 10% notify a campus official, and even fewer report such misconduct" (Lundy-Wagner & Winkle-Wagner, 2013, p. 52). Reporting the hazing would rock the foundation of their teams, athletic departments, and institutions. In addition, these student-athletes were ambivalent over how their administrations would handle these delicate situations. Student-athletes, coaches, and administrators would be implicated in the hazing. The culture of secrecy in hazing and college athletics, paired with a lack of assistance for those who suffer abuse, is not conducive for student-athletes to step forward and to seek help.

Beyond the fear of retribution, student-athletes may not report hazing because of an institution's inability to address the issue in a comprehensive way. Even if the abused women in these cases wanted to report the incident, they may not have known to whom they could speak in a safe and open way. Several studies have indicated that, as hazing and other forms of abuse occur, "some colleges are not well equipped to address the challenges with processing these offenses" (Lundy-Wagner & Winkle-Wagner, 2013, p. 52). If Peay or Burns knew that there was a person in the athletics department with whom they could discuss hazing, they might have reported their abuse sooner and without the fear of retribution for themselves and others. It is the responsibility of athletic departments to make their student-athletes aware they have resources available to help victims of hazing rituals and sexual harassment and, when this does not occur, incidents of abuse are either not reported or not reported in a timely fashion to assist victims of abuse.

Governance

The resolve to fund collegiate sports committed OU, Northwestern, and F&M to providing a positive environment for their student-athletes. When hazing occurred on their campuses, as a matter of due diligence and a commitment to good governance, they were liable for the hazing of their student-athletes (Crow & Rosner, 2002).

However, the hazing scandals that engulfed these campuses challenged how these institutions remained committed to good governance.

What was in dispute in the F&M case, as well as in the OU and Northwestern cases, was how the institution communicated its processes and findings when it investigated the hazing incident. Institutional communication was essential for good governance to ensure that consultation "by the administration with faculty leadership allow[ed] time and a mechanism for leadership to consult with their constituents" (American Association of University Professors [AAUP], 1966). A breakdown in institutional communication left the F&M coaching staff shocked when they were fired without knowing about the college's investigative process or its findings. F&M's decision to fire its coaching staff but offer a way for previously suspended players to return to the team did not project a consistent message. How could members of a team who were present at a hazing event no longer be deemed culpable, but a coaching staff that was not present and had a history of success be considered responsible? The personal and secretive nature of hazing does not lend itself well to a transparent investigation, but F&M was obliged to effectively communicate to all its constituents to ensure good governance was upheld as punishments were handed down. Yet the communication and decision-making processes at F&M remained opaque. The lack of transparency at F&M frustrated many, as questions persisted over how decisions were made and what exactly happened at the Freshmen Fun Night.

Administrators', coaches', and other higher education staff's perceptions of hazing vary widely across institutions. Failure to effectively disseminate information and to include relevant individuals when determining policy have hampered decision-making on hazing incidents and punishments among these stakeholders. Yet collective decision-making is critical when determining hazing policy and navigating incidents, as these issues touch all parts of higher education. The idea within higher education that hazing is not a common problem or that it is relegated to one small population further hampers collective decision-making on hazing incidents. Institutions continue to be shocked when hazing is found on their campuses, despite that more than a quarter million student-athletes have experienced some form of hazing (Hoover, 1999).

Many coaches and administrators do not comprehend the prevalence of hazing, which limits their willingness to diagnose and challenge the embedded hazing practices. In the 1999 report by Hoover, only 10 percent of all coaches knew hazing existed on their campuses, and even less than 10 percent reported knowledge of alcohol consumption during such activities. This lack of knowledge reached even the highest administrators, as some athletics directors perceived it as a nonissue, relegated only to Greek life, or as the responsibility of the student affairs office on their campus (Hoover, 1999). The incidents at OU, Northwestern, and F&M occurred because of a failure to effectively collaborate across campus and to develop policy that utilized the experience and expertise of faculty and staff. While it remains difficult to completely prevent hazing, improved institutional communication and collective decision-making are the best means to diminishing hazing.

The Internet

The scandal that occurred on Northwestern's women's soccer team could have happened to any number of collegiate programs around the country. But in this particular case, the Internet turned what had historically been a secretive practice into a national scandal. The pictures detailing the incident at Northwestern not only brought the hazing of women to the forefront of the discussion on hazing, but it also ushered in the expectation that Northwestern conduct its investigation and discipline of its student-athletes with transparency. The media's coverage of this incident and the role of the Internet changed the world in which college student-athletes and higher education existed. The Northwestern incident revealed a truth for all of college athletics – all teams and athletics departments are open to public scrutiny because of the ease of sharing information on the Internet.

The hazing incident at Northwestern situated the Internet as a higher education watchdog and exposed the external pressure it could apply to institutions as they make decisions about hazing. How Northwestern dealt with its hazing incident reflected on the institution and its athletics department and indicated the values it chose to uphold. The secretive nature of hazing could not persist in such an open environment. This era of information sharing forced Northwestern and subsequent athletics departments to no longer tolerate "cover-ups" and in-house mishandling.

What was also significant in the Northwestern case was the role that the institution played in protecting its student-athletes, as the line between what was public and private became blurred (Nelson, 2006). Badjocks.com viewed posting the pictures as its responsibility, even when student-athletes had not "anticipated [that] what was said or posted (online) [would] be made public" (Nelson, 2006). Both the willingness of students to post pictures online and websites to exploit them eliminated any chance for Northwestern or any institution in the future to discipline and protect its student-athletes without the entire nation watching. While it is important that institutions have checks and balances to ensure that student-athletes and athletics departments do not violate institutional, conference, or NCAA policies, let alone break the law, athletics departments do have some responsibility to protect their student-athletes from excessive exposure to and critique from outsiders. Student-athletes are young adults learning how to become respectful members of society and, while this cannot occur in a bubble, institutions must ensure that its student-athletes can exist in an environment that is free from continual scrutiny.

The Internet has altered how athletics departments operate. The ease with which information can be shared on the Internet has forced departments to strategize how to curb student-athletes' hazing, protect their athletics programs from outside scrutiny, and also maintain transparency when making decisions about hazing incidents when they occur. Transparency will continue to be demanded as higher education officials, alumni, and the greater public push for clarity when incidents occur in college athletics (Pennington, 2006).

Alternate Ending

Time and time again in college athletics at the most successful programs, coaches, team members, and even administrators speak to the feelings of unity and belonging that student-athletes share with teammates. It can easily be said that cultivating a team spirit and identity is key to propelling teams to success. The programs at OU, Northwestern, and F&M desired this unity, but their decision to use hazing as the platform for bonding alienated team members. It was no surprise, however, that these programs chose to initiate new team members of their squads through hazing. Student-athletes ascribe great significance to the hazing traditions that had forged team identities in the past.

Separating tradition and team unity out from hazing at OU, Northwestern, and F&M would have required intervention from the coaches and administration. If these institutions had understood the hazing traditions, they would have known that hazing was the method of choice to bond student-athletes. Educating student-athletes and coaches about hazing practices, as well as adopting strict zero-tolerance policies, could have reformed team-bonding practices, but it would not have been enough. These teams needed the guidance of their coaches and athletics departments. Institutional involvement and educating athletes and athletics staff could have helped to steer the hazing practices before they became outright abusive.

As women's athletics have grown and developed their identity within the world of sports, they have gravitated toward the secretive culture of hazing that continually debased young student-athletes before them. OU, Northwestern, and F&M promoted hazing cultures, where abuse of power and the degradation of women were the norm. Furthermore, the hazing cultures polarized those who felt abused in sexual and physical ways from the rest of the team, discouraging these women from reporting the incidents. Sexual and physical harassment in college athletics and higher education remain taboo subjects, in turn strengthening the role of hazing in team sports and denying those who have been abused the help they may need. Open cultures at these institutions would have encouraged physically and emotionally abused student-athletes to report hazing without the fear of alienating themselves from their teammates and coaches. Eliminating the positive stigma associated with enduring hazing (quietly) and the negative connotation associated with reporting hazing is the only path to true reform within college athletics and higher education in general.

References

American Association of University Professors (AAUP). (1966). Evaluation of shared governance. Retrieved from www.aaup.org/issues/governance-colleges-universities/resources-governance

AP. (2012, April 18). Franklin and Marshall College lacrosse coach Lauren Paul, players dismissed over hazing complaint. Retrieved from www.huffingtonpost.com/2012/04/18/franklin-marshall-college_n_1434111.html

Bannon, T. (2006a, May 16). NU probes alleged hazing. Retrieved from http://articles.chicagotribune.com

Bannon, T. (2006b, June 10). NU will discipline women's soccer players. Retrieved from http://articles.chicagotribune.com

Berman, Z. (2012, July 6). Lacrosse program shaken by hazing inquiry. Retrieved from www.nytimes.com

Crow, R. B., & Rosner, S. B. (2002). Institutional and organizational liability for hazing in intercollegiate and professional team sports. *St. John's Law Review*, 76(1), 87–114.

Crowley, E. (2000, June 22). Title IX levels playing field for funding women's sports. Retrieved from http://on.wsj.com/1x6BBch

Evans, M. (1999, October 29). Ex-sooner alleges sorid soccer ritual. Retrieved from http://newsok.com/ex-sooner-alleges-sordid-soccer-ritual/article/2672884/?page=2

Garber, G. (2002). It's not all fun and games. Retrieved from http://espn.go.com/otl/hazing/wednesday.html

Goldberg, C., and Goldberg, K. N. (2012, May 8). Former F&M women's coach Paul speaks out against firing for alleged hazing incident; university maintains position. Retrieved from http://phillylacrosse.com

Harper, S. R., & Harris III, F. (Eds.). (2010). *College men and masculinities: Theory, research, and implications for practice.* San Francisco: Jossey-Bass.

Hightower, K. (2013). FAMU hazing case: 12 charged with manslaughter in Robert Champion's death. Retrieved from www.huffingtonpost.com

Hogshead-Makar, N., & Steinbach, S.E. (2003). Intercollegiate athletics' unique environments for sexual harassment claims: balancing the realities of athletics with preventing potential claims. *Marquette Sports Law Review*, 13(2), 173–193.

Hoover, N. C. (1999). *National survey: Initiation rites and athletics for NCAA sports teams.* Retrieved from www.alfred.edu/sports_hazing/docs/hazing.pdf

Lochary, C. (2012, April 27). F&M cancels season, former coach speaks out. Retrieved from www.laxmagazine.com

Lundy-Wagner, V., & Winkle-Wagner, R. (2013). A harassing climate? Sexual harassment and campus racial climate research. *Journal of Diversity in Higher Education*, 6(1), 51–68.

Matuszewski, E. (2012, April 18). Franklin and Marshall fires women's lacrosse coach in hazing case. Retrieved from www.bloomberg.com

Morrison, D. (2006, May 21). Women's soccer team releases apology for negative attention. Retrieved from http://dailynorthwestern.com

Nelson, L. (2006, May 24). Hazing scandal raises debate on web ethics. Retrieved from http://dailynorthwestern.com

Nuwer, H. (1999). *Wrongs of passage: Fraternities, sororities, hazing and binge drinking.* Bloomington: Indiana University Press.

The Oklahoman. (1999, October 8). Soccer player sues OU. Retrieved from http://newsok.com/soccer-player-sues-ou/article/2670376

The Oklahoman. (2000, April 13). Soccer abuse suit dropped. Retrieved from http://newsok.com/soccer-abuse-suit-dropped/article/2693524

Pennington, B. (2006, October 15). After Duke case, college athletes are put on notice. Retrieved from www.nytimes.com

Rosner, S. R., & Crow, R.B. (2003). Institutional liability for hazing in interscholastic sports. *Houston Law Review*, 39(2), 275–305.

Sprow, C. (2006, May 16). Northwestern women's soccer team suspended after hazing. Retrieved from www.nytimes.com/2006/05/16/sports/soccer/16hazing.html

Sullivan, E. (2006, June 26). Soccer coach resigns, NU starts replacement search. http://dailynorthwestern.com

Waldron, J. J., & Kowalski, C. L. (2009). Crossing the line. *Research Quarterly for Exercise and Sport*, 80(2), 291–302.

17

"NUMEROUS AND REPEATED CONCUSSIONS" AT EASTERN ILLINOIS UNIVERSITY

Adrian Arrington's Lawsuit Against the NCAA

Whitney N. Griffin

Football almost died in 1905. Clad with leather helmets and a routine disregard of rules, amateur and intercollegiate football watched over 18 people die, sometimes right on the field (Greene, 2012). The fatal skull fractures and hundreds of head injuries that year received national attention, causing President Roosevelt to call a White House conference to review football rules. Thus, the Rules Committee was formed, later named the National Collegiate Athletic Association (NCAA) in 1910 (Smith, 2000). Just over a century later, four former student-athletes are currently suing the NCAA for concussion management negligence and concealment of brain trauma information. In 2011, Adrian Arrington, Derek Owens, Mark Turner, and Angela Palacios filed an ongoing class action complaint against the NCAA in the United States District Court in the Northern District of Illinois. The plaintiffs seek to represent two nationwide classes: The first consists of NCAA student-athletes who have sustained sport-related concussions or suffered from concussion-like symptoms and are still experiencing the effects. The second is a medical monitoring subclass that seeks to track former student-athletes' health after they leave school if they have sustained concussions or suffered concussion-like symptoms while playing college sports.

The Case

During the 2009 fall season, Adrian Arrington was a strong safety and captain of the Eastern Illinois University (EIU) football team, ending his athletic career with 48 solo tackles (Arrington et al. v NCAA, 2011). Somewhere in his 154 total tackles between 2006–2009, Arrington received his first three concussions and was told by the EIU team doctor that he could return to play the very next day. After his third diagnosed concussion, Arrington started experiencing seizures and memory loss unrelated to one specific traumatic event. Only after these cumulative symptoms manifested did EIU finally send Arrington to a neurologist. Two concussions later, Arrington finally left his football team and dropped out of several classes due to memory loss, depression, and regular migraines. A Magnetic Resonance Imaging (MRI) scan revealed scarring in the frontal lobe of his brain.

Arrington revealed that at no time was he coached on how to make safer tackles, nor was he given literature or lectures about concussions or other head injury prevention. The message he received from EIU was to either "play hard and play fast" (Arrington et al. v NCAA, 2011, p. 7) or be cut from the team. Since then, EIU officials have said that the school treated concussions in accordance with the NCAA Sports Medicine Handbook, which offered no specific direction about how long an athlete should be benched (Keilman, 2013).

Arrington claims the NCAA "has failed its student-athletes – choosing instead to sacrifice them on an altar of money and profits" (Hawkins, 2011) through an insidious combination of neglect and inaction regarding tackling techniques that are most likely to avoid head injuries. While the altar of NCAA profits accrues to one billion dollars in revenue in 2013, today Arrington is unable to drive a car or work; he relies on disability payments for himself, his three young children, and his girlfriend. Along with daily migraines, Arrington's frequent seizures are so severe that they resulted in a torn rotator cuff in his shoulder that required surgical repair. In 2013, 27-year-old Arrington told USA Today Sports: "My life is in shambles right now. I was a student-athlete. I was captain of the team. I'm on welfare now . . . . $430 a month is really nothing for a family" (Axon, 2013). Arrington's lasting neurological damage has left him asking questions that are not considered during college recruitment trips: "Am I going to be here for my kids? Am I gonna get too depressed where I end up trying to hurt myself?" (Keilman, 2013).

The second plaintiff, Derek Owens, was a star receiver on an academic scholarship at the University of Central Arkansas (UCA) and was named one of the top scholar-athletes in the state of Arkansas. In the summer of 2008, Owens attended a "voluntary practice" offered by UCA to incoming freshmen football players and other members of the team, but without coaches, to get acquainted with the school. Owens was hit in the head from behind without pads or helmets. Treatment was not provided. Owens called his parents after practice was over, telling them he was dizzy, was having difficulty seeing, and did not think he could drive. He did not return to summer practices and no one at UCA followed up with him. Owens believed that a concussion only occurred if he "blacked out" or was "knocked out" (Arrington et al. v NCAA, 2011, p. 9). While Owens suffered from headaches, ringing in his ears, pressure in his head, vomiting, and felt as if his head was swollen, he still did not recognize these symptoms as indicative of a concussion because he had not lost consciousness. His understanding of concussions was full of misinformation and useless clichés. He recalled thinking, "You get your bell rung. You get smoked. And then you go back in" (Vecsey, 2011). He continued to believe this throughout the fall football season since he never received (a) proper preventative tackling and blocking techniques, (b) information on all known symptoms that might signify a concussion, and (c) education on the possible long-term effects of concussions.

In just the second week of official fall practice season, Owens was hit by a linebacker and was knocked unconscious. The UCA trainers returned Owens to his dorm room, told his roommates that Owens had a severe concussion, and asked his roommates to wake him up every couple of hours to make sure he was okay. After receiving several strange texts from her son, Owen's mother called his phone and was informed by one of his roommates that Owens was unable to talk as a result of the severe concussion. Owens' mother intervened and called the UCA athletic trainer to report that this was, in fact, Owens' second concussion. By the fall of 2010, Owens was experiencing a maelstrom of cognitive, emotional, and physical symptoms: memory loss, an inability to concentrate or focus, anxiety, depression, headaches, and trouble sleeping. These symptoms seemed to exacerbate each other: if Owens went to sleep after studying for a test, he would forget the information and, out of fear of failing, forced himself to stay up all night (Arrington et al. v NCAA, 2011). This tautological method led to plummeting grades and a loss of academic scholarship. Only when Owens visited his family doctor in May 2011 for fear of having ADHD did his physician diagnose his problems as being related to the multiple sport concussions he had suffered.

The NCAA's Constitution states: "An active member institution shall have a concussion management plan for its student-athletes" (NCAA Constitution, 2011), followed by four protocols for educating student-athletes about the signs and symptoms, removal from play for the day, diagnosis, and required medical clearance for return to play. Assuming that the NCAA's rules provided more guidance than their current schools-should-have-a-plan design, at least two more underlying issues need to be tackled (pun intended). Why is the onus on the athlete to seek out proper medical attention? And if said medical attention is provided, why then should the athlete be expected to regenerate enough brain cells to remain physically eligible? When Owens informed his coach about his medical issues and inability to continue playing football, his coach responded with, "so what's your plan?" (Arrington et al. v NCAA, 2011, p. 12). The coach probably meant to say, "So what's *our* plan?" Joseph Siprut, Arrington's attorney, makes another excellent point regarding the lack of an organizational contingency plan: "The question is, do you have procedures in place that are proactive or reactive and they don't. They don't really have anything in place" (Dodd, 2013). The deleterious gap between policy and practice continues to swallow student-athletes whole and spit out the mangled remains while moving on to the next batch of recruits.

In each of these cases as well as with football player Mark Turner at Fordham University and soccer player Angela Palacios at Ouachita Baptist University, the NCAA failed to:

(1) Address and/or correct the coaching of tackling, checking or other playing methodologies that cause head injuries; (2) educate coaches, trainers and student-athletes as to the symptoms indicating possible concussions; (3) implement system-wide "return to play" guidelines for student-athletes who have sustained concussions; (4) implement system-wide guidelines for the screening

and detection of head injuries; (5) implement regulations addressing the treatment and eligibility of student-athletes who have sustained multiple concussion in the course of play; and (6) implement a support system for student-athletes who, after sustaining concussions, are left unable to either play their sport or even lead a normal life.

(Rivera, 2013, p. 3)

Without requiring proper education of true concussion symptoms, mandating student-athletes to report symptoms is meaningless (Arrington et al. v NCAA, 2011). To add injury to insult, all plaintiffs have incurred substantial out-of-pocket costs and continue to pay for ongoing medical treatment directly related to their diagnosed post-concussion syndrome.

On behalf of the class, the NCAA faces four counts of negligence (i.e. failing to disclose the role of repeated concussions in causing chronic lifelong cognitive decline), fraudulent concealment (i.e. the NCAA helped pay for studies that associated a history of multiple concussions with greater risk of future brain damage in student-athletes), unjust enrichment (i.e. earning billions in revenue and retaining the benefits of student-athletes' service while refusing to pay medical expenses of sports-related injuries whose treatment is required post-college career), and medical monitoring (i.e. student-athletes who have not yet fully manifested the long-term physical and mental effects of the NCAA's misconduct and require specialized testing that is not generally given or available to the public at large for the early detection of the long-term effects of concussions and sub-concussive blows).

It is exceedingly difficult to sympathize with the NCAA, especially in light of certain powerful members' casual attitude toward the absence of concussion management implementation. In response to the push for stronger guidelines regarding concussions in early 2010 by David Klossner, the NCAA's director of health and safety, Ty Halpin, the director of playing rules administration, wrote to a colleague, "Dave is hot/heavy on the concussion stuff. He's been trying to force our rules committees to put in rules that are not good – I think I have finally convinced him to calm down" (Axon, 2013). What was Klossner so hot and heavy about? He was exasperated in emails about the internal obstacles to implementing concussion rules and legislation that would affect return-to-play guidelines (Fenno, 2013). When the managing director of government relations asked if youth sport guidelines would go beyond what was required at the college level, Klossner blatantly responded, "Well since we don't currently require anything all steps are higher than ours. It seems the federal act is mandating baseline and post-concussive testing" (Fenno, 2013). Shockingly, Pop Warner football guidelines are currently higher and better mandated than the NCAA's.

Additionally, in an April 2013 deposition, Klossner said schools are not required to submit their concussion management plans to the NCAA and the NCAA offers no oversight (Solomon, 2014). This information stands in harsh juxtaposition to NCAA spokeswoman Stacey Osburn's statement: "Despite this new filing, we continue to believe our policies and rules address student-athlete safety" (Axon,

2013). These beliefs are hardly comforting, especially when Klossner was asked if any schools have been disciplined regarding concussion management plans or whether the NCAA has considered punishing any schools, to which he responded, "Not to my knowledge" (Solomon, 2014). With no plans for punitive measures in place and no oversight, implementing concussion management plans is little more than lip service to a larger set of sociocultural headaches.

Sociocultural Context

Ignoring Research

Considered a subset of mild traumatic brain injury (mTBI), a concussion is defined by the American Medical Society for Sports Medicine as "a traumatically induced transient disturbance of brain function and involves a complex pathophysiological process" (Harmon et al., 2013, p. 15). Of the 3.8 million estimated concussions that occur in the USA per year during competitive sports and recreational activities (Langlois, Rutland-Brown, & Wald, 2006), as many as 50 percent may go unreported (Harmon et al., 2013). In 2002, a seminal study entitled "Enduring effects of concussion in youth athletes" explored the mild effects of repeated concussion on cognitive functioning (Moser & Schatz, 2002). The authors concluded that the youth athletes who had incurred two or more concussions may have experienced decreased overall neuropsychological functioning, attention, and mental speed. While this study offered only a glimpse into postconcussion sequelae (a condition that is the consequence of a previous disease or injury), it catalyzed a shift in how researchers examined recovery from more than one concussion. Previous research noted concussion recovery of college athletes within 5–10 days (Barth et al., 1989). The new researchers expanded upon this: athletes who had sustained one or more concussions 6 months prior to the study had similar cognitive performances to those athletes who had sustained a concussion within one week of the study. In light of this new information, what happens during cognitive recovery time merits further inquiry.

McCrea et al. (2003) studied the acute effects and recovery time following concussions among NCAA football players. Specifically, they measured processing speed, new learning and memory, and mental flexibility. On average, they found that players' cognitive functioning returned to normal within 5–7 days, but student-athletes required a full 7 days for postconcussive symptoms to completely return to baseline levels. Furthermore, the researchers emphasized that not all players demonstrated the same pattern of recovery regarding symptoms, cognition, and balance. A second NCAA concussion study published that same year suggested that players with a history of previous concussions are more likely to have future concussive injuries than those with no history, 1 in 15 players with a concussion may have additional concussions in the same playing season, and previous concussions may be associated with slower recovery of neurological function (Guskiewicz et al., 2003). Since then, researchers have identified recurrent concussions and sub-concussive contacts to the head as potential risk factors for the expression of dementia-related syndromes, late-life memory impairment, Alzheimer's disease, Chronic Traumatic Encephalopathy and clinical depression (Guskiewicz et al., 2005; Guskiewicz et al., 2007; Omalu et al., 2010).

Arrington began playing college football in 2006, Owens in 2008, Turner in 1988; Palacios started playing soccer in 2010. For three out of the four cases, the NCAA had its own commissioned studies to use as empirical evidence regarding return-to-play guidelines plus additional information by the same university researchers. Instead of sitting players out 5–7 days to regain normal cognitive functioning, Arrington was returned to play the next calendar day after each of his first three concussions. If players are returning the next calendar day after one concussion, they may return to the field less than 24 hours later, when the risk of sustaining a second concussion is 5.8 times greater (Zemper, 2003). By 2008, published evidence existed regarding the risks of multiple concussions. However, Owens's cognitive, emotional, and physical symptoms that caused him to lose his academic scholarship were not related to his multiple concussions until he saw his family doctor.

Dr. Robert Cantu, arguably one of the nation's leading voices on sport concussions, supported the adage "if in doubt, sit them out" in his paper entitled "When to disqualify an athlete after a concussion" (2009). One researcher specializing in pediatrics noted that Cantu's work "has been so overpowering it's crowded out" other research (Wolken, 2014). Don't like what the research says? Crowd it out with your own.

Omnipotent Powers of the Coach

Palacios's experience with concussions was exacerbated by a learned position of powerlessness. After her face collided with another team member's during a practice drill, Palacios was kept out of practice for 3 days. Despite her lingering side effects (i.e. daily headaches and vomiting), and without any clearance from the training staff, the coach made her participate in running drills even though Palacios reported that she wasn't feeling well. According to the lawsuit, Palacios asked the trainer for help, to which the trainer replied: "you don't want to make the coach mad" (Arrington et al. v NCAA, 2011, p. 16). Palacios was finally excused from practice after her mother contacted the coach. Still, the coach's position of power had dominated and silenced Palacios's physiological health.

A coach's frustration at not being able to play an injured athlete should not determine the length of concussion recovery. This is hardly an isolated case, since the coach sets the tone for approachability for the whole team, especially in issues with sport concussions:

> [Some coaches] view the medical staff as a necessary evil. If the coach recognizes the importance of careful management of concussions, the players will also appreciate the importance of the injury and more accurately report their symptoms. If, on the other hand, a coach does not believe in concussions, then detection and management of concussions becomes a very difficult process

because players are encouraged to play through their symptoms and not report symptoms to medical staff.

(Echemendia & Cantu, 2003, p. 50)

Furthermore, there is evidence that coach approachability is a barrier for reporting concussive symptoms in high school (Chrisman, Quitiquit, & Rivara, 2013). Even though perceptions and attitudes regarding concussion reporting among athletic trainers, coaches, and parents are important for shaping the culture surrounding concussions among collegiate athletes (Torres et al., 2013), coaches are granted immunity by the NCAA. Schools are only legislated to have a plan in place, and as the director of enforcement wrote in an internal email: "As a result, it would not be appropriate for enforcement to suspend or otherwise penalize a coach pursuant to the current legislation even if the student-athlete was required to participate after having been diagnosed with a concussion" (Fenno, 2013).

Tragedy of the Commons Theorem

The real travesty is getting lost in the blame game. At its root, the issue is that student-athletes are playing sports to the point of physical, mental, and emotional deterioration. The level of exploitation on each bureaucratic rung of power trickles down from the candid reign of the NCAA to the exorbitant salaries of the coaches. While money and power tip the scales in favor of a few, the health of many college athletes degenerates. One way of accounting for the overexploitation of student-athletes' mental, emotional, and physiological health is the tragedy of the commons, an economic theory that argues that most people who are trying to find a way to avoid the evils of a common problem want to do so without relinquishing any of the privileges they currently enjoy (Hardin, 1968). An example of this is when a Division III football player emailed Klossner because his school didn't have an athletic trainer at practice and most games for the previous 2 years. Klossner responded in an email, "'We do not have rules pertaining to the use of an Athletic trainer,' he wrote. 'The health and safety principle of the NCAA Constitution states that it is the responsibility of each member institution to protect the health and provide a safe environment for each of its participating student-athletes'" (Fenno, 2013). With that statement, the NCAA had absolved itself from action.

> Klossner followed with a discussion of legal liability and suggested the player approach his athletic department about applying for a grant to cover the cost of a trainer. He closed with links to concussion return-to-play guidelines and a concussion-awareness video put out, ironically, by the National Athletic Trainers' Association.
>
> *(Fenno, 2013)*

With this next statement, the NCAA had justified its inaction and simultaneously placed the onus on the student-athletes to write a grant and solve their problem.

The tragedy of the commons illuminates the larger athletic culture as a system where human brains and lives are treated as inexhaustible resources.

Alternate Ending

The NCAA announced a $399,999 donation to study the long-term impact of concussions just hours before the filing of the Arrington case (Fenno, 2013). If only they had commissioned and supported research in 2003, acknowledged the findings, and adjusted existing head safety policies accordingly, perhaps we could have skipped the last decade and jumped straight to the $399,999 study in 2004. The resources and time dedicated to protecting the disregard of student-athletes with head injuries could instead be used to implement policies that would actually be policed. Neglecting to care for all student-athletes should be exposed until a remedy is created, not just until the lawsuit reaches a settlement. It should go without saying that athletes have the right to be monitored medically, strengthened intellectually, and fed regularly in college. Perhaps this is the case that sets those assumptions into law.

Since the lawsuit is currently open, any alternate ending is therefore an optimistic prediction of events to come. At some point, does it matter who is responsible or not for explicitly communicating concussion information and return-to-play guidelines? Would not both parties be purposefully interested in the optimal performance and recovery of its moneymakers? Both the NCAA and member institutions are capable of enacting policies at their respective levels within a cogent system of checks and balances. Coaches, athletic trainers, advisors, and physicians are all sent to specialized conferences every year for their professional development. The NCAA is a self-governing institution that commissions concussion research. With their powers combined, different results are a reality. It just so happens that the NCAA got caught slipping first with its laissez-faire approach to bureaucratic loopholes. According to Klossner's knowledge, there are currently no punitive measures in place for institutions that do not create and adhere to concussion protocols and return-to-play guidelines. That might be a helpful first step.

With these scenarios in mind, athletes might have a better chance of improving their quality of life during and after their playing days. There is no perfect concussion protocol yet, but there are certainly better ways than the status quo of scapegoating blame. In the tragedy of the commons, a preferable plan is more useful than a perfect plan (Hardin, 1968).

References

Adrian Arrington, Derek Owens, Mark Turner, and Angela Palacios, et al. v. NCAA. No. 1:2011cv06356, Northern Illinois District (Chicago), available at www.scribd.com/doc/78428992/NCAA-Complaint

Axon, R. (2013, July 25). Does NCAA face more concussion liability than NFL? Retrieved from www.usatoday.com/story/sports/ncaaf/2013/07/25/ncaa-concussion-lawsuit-adrian-arrington/2588189/

Barth, J. T., Alves, W. M., Ryan, T. V., Macciocchi, S. N., Rimel, R. W., Jane, J. A. & Nelson, W. E. (1989). Mild head injury in sports: Neuropsychological sequelae and recovery of function. In H. S. Levin, H. M. Eisenberg, & A. L. Benton (Eds.), *Mild head injury* (pp. 257–275). New York: Oxford University Press.

Cantu, R. C. (2009). When to disqualify an athlete after a concussion. *Current Sports Medicine Reports*, 8(1), 6–7.

Chrisman, S. P., Quitiquit, C., & Rivara, F. P. (2013). Qualitative study of barriers to concussive symptom reporting in high school athletics. *Journal of Adolescent Health*, 52(3), 1–6.

Dodd, D. (2013, April 19). NCAA considering settlement of Arrington concussion suit. Retrieved April 17, 2014 from www.cbssports.com/collegefootball/writer/dennis-dodd/23222960/ncaa-considering-settlement-of-arrington-concussion-suit

Echemendia, R. J., & Cantu, R. C. (2003). Return to play following sports-related mild traumatic brain injury: the role for neuropsychology. *Applied Neuropsychology*, 10(1), 48–55.

Fenno, N. (2013, July 20). Internal NCAA emails raise questions about concussion policy. Retrieved April 24, 2014 from www.washingtontimes.com/blog/screen-play/2013/jul/20/internal-ncaa-emails-raise-questions-about-concuss

Greene, B. (2012, February 5). The president who saved football. Retrieved from www.cnn.com/2012/02/05/opinion/greene-super-bowl/

Guskiewicz, K. M., McCrea, M., Marshall, S. W., Cantu, R. C., Randolph, C., Barr, W., . . . Kelly, J. P. (2003). Cumulative effects associated with recurrent concussion in collegiate football players: The NCAA concussion study. *Journal of the American Medical Association*, 290(19), 2549–2555.

Guskiewicz, K. M., Marshall, S. W., Bailes, J., McCrea, M., Cantu, R. C., Randolph, C., & Jordan, B. D. (2005). Association between recurrent concussion and late-life cognitive impairment in retired professional football players. *Neurosurgery*, 57(4), 719–726.

Guskiewicz, K. M., Marshall, S. W., Bailes, J., McCrea, M., Harding, H. P., Matthews, A., . . . Cantu, R. C. (2007). Recurrent concussion and risk of depression in retired professional football players. *Medicine & Science in Sports & Exercise*, 39(6), 903–909.

Hardin, G. (1968). The tragedy of the commons. *Science*, 162(3859), 1243–1248.

Harmon, K., Drezner, J., Gammons, M., Guskiewicz, K., Halstead, M., Herring, S., . . . Roberts, W. (2013). American medical society for sports medicine position statement: Concussion in sport. *British Journal of Sports Medicine*, 47(1), 15–26.

Hawkins, K. (2011, September 16). Ex-ill athlete sues NCAA over concussion rules. Retrieved from www.cnsnews.com/news/article/ex-ill-athlete-sues-ncaa-over-concussion-rules

Keilman, J. (2013, January 4). Ex-college football player claims concussions ruined his life. Retrieved April 17, 2014 from http://articles.chicagotribune.com/2013-01-04/news/ct-met-college-concussion-20130104_1_multiple-concussions-concussion-policies-class-action-status

Langlois, J. A., Rutland-Brown, W., & Wald, M. M. (2006). The epidemiology and impact of traumatic brain injury: A brief overview. *The Journal of Head Trauma Rehabilitation*, 21(5), 375–378. Retrieved from www.ncbi.nlm.nih.gov/pubmed/16983222

McCrea, M., Guskiewicz, K. M., Marshall, S. W., Barr, W., Randolph, C., Cantu, R. C., . . . Kelly, J. P. (2003). Acute effects and recovery time following concussion in collegiate football players: The NCAA concussion study. *Journal of the American Medical Association*, 290(19), 2556–2563.

Moser, R. S., & Schatz, P. (2002). Enduring effects of concussion in youth athletes. *Archives of Clinical Neuropsychology*, 17(1), 91–100.

NCAA Constitution (2011), Article 3, at 2.4.17 (Adopted: 8/12/10), available at www.ncaapublications.com/productdownloads/D112.pdf

Omalu, B. I., Hamilton, R. L., Kamboh, M. I., DeKosky, S. T., & Bailes, J. (2010). Chronic traumatic encephalopathy (CTE) in a National Football League Player: Case report and emerging medicolegal practice questions. *Journal of Forensic Nursing*, 6(1), 40–46.

Rivera, A. G. (2013). The big hit: NCAA concussion policy a nightmare for student-athletes. Retrieved from www.law.uh.edu/healthlaw/perspectives/2013/Rivera_The%20Big%20Hit_NCAA%20Concussions%20Policy%20a%20Nightmare%20for%20Student-Athletes.pdf

Smith, R. K. (2000). A brief history of the National Collegiate Athletic Association's role in regulating intercollegiate athletics. *Marquette Sports Law Review*, 11(1), 9–22.

Solomon, J. (2014, February 6). NCAA concussion defense: Sporting event organizers aren't liable for obvious injury risks. Retrieved from www.al.com/sports/index.ssf/2014/02/ncaa_concussion_defense_sporti.html

Torres, D. M., Galetta, K. M., Phillips, H. W., Dziemianowicz, E. M. S., Wilson, J. A, Dorman, E. S., & Balcer, L. J. (2013). Sports-related concussion: Anonymous survey of a collegiate cohort. *Neurology Clinical Practice*, 3(4), 279–287.

Vecsey, G. (2011, November 29). College athletes move concussions into the courtroom. Retrieved April 17, 2014 from www.nytimes.com/2011/11/30/sports/ncaafootball/college-players-move-concussions-issue-into-the-courtroom.html?pagewanted=all&_r=0

Wolken, D. (2014, January 13). Analysis: A conflicting voice in concussion dialogue. Retrieved April 26, 2014 from www.usatoday.com/story/sports/ncaaf/2014/01/13/college-football-concussions-afca-convention-sandra-chapman/4463025

Zemper, E. D. (2003). Two-year prospective study of relative risk of a second cerebral concussion. *American Journal of Physical Medicine & Rehabilitation*, 82(9), 653–659.

FOURTH QUARTER

Sexual Misconduct and Gender Discrimination

18

WRESTLERS GONE WILD

Gay Porn Starring University of Nebraska Student-Athletes

Shaun R. Harper and Charles H.F. Davis III

Varsity wrestling has long been a powerhouse sport at the University of Nebraska. By the numbers, the University has produced four academic All-Americans, five Olympic medalists, ten NCAA individual national champions, 88 NCAA All-Americans, and seven team conference championships in wrestling. In 2008, this storied program wrestled with an Internet scandal. *The Scarlet Project*, a gossip blog, broke the story on two University of Nebraska wrestlers, Paul Donahoe and Kenny Jordan, who separately appeared on FratMen.com, a pornographic website frequented mostly by gay and bisexual men. Specifically, the blog reported the wrestlers were depicted in both photos and videos undressing, showering, and masturbating. Both were alone in their video shoots. Although they were given aliases on the site, one student-athlete had the University's logo tattooed on his thigh, which is how someone discovered him in the video. Both wrestlers were paid approximately $2,000 and provided an all-expense-paid trip to Los Angeles to participate in the website shoot. In an ESPN interview, Paul and Kenny explained that they performed for the gay porn site because they needed the money; both said they were heterosexual (Lavigne, 2009). This scandal revealed much more than a pair of penises on the Internet; it uncovered a larger, more persistent set of problems in the Nebraska wrestling program.

The Case

Paul, a rising senior, was the 2007 NCAA Individual Champion at 125 pounds, and among the ten national champions in the program's history. A standout performer in both the 2007 and 2008 seasons, he earned All-Conference (Big XII) and All-American honors. Kenny was a previous high school state champion in Illinois and national junior college champion at 133 pounds prior to transferring to the University of Nebraska. Despite their achievements on the mat, both young men had several run-ins with the law prior to their appearances on FratMen.com. While in Lincoln, Donahoe was cited for a noisy house party and had previously pleaded guilty to having an open container in a motor vehicle (Associated Press, 2008). Perhaps a bit more rebellious, Jordan pleaded or was found guilty on five separate occasions for a range of legal infractions, two of which included assault charges. Additionally, the NCAA had previously sanctioned both wrestlers for selling iPods the Big XII Conference provided them.

Despite their legal and disciplinary troubles, Paul and Kenny were allowed to compete on the University's wrestling team without any long-term penalties. Both received single-match suspensions in 2008, a penalty imposed by the NCAA for selling the iPods. Jordan was temporarily dismissed after his second assault charge in 2005, only to be reinstated the following season. Beyond this, no long-standing institutional penalties had been enforced for either wrestler prior to the FratMen.com incident. Donahoe and Jordan both publicly acknowledged, in a compelling set of interviews with ESPN's *Outside the Lines* (Lavigne, 2009), that the disciplinary action they received was lenient. In particular, Jordan noted that Donahoe repeatedly "got away" with offenses due to his status as a national champion; he felt the coach showed Paul favor.

When the news of their participation in gay porn reached Nebraska Head Coach Mark Manning's desk, Donahoe and Jordan were reportedly issued an ultimatum: either they had to make sure the videos were immediately removed from the website, or they would not be allowed to continue wrestling. However, on August 12, 2008, after Manning met with University of Nebraska Athletics Director Tom Osborne, the two wrestlers were swiftly dismissed from the elite program. In a phone interview, Osborne insisted the decision to kick Paul and Kenny off the team was not solely attributable to their performances on the gay porn site. "Believe me, if this had been a standalone event, first time deal, or there was no premeditation, that there had not been adequate warning, we quite likely would have tried to work with these guys" (Lavigne, 2009). According to Josh White, Nebraska's Assistant Athletic Director for Compliance, "Donahoe and Jordan were declared ineligible because they violated an NCAA rule that prohibits athletes from appearing in pictures for commercial use" (Associated Press, 2008). The challenge in this case is that the two student-athletes appeared in their FratMen.com videos under pseudonyms – "Nash" and "Cal" – and did not represent themselves as members of the Nebraska wrestling team; there was no mention of their affiliation with the University on the pornographic website (Crowl, 2002).

In their ESPN interviews, Paul and Kenny spoke about the unfairness of their dismissal. Both named various instances in which teammates and coaches were protected from adjudication by the institution and the NCAA for much more problematic offenses. These included engaging in fights that resulted in serious injuries, destruction of public property, the consumption of alcohol, the use of drugs, and gambling, to name a few. Donahoe and Jordan believed that because what they had done was not actually illegal, and because those athletes who had committed actual crimes suffered lesser penalties (if any), the University was wrong in its decision to let them go. Further investigation by ESPN uncovered a 2006 incident in which Coach Manning invited some wrestling team members to his wedding in Oklahoma. Following the reception, two student-athletes, Brandon Browne and Mike Rowe, got into an altercation. In the end, Browne needed reconstructive surgery as a result of being struck in the head with a beer bottle by Rowe, his teammate. Manning acknowledged that the two students were drinking alcohol that evening but said they were not doing so at his wedding reception. No criminal charges were filed in the matter, though a civil suit on Browne's behalf moved forward. A civil judgment was awarded to Browne in the amount of $6,000. Browne and Rowe were allowed to stay on the team after temporary suspensions. On a multitude of other occasions, Head Coach Manning and his two assistant coaches hosted poker games at their homes. According to Jordan and other student-athletes, games often involved large sums of money, upward of $1,000. In addition, students and coaches played poker games for money on team buses during travel to and from various wrestling matches.

Donahoe felt the same-sex nature of his and Jordan's offense is the reason the University was unwilling to afford them the same protections that teammates of theirs had been given in other situations. "You can't cover up what I did. . . . . Once my pictures were out, people knew I posed nude. Someone gets in a fight, someone gets rape charges, someone gets sexual harassment charges – you can cover that up," he said (Lavigne, 2009). Jordan agreed that neither the University nor Lincoln was ready for two wrestlers to appear on a gay porn site.

The ESPN interviews also revealed some additional underlying politics concerning the University of Nebraska's terms and conditions for dismissal, which differed for Paul and Kenny. The NCAA transfer policy makes clear that student-athletes "must spend one academic year in residence at your new school before you are eligible to compete" (National Collegiate Athletic Association, 2014, p. 12). In this case, both wrestlers were told they would be released from the University of Nebraska but would not be able to compete the following season. Donahoe, a senior eager for another NCAA title, made a play. After being told the University would only release him to compete at three schools of *their* choosing, Donahoe responded with a threat to blow the whistle on the program's various illegal operations and practices. As such a highly competitive athlete, the institution would likely have wanted to ensure Donahoe would not compete against the Huskers in the Big XII, if at all. The compromise, Donahoe suggested, was his release without penalty to the schools of *his* choice. Donahoe immediately matriculated to Edinboro University, which has a perennial powerhouse wrestling program. Jordan was not released to participate at another Division I program. Upon transferring to Purdue, he had to sit out the 2009 season and jump through a series of loopholes to join the Boilermakers team the following year.

Sociocultural Context

Scholarship on the social construction of masculinities and homophobia in sport, together, help explain why several wrestlers at the University of Nebraska were allowed to break so many rules over time, yet the two student-athletes who performed for a gay pornographic website were kicked off the team.

A "Boys Will Be Boys" Culture

Masculinities scholars have written extensively about the ways in which boys and men are socialized to perform their gender identities in particular ways. Accordingly, most are taught to adhere to traditional notions of manhood – toughness, risk taking, fearlessness, competition, thrill seeking, power and dominance over women, and suppressed emotionality, to name a few (Davis, 2002; Edwards & Jones, 2009; Harris, 2010; Harris & Edwards, 2010; Harris & Harper, 2008). From birth, behavioral expectations are communicated differently along gender lines – girls should be sweet, and it is acceptable for boys to be rugged and rowdy. Rambunctiousness and rule breaking are usually excused by a "boys will be boys" explanation. Children receive these messages from their parents and families through assorted forms of media (e.g. movies, cartoons, and toy store advertisements) and in schools. Mahalik, Good, and Englar-Carlson (2003) present seven masculine "scripts" that often shape and govern men's gender performativity. Fighting and being physically aggressive, for example, is part of the "Give-'em-Hell" script.

> Sports such as boxing and wrestling directly encourage male violence against other males. Additionally, coaches' support of violence in practices and games may lead to an admiration of violence . . . . Boys and men may learn that violence is, at least to some extent, a socially acceptable way to behave and work out problems, and they may not learn to separate aggression and violence that occur within the context of a sporting event from aggression and violence against others outside of the sports arena.
>
> *(p. 125)*

Mahalik et al. posit that boys and men deal with feelings such as hurt, shame, and inadequacy through aggressive acts like physical assault and property destruction. All-male groups, they contend, are frequently environments in which boys and men are initiated into cultures that are violent, sexist, homophobic, and otherwise unhealthy.

Many undergraduate men, including those who play intercollegiate sports, come to college having been socialized to behave in problematic ways (Harper, Harris, & Mmeje, 2005; Harris & Harper, 2015). Harris and Harper found that youth sports are among the most powerful spaces in which gender socialization occurs for boys. Coaches and teammates co-construct and sustain cultural norms that often excuse (and at times reward) bad behaviors. Homophobic joking, misogynistic and sexist comments that degrade women, and heterosexist stories of sexual conquests are commonplace in many locker room settings, especially among boys who play on high school sports teams (Harris & Harper, 2015; Katz, 1995; Whitson, 1990). Baird (2002) suggests that men who opt out of this locker room talk are at risk of having their heterosexuality questioned.

Men's sports teams (as well as social fraternities) tend to be gender-exclusive spaces in which undergraduate men take their cues from other men who socialize them into cultures that reward particularly destructive masculine performances. Cultural norms were clearly established within the wrestling program at the University of Nebraska. Long before Paul and Kenny were discovered masturbating on a pornographic website, they and several teammates were socialized into a culture where misbehavior and NCAA policy violations were commonplace. Wrestlers were likely excused for fighting, gambling, vandalism, and a range of other bad actions for at least two reasons: (1) Their coaches wanted to keep them eligible to compete, and (2) they were viewed as young college men who sometimes do stupid things. Regarding the latter, a "boys will be boys" mentality may have been firmly etched into the team's culture and repeatedly used to justify keeping student-athletes around who violated policies and sometimes broke laws. This culture apparently collided with another to yield an unfavorable response for the team's porn stars.

A Culture of Homophobia in Sport

In his 2005 book, *In the Game: Gay Athletes and the Cult of Masculinity*, Eric Anderson presents compelling narratives of gay athletes in high school, collegiate, and professional sports. He offers a deep sociocultural analysis of the roles of homophobia and masculinities in sports, including the following:

> The fraternity between members of sports teams bridges many relational aspects. Teammates often spend the better part of their day together, practicing, attending school, and (in the case of collegiate and professional athletes) living together, in a near-total institution. This creates a rigid and tightly policed bond between team members in accordance with the mandates of orthodox masculinity. In the hyper-heterosexual world of athletics, the presence of an openly gay athlete creates dissonance where there was once masculine heterogeneity.
>
> *(pp. 123–124)*

What Anderson so powerfully describes in his book is a culture that is sustained from year-to-year, one in which athletes who deviate from what has been socially constructed as masculine are in danger of penalties that range from teasing to alienation to physical assault. Other scholars (e.g. Baird, 2002; Bauer, 1998; Kauer & Krane, 2006; Wolf-Wendel, Toma, & Morphew, 2001) have written about homophobia and the experiences of gay, lesbian, and bisexual student-athletes in intercollegiate athletics. Like Anderson, these researchers all make note of the culture (not just homophobic individuals) that excludes non-heterosexual members of college sports teams and therefore compels many to remain closeted throughout their undergraduate years.

In a recent poll published in *ESPN The Magazine* (Feldman & Hockensmith, 2012), 49.4 percent of college football players surveyed said they believe they had at least one gay teammate; the number was higher (70 percent) among respondents on football teams in the Pac 12 Conference. Anderson (2005) notes that homophobic comments are far more likely to be reported in the media than are the homo-supportive affirmations an athlete receives from her or his teammates, coaches, and others. In his analysis of three decades of research, Anderson (2011) found an increase in the number of openly gay athletes and an evolving (albeit slowly) sense of support for them. But in his book *In the Game*, Anderson explains how support for gay athletes in sports programs depends largely on coaches. Accordingly, coaches have the most "masculine capital" in men's sports – meaning, they are the men that student-athletes most respect and admire. If coaches foster safe, respectful, and gay-affirming cultures, students are more likely to adhere to those cultural norms. In their study of 289 coaches of intercollegiate sports teams, Oswalt and Vargas (2013) found that most survey respondents were "tolerant" of gay, lesbian, and bisexual (GLB) student-athletes. It is plausible, though, that tolerance does not effectively translate into coaches deliberately cultivating team cultures in which non-heterosexual players feel comfortable and supported.

Paula Lavigne, an ESPN staff writer, wrote this in her 2009 article:

> Donahoe says he is straight, as does Jordan, and suggests the mere association with a gay Web site was too much to handle for the university – and especially for Osborne [the Nebraska Athletics Director], a devout Christian and former Republican congressman.

Paul Donahoe said the following in an interview with *The Boston Globe*:

> I am straight, but on the forums people make a lot of gay jokes about me . . . . Obviously, I did it for the money. We kept thinking no one would ever find out because it was a gay website.
>
> *(Grossfeld, 2009)*

Their appearance on a gay pornographic website most assuredly got Paul and Kenny kicked off the team. Despite repeatedly saying they both were heterosexual, what they did was likely viewed as inexcusably gay. Perhaps they would have been treated differently had they appeared on a heterosexual porn site – teammates (and perhaps coaches) may have celebrated and congratulated them had they been filmed having sex with women. Even though these two student-athletes and others on their team had repeatedly violated laws and less ambiguous NCAA policies, being on a gay site put the team's masculine reputation at risk, hence the two porn stars were disqualified from future bouts as Huskers.

Alternate Ending

The outcome of this case likely would have been different had the University of Nebraska wrestling team coaches established a culture that promoted productive masculinities and consistently disciplined those who violated team, university, conference, and NCAA policies. It was the inconsistency of the coaches' disciplinary actions that seems to suggest their response to Paul and Kenny doing gay porn was excessive and likely homophobic. These two student-athletes and teammates of theirs repeatedly broke the law and violated policies, yet were still allowed to compete. Wrestling team members' past wrongdoings were clear, whereas performing on a pornographic website as an individual actor using a pseudonym (as opposed to representing oneself as an NCAA Division I student-athlete) was not clearly spelled out as a policy infraction. Clear policy articulation and compliance, as well as the consistent application of disciplinary procedures, would have made the outcome of this case seem less homophobic.

References

Anderson, E. (2005). *In the game: Gay athletes and the cult of masculinity.* Albany: State University of New York Press.

Anderson, E. (2011). Masculinities and sexualities in sport and physical cultures: Three decades of evolving research. *Journal of Homosexuality, 58*(5), 565–578.

Associated Press. (2008, August 12). Nebraska wrestlers dismissed after posing nude. Retrieved from http://espn.go.com/ncaa/news/story?id=3532146

Baird, J. A. (2002). Playing it straight: An analysis of current legal protections to combat homophobia and sexual orientation discrimination in intercollegiate athletics. *Berkeley Journal of Gender, Law & Justice, 17*(1), 31–67.

Bauer, D. (1998). Athletics and gay male identity: The loneliness of the long distance runner. In R. L. Sanlo (Ed.), *Working with LGBT college students: A handbook for faculty and administrators* (pp. 213–220). Westport, CT: Greenwood Press.

Crowl, J. (2002, August 22). Nebraska wrestlers dismissed for posing nude online might not go quietly. Retrieved from www.cbsnews.com/news/nebraska-wrestlers-dismissed-for-posing-nude-online-might-not-go-quietly

Davis, T. L. (2002). Voices of gender role conflict: The social construction of college men's identity. *Journal of College Student Development, 43*(4), 508–521.

Edwards, K. E., & Jones, S. R. (2009). "Putting my man face on": A grounded theory of college men's gender identity development. *Journal of College Student Development, 50*(2), 210–228.

Feldman, B., & Hockensmith, R. (2012, July 10). The only preseason poll that matters. Retrieved from http://espn.go.com/espn/magazine/archives/news/story?page=magazine-20090824-article35

Grossfeld, S. (2009, March 17). Grappling with scandal: Unapologetic wrestler starts over after controversial website shoot. Retrieved from www.boston.com/sports/colleges/articles/2009/03/17/grappling_with_scandal

Harper, S. R., Harris III, F., & Mmeje, K. (2005). A theoretical model to explain the overrepresentation of college men among campus judicial offenders: Implications for campus administrators. *Journal of Student Affairs Research and Practice, 42*(4), 565–588.

Harris III, F. (2010). College men's conceptualizations of masculinities and contextual influences: Toward a conceptual model. *Journal of College Student Development, 51*(3), 297–318.

Harris III, F., & Edwards, K. E. (2010). College men's experiences as men: Findings from two grounded theory studies. *Journal of Student Affairs Research and Practice, 47*(1), 43–62.

Harris III, F., & Harper, S. R. (2008). Masculinities go to community college: Understanding male identity socialization and gender role conflict. In J. Lester (Ed.), *Gendered perspectives in community colleges. New Directions for Community Colleges* (No. 142, pp. 25–35). San Francisco: Jossey-Bass.

Harris III, F., & Harper, S. R. (2015). Matriculating masculinity: Understanding undergraduate men's precollege gender socialization. *Journal of the First-Year Experience & Students in Transition,* 27(2), 49–65.

Katz, J. (1995). Reconstructing masculinity in the locker room: The Mentors in Violence Prevention Project. *Harvard Educational Review,* 65(2), 163–174.

Kauer, K. J., & Krane, V. (2006). "Scary dykes" and "feminine queens": Stereotypes and female collegiate athletes. *Women in Sport & Physical Activity Journal,* 15(1), 42–55.

Lavigne, P. (2009, June 14). Naked in Nebraska: A wrestler's story. Retrieved from http://espn.go.com/espn/otl/news/story?id=4242983

Mahalik, J. R., Good, G. E., & Englar-Carlson, M. (2003). Masculinity scripts, presenting concerns, and help seeking: Implications for practice and training. *Professional Psychology: Research and Practice,* 34(2), 123–131.

National Collegiate Athletic Association. (2014). *Transfer 101: Basic information you need to know about transferring to an NCAA college, for Divisions I/II/III (2014–15).* Indianapolis, IN: Author.

Oswalt, S. B., & Vargas, T. M. (2013). How safe is the playing field? Collegiate coaches' attitudes towards gay, lesbian, and bisexual individuals. *Sport in Society,* 16(1), 120–132.

Whitson, D. (1990). Sport in the social construction of masculinity. In M. Messner & D. Sabo, (Eds.), *Sport, men, and the gender order: Critical feminist perspectives* (pp. 19–29). Champaign, IL: Human Kinetics.

Wolf-Wendel, L. E., Toma, J. D., & Morphew, C. C. (2001). How much difference is too much difference? Perceptions of gay men and lesbians in intercollegiate athletics. *Journal of College Student Development,* 42(5), 465–479.

19

ILLEGAL CONTACT? PLAYER-COACH SEXUAL RELATIONSHIPS AT LSU AND BOSTON COLLEGE

Willis A. Jones and Neal H. Hutchens

In 2007, the world of women's intercollegiate athletics was shocked by two eerily similar coaching resignations. Both coaches were in their late 30s. Both coaches were at high-profile institutions and experiencing extraordinary on-field success. Both issued statements proclaiming that their resignation was to "pursue other career interests" (Associated Press, 2007). However, each coach also resigned amid allegations of inappropriate sexual relationships with a player. On March 7, 2007, Louisiana State University (LSU) head women's basketball coach Dana "Pokey" Chatman resigned after the university became aware of an alleged sexual relationship between Chatman and one of her players. On April 24, 2007, the head coach of the Boston College (BC) women's ice hockey team, Tom Mutch, resigned after allegations surfaced of a sexual relationship between him and a 19-year-old player on his team.

These cases serve as the foundation for this chapter. After describing each case, we attempt to analyze these situations from a broader sociocultural and legal context. As part of this analysis, we consider institutional consensual relationship policies, the larger issue of player-coach sexual relationships, and institutional reactions in each case.

The Cases

Pokey Chatman, Louisiana State University Women's Basketball

In February 2007, Pokey Chatman was arguably at the top of her profession. A native of Ama, Louisiana, Chatman was a decorated high school point guard who won several All-American honors at Hahnville High School in Louisiana. She continued her playing career at LSU from 1987 to 1991, where she scored more than 1,800 points, set school records for steals and assists in a career, was a three-time All-Southeastern Conference (SEC) selection, and helped the Lady Tigers win their first SEC tournament championship. In recognition of her athletic career, she was inducted into the LSU Athletics Hall of Fame in 1999.

A year after graduating from LSU, Chatman accepted a position as an assistant basketball coach at the school. She would serve in that role for 13 years before assuming the head coaching position. During the 2003–2004 season, Sue Gunter (then–head coach of the women's basketball team) took a medical leave of absence due to respiratory illness. The school appointed Chatman as interim head coach for the remainder of the 2003–2004 season. As the interim head coach, Chatman led the team to a 15–5 record and the team's first ever NCAA Women's Final Four appearance. After Gunter announced her retirement in April 2004, LSU named Chatman the permanent head coach of the woman's basketball team.

During her two-and-a-half years as the head coach, Chatman experienced unprecedented on-court success. In the 2004–2005 season, her team had a 33–3 record and earned a trip to a second consecutive Women's Final Four. In 2005–2006, Chatman's Lady Tigers went 31–4, won a second consecutive conference championship, and made it to a third consecutive Women's Final Four. Chatman's coaching accomplishments earned her numerous awards, including the 2005 Naismith National Coach of the Year, the 2005 United States Basketball Writers Association (USBWA) National Coach of the Year, and the 2005 Black Coaches Association Coach of the Year. Chatman's 47–3 record in her first 50 games as a head coach was the second-best record to start a coaching career in women's college basketball history.

The LSU Lady Tigers would make it to their fourth consecutive Women's Final Four in the 2006–2007 season. Pokey Chatman, however, would not be the coach during the team's NCAA tournament run. On March 7, just ten days before the start of the 2007 NCAA Women's Division I Basketball Tournament, Chatman abruptly resigned as LSU's women's basketball coach.

Within days of this announcement, reports began to circulate regarding the circumstances surrounding Chatman's resignation. Various news outlets reported that Chatman quit amid allegations of an inappropriate sexual relationship between her and a player that had been on her team during her time as an assistant coach (ESPN, 2007; Longman, 2007; Thompson, 2007). While details of the allegations remain shrouded in secrecy, it was reported that LSU learned about Chatman's alleged relationships from Carla Berry, one of Chatman's assistant coaches. Then–athletic director Skip Bertman initially conducted an informal investigation into the allegations. Chatman was made aware of the allegations on March 4, and three days later made the decision to resign (Brittain, 2007).

Whether the resignation was voluntary or forced remains a matter of debate. Chatman contended that her resignation was prompted by an ultimatum from the institution. Six weeks after resigning, Chatman, through her lawyer Mary Olive Pierson, sent a letter to members of the media detailing her version of the circumstances surrounding her resignation. Chatman says that she was asked to meet with LSU general counsel Ray Lamonia on the morning of March 7. During that meeting she claims she was told to resign as the women's head basketball coach or that she would be fired for violating what the university called an absolute zero-tolerance policy involving coach-player relationships. Chatman alleges that she was given just two hours to make the decision. Chatman's lawyer described the situation in the following way:

> Frankly, it was my clear impression that the university had taken about two weeks to a) get one version of the story from Ms. Berry; b) make no effort to contact Coach Chatman to seek her input into the situation; c) make no effort to validate the unsubstantiated stories being told by Ms. Berry; d) rush to judgment; and e) terminate Coach Chatman and try to make it look like a voluntary resignation.
>
> *(Merrill, 2007, par. 20)*

The letter from Chatman also alleges that the institution's "absolute zero tolerance policy involving coach-player relationships" did not actually exist at the time of Chatman's resignation. "If I'd have known on March 7th they didn't have a policy," Chatman's lawyer said, "she would not have resigned" (Merrill, 2007, par. 12).

LSU disputed several aspects of Chatman's description. Ray Lamonica, the university's general council, said in an interview with ESPN that the university gave Chatman two options during the March 7th meeting: resign as head coach or be put on administrative leave while the investigation of the situation continued. LSU system spokesman, Charles Zewe, said "the notion that Coach Chatman was somehow ambushed and given two hours to make up her mind and fire or be fired or quit or resign is simply not true" (Meriwether, 2007, par. 9). Athletic Director Bertman echoed those sentiments, saying of Chatman's resignation: "The girl did what she did and LSU had no control over that" (Longman, 2007, par. 10).

The university also contended that their investigation went beyond hearsay from one individual. Zewe said of the situation:

> We had substantial indications that it went well beyond – well beyond – Coach Berry's assertions about what had gone on here. We had other assertions, admissions. Coach Chatman had made admissions about her conduct to multiple people on this campus including her colleagues in the athletic department. Those have all been documented and so it's not just one assistant coach's word against Coach Chatman.
>
> *(Meriwether, 2007, par. 7)*

Chatman and LSU avoided litigation in the case after reaching a $160,000 financial settlement regarding performance bonuses in her contract (Associated Press, 2001). Chatman later resumed her coaching career in professional women's basketball overseas and in the WNBA.

Tom Mutch, Boston College Women's Ice Hockey

The circumstances surrounding the resignation of Tom Mutch as head coach of BC's women's ice hockey team share many similarities to the situation involving Pokey Chatman. Mutch was a native of Canton, Massachusetts, who played hockey at Northeastern University from 1986 to 1988. After playing professional hockey for several years, Mutch began his coaching career as an assistant coach for the United States women's Olympic ice hockey team. Following the 1998 Olympics, Mutch served as an assistant men's hockey coach for the Omaha Lancers hockey club and the University of Nebraska-Omaha. He returned to Boston in 2002 to become a men's hockey assistant coach at his alma mater before taking over as the head coach of the BC women's hockey team in 2003.

During his four years at BC, Mutch, like Chatman, experienced a very high level of success. After finishing his first season 6–22–3, the team improved to 10–20–4 in the 2004–2005 season. This improvement landed Mutch the Hockey East Co-Coach of the Year Award. In the 2005–2006 season, BC doubled its win total and finished with a 20–11–4 record and won the team's first ever Beanpot Tournament trophy.

Mutch's most successful season occurred during 2006–2007. The team won its second consecutive Beanpot Tournament and finished the regular season with a 23–9–2 record. This record landed the program its first ever appearance in the NCAA Division I Women's Hockey Tournament. During the tournament, BC defeated Dartmouth to earn an appearance in the Women's Frozen Four. Mutch had implemented one of the biggest turnarounds in women's collegiate hockey history. In recognition of this, he received numerous awards in 2007. He was named the Hockey East Coach of the Year and the New England Hockey Writers Division I Women's Coach of the Year. He would be named runner-up for the American Hockey Coaches Association (AHCA) Division I Women's Coach of the Year Award.

Just 45 days after appearing in the Frozen Four, however, Mutch abruptly resigned as head coach of the women's hockey team. While the school initially stated that Mutch resigned to "pursue other interests" (Associated Press, 2007), it quickly became known that the resignation was in response to allegation of inappropriate sexual conduct between Mutch and one of his players. Then-BC athletic director Gene DeFilippo said in a statement:

> An allegation of inappropriate conduct has been raised involving Boston College women's hockey coach Tom Mutch. The university takes any such matters very seriously. As a result, the Athletics Department began an investigation of the alleged incident as soon as it was brought to our attention. Coach Mutch subsequently submitted his resignation, and his resignation was accepted.
>
> *(Associated Press, 2007, par. 3)*

As with Chatman's case, details of Mutch's story remain somewhat unclear. Mutch, who at the time was married and the father of a newborn baby girl, is alleged to have sent sexually graphic text messages to 19-year-old Kelli Stack. Stack was a star freshman on the 2006–2007 BC women's hockey team who set a school record for assists in her freshmen year. After Stack loaned a teammate her cell phone, the teammate discovered sexually explicit text messages between Stack and Mutch. The teammate reported these messages to the athletic department, and soon an investigation began into the relationship between Mutch and Stack. Once Mutch became aware of the investigation, he resigned his position.

Subsequent investigation into the Mutch situation by the school uncovered no evidence of an inappropriate relationship between Mutch and Stack, beyond the alleged phone text messages (Labbe, 2008). In subsequent interviews with *The Boston Globe*, Stack acknowledged that there had been sexually explicit text messages exchanged between her and her coach, but that nothing inappropriate occurred beyond that. She maintained that there was no romantic or physical contact between the two. Mutch has refused all interview requests related to the incident (Springer, 2011).

Sociocultural Context

Consensual relationships between players and coaches are by no means isolated to the instances discussed here. Many in the athletic community have noted a rise in the number of coaches engaged in romantic relationships with the players they train or coach. Track stars such as Marion Jones and Jackie Joyner-Kersee famously married their former coaches. Soccer players Brandi Chastain and Julie Foudy each married one of their former coaches. *Sports Illustrated* reported that, in 2000, at least 12 of the top 100 women tennis players in the world were romantically linked with their coaches (Wahl, Wertheim, & Dohrmann, 2001). Tom Mutch, at the time of his alleged transgressions at BC, was himself married to a woman whom he coached on the 1998 Women's Olympic hockey team (Matson, 2007).

The prevalence of these player-coach relationships in sports is complicated by the fact that there are no consistent policies and guidelines within sports regarding what is and is not proper in coach-athlete relationships. Many athletic governing bodies and coaching organizations, such as the American Swimming Coaches Association (ASCA), the governing body of USA Volleyball, and the United States Olympic Committee, prohibit player-coach relationships (Bringer, Brackenridge, & Johnston, 2006; Wahl et al., 2001). Other amateur athletics organizations have remained fairly quiet on the topic. At the time of the Chatman and Mutch cases, for example, the NCAA did not have a policy explicitly banning sexual relationships between coaches and players (Shelburne, 2007).

Some scholars argue that policies restricting consensual relationships needlessly intrude into the private lives of adults (Jafar, 2003; Potter, 2007). Sherry Young (1996), for example, argues that restricting consensual relationships between adults has an unwritten paternalistic characteristic that treats females as less than competent adults. Her argument is that, because many supporters of such a policy would concede that the intent of this restriction is the desire to protect women from male professions, these policies create an "absolute presumption of harm" that "implicitly decides that a woman will always be incapable of giving informed consent to a sexual relationship once she comes under the domineering influence of a male professional" (Young, 1996, p. 270). Young also argues that consensual relationships fall outside the purview of Title IX, and thus an institution of higher education would not have legal liability regarding potential fallout from these relationships.

Advocates of policies restricting coach-player relationships often cite issues of power, potential harm to third parties, and concern over legal liability from sexual harassment lawsuits. For these advocates, consensual relationship policies are needed to address the inherent power differential that exists between coaches and student-athletes. The American Association of University Professors' (AAUP) Statement on Professional Ethics warns of the possibility of the exploitation of a student in a seemingly consensual relationship because "the power exercised by the professor in an academic or evaluative role, make voluntary consent by the student suspect" (2006, p. 247). The uneven power dynamic discussed in the AAUP statement is arguably even more prevalent in a coach–student-athlete relationship. Heckman (2009), citing ethical considerations and power dynamics, argues that a coach can never ethically engage in a consensual relationship with a student-athlete. O'Brien and O'Brien (2011) state that "relationships between coaches and student-athletes clearly represent [such a] power differential" (p. 4). Accordingly, institutional policies on consensual relationships, including in relation to athletics, are often grounded in the notion of addressing the disparate power relationships that generally exist between educators/coaches and students/student-athletes.

Another reason a college or university may enact a consensual relationship policy is to safeguard the overall integrity of programs and to protect third parties who may feel that an individual is receiving preferential treatment as the result of a consensual relationship. One rationale for this policy is that it promotes an environment where other individuals are not adversely affected by a (consensual) relationship between a player and a coach. Given concerns about complying with NCAA standards, and when scholarship renewals, playing time, and future career opportunities are at stake, athletics programs may enact a consensual relationship policy to protect the interests of other student-athletes and the status of an institution's athletics program in general.

Legal liability, particularly in relation to sexual harassment, may also be a concern of institutions (Hutchens, 2003). Apprehension over legal liability may not only encompass students engaged in consensual relationships but also extend to third parties who feel that they have been treated unfairly because of a relationship between a coach and an athlete or feel pressure to engage in such relationships to remain in favor with their coaches or other officials.

The issue of potential legal liability stemming from a player-coach consensual relationship raises an important legal distinction regarding consensual relationships and instances of sexual harassment. Title IX of the Higher Education Amendments of 1972 prohibits educational institutions, including colleges and universities that receive federal funds, from discriminating against students on the basis of sex. Title

IX provides that "no person in the United States shall, on the basis of sex, be excluded from participation in, be denied the benefits of, or be subjected to discrimination under any education program or activity receiving federal financial assistance." (Wulf, 2012, par. 10).

Under Title IX, an institution may be held legally liable for sexual harassment committed by an employee if it does not take adequate steps to respond to incidents of sexual harassment about which it knows or should have known (Hutchens, 2003). Title IX does not, however, apply to relationships of a consensual nature; instead it covers unwanted attention or behavior that constitutes sexual harassment for purposes of the law. At the same time, the existence of a consensual relationship would not bar a student-athlete from claiming sexual harassment if the consensual nature of the relationship ended and a coach then engaged in behavior that was sexually harassing in nature. Accordingly, while a college or university may view a consensual relationship policy as a useful mechanism to help deter instances of sexual harassment, such a policy alone does not shield a school from potential legal liability. Even if a consensual relationship once existed between a student-athlete and a coach, a school would still have a responsibility to respond to any allegations of sexual harassment by the player.

A further rationale for a college or university to adopt a consensual relationship policy for coaches and student-athletes is that it discourages situations that might later give rise to incidents involving sexual harassment. Concerns over the unequal power relationship between coaches and student-athletes and the possibility of exploitation often undergird fears related to consensual relationships between players and coaches. Such a policy would provide a school with a mechanism to sanction a coach who violated the policy without the coach being able to argue that a consensual relationship once existed should a claim of sexual harassment arise. An institution may also be motivated to enforce a consensual relationship policy if it determines that such policy contributes to a culture in its athletics program that prohibits sexual harassment.

For these reasons, many institutions have attempted to prohibit player-coach sexual relationships (O'Brien & O'Brien, 2011). An athletics program's policies and practices related to consensual relationships between student-athletes and coaches will often fall under the umbrella of the institution's general sexual harassment or consensual relationship policies. For example, the Stanford University Department of Athletics student-athlete handbook for 2010–2011 encourages student-athletes to become familiar with the university's general sexual harassment and consensual relationship policy (Stanford University Department of Athletics, 2010). The handbook also includes a statement in its section on sexual harassment that "discourages fraternization between staff members/coaches and student-athletes" (Stanford University Department of Athletics, 2010, p. 8). The handbook also states that problems or issues resulting from such fraternization should be brought to the attention of appropriate officials to ensure that no university or NCAA regulations are violated.

Some universities have opted to include specific consensual relationship policies as part of their athletics regulations. For example, Arizona State University's athletics regulations contain a specific prohibition of consensual relationships between coaches and student-athletes, with the policy also applicable to other employees or student assistants in the athletics department. The policy does provide an exception for pre-existing relationships, which must be reported to an appropriate athletics official, and the policy provides that an individual in such a pre-existing relationship must not be placed in a position to provide any improper extra benefits to the student-athlete.

According to the regulation, the policy is meant:

> [...] to maintain the integrity of the professional relationship between university coaches and staff members and the students for whom they are responsible, and to prevent the giving of impermissible benefits or advantages to student-athletes by ICA coaches, staff members, or student-assistants.
>
> (*Arizona State University Department of Intercollegiate Athletics, n.d.*)

The policy also provides that, "while friendships are not prohibited (unless an impermissible benefit or advantage is realized), sexual relationships, which increase the likelihood of an improper extra-benefits violation, are prohibited" (Arizona State University Department of Intercollegiate Athletics, n.d.).

Alternate Ending

Given this backdrop, several interesting questions can be asked regarding how LSU and BC handled the Pokey Chatman and Tom Mutch incidents, respectively. In each instance, it appears that the institution created a situation where the coach was encouraged to resign as opposed to the school firing the coach. One explanation for this action may be the lack of written institutional policy regarding coach-player romantic relationships. At the time of the Chatman incident, LSU spokesman Charles Zewe admitted that the institution had no written rule prohibiting student relationships with higher authorities at the institution (Brittain, 2007). Zewe also noted:

> It's absolutely preposterous to suggest that the University should condone relationships between professors, deans, or whomever and students just because there isn't a written policy. How could anyone consider that having an alleged sexual or romantic relationship or some kind of alleged intimate relationship would be in high morals?
>
> (*Brittain, 2007, par. 10*)

At BC, there was nothing from the university administration explicitly stating the institution's policy toward student-coach relationships; many news reports about the case indicated that BC, too, had no written policy on the matter.

Without a written policy prohibiting coach–student-athlete romantic relationships, firing the coaches for their alleged transgressions could have made the institution potentially liable under a wrongful termination lawsuit.[1] To avoid such a possibility, negotiating to receive a resignation rather than firing the coach likely helped to shield the institution from legal liability for not having a clear, explicit policy in this area. In the case of Mutch, for instance, it may have been unclear whether an exchange of text messages violated any applicable policies. Uncertainty about the existence or the specific nature of a policy may help to explain why LSU was so adamant that Chatman voluntary resign from her coaching position. If this were the scenario that played out at each school, it suggests that athletics departments should strongly consider adopting a policy explicitly stating that player-coach romantic relationships are prohibited. Another way institutions can establish legally enforceable standards to dismiss coaches who engage in consensual relationships with players is through the inclusion of "character clauses" in coaches' contracts – these clauses allow a university to dismiss a coach who engages in acts that negatively affect the reputation of the university as solely determined by the university. Private institutions such as BC, like many private schools, may also claim a religious dimension to its institutional mission. Such institutions possess even more legal leeway than public colleges and universities in defining behaviors that could lead to a coach's termination.

In the Tom Mutch situation, questions also arise regarding what exactly constitutes an inappropriate relationship with a student and whether the student involved in the case should be subject to disciplinary action. Based on interviews with Kelli Stack, it appears that, while sexually explicit text messages were exchanged between her and her coach, no romantic or physical contact occurred between the two. The institution itself acknowledged that investigations uncovered no evidence that the Mutch incident involved anything more than text messages (Labbe, 2008). Does the exchange of sexually explicit text messages constitute a relationship? What is the bar for determining whether a consensual "relationship" took place? One way an institution may choose to navigate such an issue is to include language in its consensual relationship policies similar to that adopted by Stanford University. As noted earlier, the Stanford University policy discourages consensual physical relationships as well as "fraternizing" between coaches and student-athletes. This type of language may help clarify the somewhat ambiguous nature of what constitutes a relationship.

If we assume that Mutch engaged in an activity that warranted institutional disciplinary action, a question may be asked about whether Kelli Stack should have been subject to discipline for her role in the relationship. All indications are that, after the resignation of Mutch, Stack was able to continue her career at BC without any school-administered disciplinary action. This is not unusual with regard to consensual relationship policies in higher education. In discussing an informal survey of 156 institutions, O'Brien and O'Brien (2011) found that only 14 percent of administrators said their institution's consensual relationship policy included sanctions for both the faculty member and the student in question. The majority (52 percent) of respondents noted that their school's policy included disciplinary sanctions for only the professor involved.

Whether one believes Stack should have been punished for her role in the Mutch affair in part depends on how you believe a consensual relationship policy should be grounded. If the policy is grounded in issues of power, and there is a belief that coach–student-athlete relationships exploit students who hold considerably less power than the presumed authority figure, Stack would be viewed as a victim and no disciplinary action would be expected. If, on the other hand, a policy is grounded in protecting third parties who may feel that an individual is receiving preferential treatment as a result of the consensual relationship, one may argue that Stack could have been looking to foster this relationship to further her career and should be subject to discipline. It appears, based on the survey from O'Brien and O'Brien (2011), that most institutions ground their policy in the power dynamic.

Another aspect of the Chatman and Mutch cases, which arguably impacted institutional response, revolves around issues of gender and sexuality. Some have argued that, while coach-player relationships in sports are typically seen as a bad idea, same-sex relationships between coaches and players are viewed even more negatively. Mary Jo Kane of the University of Minnesota has noted that "because of homophobia in and around women's sports, if it's a lesbian relationship, the negative perception is exacerbated – it quietly moves from the arena of poor judgment to the arena of deviance and immorality" (Wahl et al., 2001, p. 3). Observers have suggested that this is somewhat evident in the coverage and institutional reactions to the Chatman and Mutch cases (Redden, 2007). Quantifying the impact of gender and sexual orientations on these incidents, however, is very difficult. Considering the similar course of action taken by both institutions in handling the respective cases, it would be difficult to proclaim that, in these particular situations, Chatman and Mutch were treated differently due to their gender or sexual orientation. Administrators should be well aware, however, that consensual relationship standards must be applied equally regardless of gender or sexual orientation. Policies or standards that are enforced unevenly or unfairly based on gender or sexual orientation, or on other factors, could well leave a college or university more open to a legal challenge from a coach (or player) disciplined for a consensual relationship. Institutions and their athletics departments should take care that consensual relationship standards are enforced in an evenhanded manner across all athletics programs and that special exceptions are not made for particular sports or coaches, including those who are very successful in high-profile sports.

Note

1 This appeared to be the case Chatman planned to make were she to follow through on the threat to sue LSU.

References

American Association of University Professors. (2006). *Policy documents and reports* (Tenth ed.). Washington, DC: American Association of University Professors.

Arizona State University Department of Intercollegiate Athletics. (n.d.). Intercollegiate athletics manual: ICA 406: Consensual relationships. Retrieved April 3, 2012 from www.asu.edu/aad/manuals/ica/ica406.html

Associated Press. (2001, June 15). LSU, ex-hoops coach Chatman agree to $160K settlement. Retrieved from http://sports.espn.go.com/ncw/news/story?id=2795145

Associated Press. (2007, April 24). Mutch resigns after probe into allegations. Retrieved from www.usatoday.com/sports/2007-04-24-2050196312_x.htm

Bringer, J. D., Brackenridge, C. H., & Johnston, L. H. (2006). Swimming coaches' perceptions of sexual exploitation in sport: a preliminary model of role conflict and role ambiguity. *Sport Psychologist,* 20(4), 465–479.

Brittain, A. (2007, March 17). News release confirms Berry as source. Retrieved from www.lsureveille.com/news-release-confirms-berry-as-source/article_c8f669ae-8f0d-5738-999c-69b919c2cc0c.html

ESPN. (2007, March 9). Sources: Chatman quit amid sexual misconduct claims. Retrieved from http://sports.espn.go.com/ncw/news/story?id=2791950

Heckman, D. (2009). Title IX and sexual harassment claims involving educational athletic department employees and student-athletes in the twenty-first century. *Virginia Sports and Entertainment Law Journal,* 8(2), 223–273.

Hutchens, N. (2003). Legal effect of college and university policies prohibiting romantic relationships between students and professors. *Journal of Law & Education,* 32(4), 411–443.

Jafar, A. (2003). Consent or coercion? Sexual relationships between college faculty and students. *Gender Issues,* 21(1), 43–58.

Labbe, D. (2008). Through a nightmare and toward a dream. Retrieved February 15, 2011 from www.cleveland.com/sports/index.ssf/2008/11/through_a_nightmare_and_toward.html#comments

Longman, J. (2007, March 9). L.S.U.'s Chatman won't coach in N.C.A.A.. Retrieved from www.nytimes.com/2007/03/09/sports/ncaabasketball/09lsu.html?_r=1

Matson, B. (2007, April 25). BC's Mutch quits amid allegations. Retrieved from www.boston.com/sports/articles/2007/04/25/bcs_mutch_quits_amid_allegations/

Meriwether, G. (2007). Pokey Chatman, lawyer demanding nearly $1 million from LSU. Retrieved from www.wafb.com/Global/story.asp?S=6383843

Merrill, E. (2007, April 18). Chatman's attorney: LSU forced resignation. Retrieved from http://sports.espn.go.com/ncw/news/story?id=2840260

O'Brien, D., & O'Brien, T. (2011). Consider adopting consensual relationship policy for coaches, student-athletes. *College Athletics and the Law,* 8(4), 4–5.

Potter, C. B. (2007). Pokey Chatman Update. Retrieved from http://chronicle.com/blognetwork/tenuredradical/2007/03/pokey-chatman-update-thnk-heaven-for/

Redden, E. (2007, April 30). "Dirty little secrets" in women's sports. Retrieved from www.insidehighered.com/news/2007/04/30/sports

Shelburne, R. (2007, April 3). LSU affair leaves questions. Retrieved from www.dailynews.com/sports/ci_5580197

Springer, S. (2011, March 4). Stack scores on the rebound. Retrieved from www.boston.com/sports/colleges/womens_hockey/articles/2011/03/04/stack_scores_on_the_rebound/?p1=News_links

Stanford University Department of Athletics. (2010). Stanford University Department of Athletics Student-Athlete Handbook 2010–2011. Retrieved April 3, 2012 from http://grfx.cstv.com/photos/schools/stan/genrel/auto_pdf/10-11StudentAthleteHandbook.pdf

Thompson, W. (2007, March 12). Chatman's assistant told LSU about relationship. Retrieved from http://sports.espn.go.com/ncw/news/story?id=2795145

Wahl, G., Wertheim, L. J., & Dohrmann, G. (2001, September 10). Passion plays. Retrieved from http://sportsillustrated.cnn.com/vault/article/magazine/MAG1023662/index.htm

Wulf, S. (2012, April 29). Title IX: 37 words that changed everything. Retrieved from http://espn.go.com/espnw/title-ix/article/7722632/37-words-changed-everything

Young, S. (1996). Getting to yes: The case against banning consensual relationships in higher education. *American University Journal of Gender, Social Policy & The Law*, 4(2), 269–302.

20

PROTECTING THE PRIDE

The Penn State Jerry Sandusky Child Sex-Abuse Scandal

Andrew Howard Nichols and Emil L. Cunningham

Established in 1855, Penn State, a multicampus system comprised of over 20 different campus locations, has its primary administrative hub at the University Park campus in State College, Pennsylvania (Penn State, 2012a). The main campus enrolls more than 45,000 students and is located in an isolated college town in central Pennsylvania, making the university the area's largest employer and most powerful entity (Penn State, 2012b). Although the university is lauded for its academics, college football is a critical centerpiece to the institution's identity, culture, and public reputation. Football has been a part of the Penn State tradition since 1887 (Prato, 1998) but became a significant cultural fascination under the tenure of head coach Joe Paterno during the 1980s. Paterno amassed a legacy that was shattered in the aftermath of a scandal involving the sexual abuse of children.

Dubbed the "most explosive scandal in the history of college sports" on the November 2011 cover of a *Sports Illustrated* special report, the child sex abuse scandal at Penn State was described as a scandal that would "make a mockery of the recent drumbeat of NCAA outrages" (Wertheim & Epstein, 2011, p. 40). Stories of recruiting violations, athlete and coach misconduct, and improper benefits afforded to athletes are quite trivial in comparison to the alleged institutional cover-up led by four of the university's most powerful administrators—an alleged cover-up that enabled Jerry Sandusky, a former Penn State coach, to sexually abuse young boys for nearly 15 years. Despite being initially reported in March 2011 by Sara Ganim of the *Patriot-News*, a Harrisburg, Pennsylvania–based newspaper, the Sandusky story began garnering national media coverage after the release of the Pennsylvania Grand Jury report on Friday, November 4, 2011, that accused the former Penn State football defensive coordinator, Jerry Sandusky, of 40 counts of sexual abuse toward minor male children from 1994 to 2009 (Viera, 2011; Pennsylvania Attorney General, 2011). Later, more counts were added, and Sandusky was eventually convicted of 45 counts of child sexual abuse in July 2012 (Boren, 2011b; Freeh, Sporkin, and Sullivan, LLP, 2012).

In response to the scandal, Penn State's Board of Trustees commissioned an independent investigation that was spearheaded by former FBI Director Louis Freeh. The report, which was released on July 12, 2012, stated that Penn State President Graham Spanier, Senior Vice President of Finance and Business Gary Schultz, Head Football Coach Joe Paterno, and Athletic Director Tim Curley, "repeatedly concealed critical facts relating to Sandusky's child abuse from the authorities, the University's Board of Trustees, the Penn State community, and the public at large" with the hope of avoiding "the consequences of bad publicity" (Freeh, Sporkin, and Sullivan, LLP, 2012, p. 16).

On July 23, 2012, a little more than ten days after the release of the Freeh report, the NCAA imposed a litany of crippling sanctions on Penn State and its football program (ESPN.com, 2011c). The university was fined $60 million, the equivalent of roughly one year of revenue generated from the football program. The athletics program was placed on a five-year probation, and the football team was placed on a four-year bowl or postseason ban. Football scholarships were also reduced from 25 to 15 for a four-year period, and players were afforded the unusual option of transferring and playing immediately at other institutions. Lastly, all football program wins (112 total victories) were vacated from 1998 to 2011. This specific penalty erased several bowl victories and conference championships and altered the career record of Coach Joe Paterno, dropping him from first to 12th on the all-time wins list. These combined sanctions were perhaps the most significant penalties levied by the NCAA against any institution since Southern Methodist University received the dreaded "death penalty" in 1987.

Although the Penn State sex abuse case is large and complex, this chapter primarily details the events between the release of the Grand Jury report and the student riots in response to the firing of Coach Joe Paterno and President Graham Spanier. During that time, Penn State experienced a chain of events accompanied by a media firestorm that would forever change the institution, the surrounding community, and the legacies and reputations of several administrators. As a result of this sex-abuse scandal, both a senior-level vice president and the athletic director stepped down, the university president and iconic head football coach were relieved of their duties, and students protested by rioting in the streets. This chapter uses the events at Penn State as a case study that can serve as a thought-provoking learning tool for higher education and student affairs professionals, particularly those involved with athletic departments. After some critical background information is presented, this chapter focuses on the details of the Grand Jury report, the resulting fallout, and the findings of the Freeh report. The case is then positioned within its sociocultural context, and an alternate administrative response that could have potentially addressed the situation is offered.

The Case

To ascertain the significance, scope, and key elements of this case, it is important for the reader to have some knowledge of the six individuals who were closely involved. Below are six brief biographical sketches of Jerry Sandusky, Graham Spanier, Joe Paterno, Mike McQueary, Tim Curley, and Gary Schultz that offer critical information relevant to the case.

Jerry Sandusky

Sandusky served under Joe Paterno as the Penn State defensive coordinator for 23 years and on the coaching staff for a total of 32 years. Sandusky is largely credited with being the chief mastermind behind the perennially tough Penn State defense that earned the team the nickname "Linebacker U." Sandusky retired from Penn State in 1999 at the early age of 55 after learning he would not succeed Joe Paterno as the head coach. As part of his retirement package, Sandusky was granted professor emeritus status with various amenities, including an office on campus, access to all football and recreational facilities, a parking pass, and a Penn State email account (Freeh et al., 2012; Press Secretary, 2011).

In 1977, while coaching at Penn State, Sandusky founded the Second Mile. The charity was designed to help cultivate positive life skills and self-esteem among at-risk youth. Although the charity was initially started in State College, Pennsylvania, it expanded throughout the Commonwealth, serving between 7,500 and 12,000 students annually (Gilliland, 2011), with an operating budget approaching $2.85 million in 2010. Sandusky was accused of using the Second Mile charity as a means to meet the children he would later be convicted of sexually abusing.

Graham Spanier

Spanier had been serving as university president since 1995 (Murphy, 2012a). The president also held academic appointments as a professor of human development and family studies, sociology, demography, and family and community medicine. Between 1972 and 1983, Spanier was a Penn State faculty member and administrator in the College of Health and Human Development. Prior to assuming the presidency at Penn State, Spanier held senior-level administrative appointments at the University of Nebraska-Lincoln, Oregon State University, and the State University of New York at Stony Brook. He was a nationally recognized leader, having chaired the Association of American Universities, the Association of Public and Land-Grant Universities, the Big Ten Conference Council of Presidents/Chancellors, and the NCAA Division I Board of Directors. In addition to his leadership accolades, Spanier was a well-respected scholar, having authored more than 100 academic publications and served as founding editor of the *Journal of Family Issues*.

Under Spanier's 16-year tenure as university president, Penn State's profile on the national scene grew tremendously as the institution became one of the elite public universities in the nation. As president, he achieved many noteworthy feats and largely avoided controversy. His long-standing track record of success secured Spanier an unusual amount of autonomy and trust from the institution's Board of

Trustees (Freeh et al., 2012). Spanier's influence and close relationship with several Board members allowed him to set the agenda, manage the message, and dictate outcomes in a way that received very little pushback from laissez-faire Penn State trustees (Frantz, 2012).

Joe Paterno

At the start of the 2011 football season, Joe Paterno, at the age of 84, was still the head football coach at Penn State. Paterno, a coaching legend, had been at the university since 1950 and in the head-coach role since 1966 (Wertheim & Epstein, 2011). Before being relieved of his duties, with 409 total wins, he held, at that time, the NCAA record for Division I-A victories as head coach. Although, prior to his termination, the only role Paterno held at the university was head football coach, he was often regarded as the most powerful man on campus, if not the Commonwealth. During his 46 years as head coach, the Penn State football program developed into a perennially competitive national powerhouse that won two national championships (1982, 1986) and appeared in 37 bowl games. Paterno's success raised the institution's profile and helped grow the university's endowment, which was barely existent at the beginning of his tenure, to nearly $2 billion (Wertheim & Epstein, 2011).

The legendary coach was well known for being both a generous donor and tenacious fundraiser (Murphy, 2012b). Although the exact amount he personally contributed to Penn State is unknown, it is suggested that Paterno and his wife donated over $4 million to the university. Additionally, the coach, who routinely met with donors and potential benefactors, was a key figure in Penn State's fundraising enterprise. His national reputation, popularity, and stature allowed university administrators to interact with donors who were previously untouchable. Some suggest that, throughout his career, he could have been responsible for helping the university raise well over $1 billion dollars.

Despite his accomplishments and status, Paterno maintained a rather modest lifestyle and a humble public persona. He was affectionately referred to as JoePa and was beloved at Penn State, throughout Pennsylvania, and within the sports community. The coach lived in a modest home several blocks from campus, and his name appeared on the main library, a university course, an on-campus sandwich shop, and an ice cream flavor at the campus creamery. A statue of Paterno was even erected outside the football stadium.

Under Paterno, the football program had a reputation for graduating and developing high-character players. Football was often recognized for running a clean program and for having never been cited for a major NCAA violation under Paterno's watch. However, the football program had recently received criticism for an uptick in unruly off-the-field behavior by players. An ESPN *Outside the Lines* investigation found that, between 2002 and 2008, 46 players were charged with 143 separate criminal counts (Lavigne, 2008). Of all players charged with crimes, 27 were found or pleaded guilty on a total of 45 separate criminal counts. Many believed this surge in off-the-field misconduct was the result of a philosophical change in recruiting that overlooked some player character issues in an attempt to sign top-tier athletes at a time when the football program was struggling between 2000 and 2004. The team's poor performance even compelled Spanier and Curley to privately suggest the then-77-year-old Paterno retire. Paterno refused and was able to restore the program's winning tradition during the latter half of the decade. In January of 2012, Paterno abruptly died of complications from lung cancer.

Mike McQueary

Mike McQueary, a State College native and former Penn State quarterback, is the primary witness named in the Grand Jury report. At the time of the scandal, he was serving as an assistant football coach at Penn State, where his major responsibilities included the coordination of recruiting efforts and coaching wide receivers. McQueary testified to the Grand Jury that he witnessed Sandusky having anal intercourse with a young boy in the shower of the Lasch Football Building on the Penn State campus in 2001 while he was a graduate assistant working with the football team. McQueary joined the Penn State staff full-time in 2004 (Freeh et al., 2012)

Tim Curley

Curley is a State College, Pennsylvania, native, who attended Penn State and walked on the football team in the 1970s. Curley remained involved with the athletic department and eventually became the athletic director at Penn State. Curley was the athletic director at the time of the alleged sex abuse crimes and was still acting in that capacity when the scandal became public. Curley reported directly to President Spanier and was Joe Paterno's immediate supervisor. It should be noted that Curley's athletic department experienced another high-profile incident when a former women's basketball player filed a racial and sexual discrimination lawsuit against Penn State, then-women's head basketball coach Rene Portland, and Tim Curley in 2005. In 2007 a settlement was reached and Portland allegedly opted to retire on her own. Still, the institution, particularly Curley and Spanier, received significant criticism for allowing Portland to remain at Penn State for nearly 20 years after it was publicly revealed that she held strong anti-gay convictions (Cyphers, 2011; Lieber, 2006).

Gary Schultz

At the time the scandal surfaced nationally, Gary Schultz was Penn State's senior vice president for finance and business, which included oversight of the university police department. He was serving in this capacity at the time several of the alleged incidents occurred on campus facilities in 1998 and 2002. Although Schultz retired in 2009, he returned to the university in fall 2011 to fill his previous position in an interim role.

The Grand Jury Report

The Grand Jury report documents, in graphic detail, claims of sexual abuse from eight alleged victims against Jerry Sandusky that occurred between 1994 and 2009. In the report, Sandusky was charged with 40 criminal counts (21 felonies), including seven counts of involuntary deviate sexual intercourse, one count of aggravated indecent assault, eight counts of corruption of minors, eight counts of unlawful contact with a minor, eight counts of endangering the welfare of a child, seven counts of indecent assault, and one count of attempt to commit indecent assault (Lieber, 2006; Pennsylvania Attorney General, 2011). At a press conference discussing the allegations on November 7, 2011, Linda Kelly – Pennsylvania's Attorney General – described Sandusky as a "sexual predator accused of using his position within the community to prey on numerous young boys for more than a decade" (Pennsylvania Attorney General, 2011). The report describes how Sandusky used the Second Mile charity he founded to meet and develop personal relationships with the young boys that he would eventually be convicted of sexually abusing.

Sandusky's victims claim he provided them with gifts (sporting equipment, electronics, clothing, and money) and took them to sporting events, restaurants, and other activities and special events. One victim indicated Sandusky would purchase him cigarettes and even marijuana on one specific occasion. The report describes how Sandusky would befriend the boys and slowly establish physical contact with them through wrestling, massaging, tickling, touching their knees and thighs, and cracking their backs. The victims separately communicated how these uncomfortable incidents transformed into encounters that included showering, fondling, oral sex, and anal sex. The victims indicated that many of the sexual encounters typically occurred at Sandusky's home, the Penn State campus football facilities, or Penn State-sponsored trips and events away from campus. Sandusky's alleged abuse of young boys finally came to light in 2009 after a mother reported the sexual assault of her son by Sandusky to officials at her son's high school, where Sandusky was serving as a volunteer assistant football coach (Wertheim & Epstein, 2011). This accusation, accompanied by the testimony of two high school coaches, prompted the launch of the Pennsylvania Grand Jury investigation. Below are summaries of four critical accounts that occurred in 1998, 1999, 2000, and 2001, contained in the Grand Jury report.

Critical Account – 1998

In 1998, a mother of an 11-year-old boy who Sandusky met through the Second Mile program reported to Penn State University police that Sandusky had taken a shower with her son on campus at the football locker room facilities. The mother indicated that both Sandusky and her son were completely naked while in the shower together. In response to the complaints, university police launched an investigation. During the investigation, lead detective Ronald Schreffler and a State College police detective eavesdropped, with the consent of the alleged victim's mother, on telephone conversations between her and Sandusky. In those conversations, Sandusky admitted to showering with her son and other boys. The alleged victim's mother attempted to secure Sandusky's word that he would not continue this practice of showering with young boys, but he would not agree. When asked if Sandusky had touched the boy's "private parts," he responded, "I don't think so . . . maybe" (Press Secretary, 2011, p. 20). Later in the conversation after the mother told Sandusky he could no longer see the boy, Sandusky responded, "I understand. I was wrong. I wish I could get forgiveness. I know I won't get it from you. I wish I were dead" (Press Secretary, 2011, p. 20). As part of the investigation, Detective Schreffler and an investigator from the Pennsylvania Department of Public Welfare also interviewed Sandusky. In that conversation, Sandusky admitted to showering with the boy and hugging him while in the shower. Eventually, the case was closed after the county district attorney, Ray Gricar, determined no criminal charges would be filed. Schreffler indicated he was instructed to close the case by the Penn State director of university police.

Critical Account – 1999

The Grand Jury report also captures the story of another alleged victim, who recalls being subjected to repeated involuntary sexual intercourse and assault by Sandusky over the course of several years during his early teenage years. According to the victim, many of the assaults:

> [...] took place on the Penn State University Park campus, in the football buildings, at the Toftrees Golf Resort and Conference Center ("Toftrees") in Centre County, where the football team and staff stayed prior to home football games and at bowl games to which he traveled with Sandusky.
>
> *(p. 14)*

After the football program moved into the Lasch football building, the victim indicated that most of the inappropriate sexual conduct occurred in the sauna at that facility. The victim, like most others, was introduced to Sandusky through the Second Mile charity.

Although he was sexually abused by Sandusky on various occasions, the victim had resisted some of Sandusky's advances. The victim testified that Sandusky would not ask permission but would simply "see what Victim 4 would permit him to do" (Press Secretary, 2011, p. 20). The victim recalls resisting Sandusky while at the 1999 Alamo Bowl and being threatened with the possibility of being sent home from the trip. Typically, the sexual abuse would include the touching of genitals and oral sex, but Sandusky did attempt to penetrate the victim with his penis and finger. Only slight penetration was achieved before the victim resisted. The victim testified that Sandusky routinely provided him with gifts, including promising him that he could be a walk-on player at Penn State and featuring him in a video about linebackers that highlighted Sandusky.

Critical Account – 2000

In fall 2000, Jim Calhoun, a janitor at Penn State, witnessed Sandusky sexually assaulting a young boy on campus. Calhoun never officially reported the incident for fear of losing his job, but immediately shared it with his co-workers after the incident occurred. During the Grand Jury's investigation, Calhoun was residing in a nursing home facility and was considered unable to testify to the Grand Jury due to dementia. According to the Grand Jury report, the janitor initially told a co-worker that he witnessed a man, later to be identified as Sandusky, performing oral sex on a young boy who was pinned up against the wall in the Lasch Building shower. Although Calhoun's co-worker did not personally witness the act, he reported seeing Sandusky and a boy holding hands while leaving the locker room with gym bags and wet hair. Calhoun's co-worker indicated that Calhoun was visibly shaking from what he witnessed. Calhoun did inform his immediate supervisor, who described Calhoun as "very emotionally upset" and "very distraught," even indicating that he "was afraid the man was going to have a heart attack or something" (p. 22). Calhoun's supervisor told the Grand Jury that he had told Calhoun that he could report the incident and provided him with the information to do so.

Critical Account – 2001

An incident of sexual assault that had occurred in 2001 was described in the report in detail; it arguably received the most public attention of all the incidents. This incident involved Mike McQueary, who was at that time a 28-year-old graduate assistant working with the Penn State football team. He told the Grand Jury investigators that he witnessed Sandusky having anal intercourse with a young boy in the shower at the Lasch Building on Penn State's campus one night after returning to the locker room to store his belongings and collect some recruiting tapes. McQueary indicated that he discovered Sandusky with the boy because the lights were on in the shower and "rhythmic, slapping sounds" (p. 6) were coming from the area. In the report, McQueary described a scene where both Sandusky and the young boy were naked and Sandusky was behind the boy, who had his hands up against the wall. Both Sandusky and the young boy noticed his presence, and McQueary left the locker room immediately, returning to his office to call his father and report what he witnessed. McQueary's father told him to leave the building and return home.

The next day the graduate assistant and his father went to Joe Paterno's home to report what McQueary witnessed to the head coach. The following day, Paterno invited Curley, the athletic director, to his home and "reported to him that the graduate assistant had seen Jerry Sandusky in the Lasch Building showers fondling or doing something of a sexual nature to a young boy" (p. 7). Nearly a week and a half later, McQueary was asked to share what he had seen in the shower with Curley and Schultz, the vice president for finance and business. During that meeting, McQueary said he told the two senior administrators that he "witnessed what he believed to be Sandusky having anal sex with a boy in the Lasch Building showers" (p. 7). The graduate assistant indicated that the administrators promised to look into the matter. McQueary was contacted a few weeks later by Curley and informed him that Sandusky's locker room keys were confiscated and the incident was reported to the Second Mile. Until he spoke to the Grand Jury, McQueary indicated that he had never discussed the matter with anyone actively investigating the incident.

In their individual testimonies to the Grand Jury, both Curley and Schultz claimed that McQueary did not explain the shower incident in graphic detail. Instead, they both said that the graduate assistant never specifically described the actions or referred to them as sexual in nature. Instead, they asserted that McQueary used terms like "inappropriate conduct" and "horsing around," (p. 8) indicating, nevertheless, that the incident made him uncomfortable. Despite corroborating the timeline of events and many of the specific details shared by McQueary, except the specific description of the shower encounter as sexual in nature, both Schultz and Curley told the Grand Jury that they "had no indication that a crime had occurred" (p. 9). Additionally, both of the senior administrators told the Grand Jury that the Penn State University president, Graham Spanier, was informed of the incident in 2001 and approved of the decision to alert the Second Mile and ban Sandusky from bringing boys on campus, a seemingly unenforceable punishment, given Sandusky's access to the campus. However, the specificity about what President Spanier was told remains unclear. Neither Curley nor Schultz reported the incident to any policing agency, not even Penn State's university police, a department under Schultz's supervision. In his testimony, Schultz indicated that he was aware of the 1998 incident involving Sandusky and another boy, yet he failed to take further action with the information provided by McQueary.

In his testimony to the Grand Jury, Spanier confirmed that Schultz and Curley informed him of the incident, but the campus leader also claimed that the information he was given failed to suggest the incident was sexual in nature. Like Schultz and Curley, Spanier recalled being apprised of an incident with Sandusky and a child in a shower that involved "horsing around" that made a staff member "uncomfortable" (p. 10). Spanier also denied being aware of the 1998 incident. Spanier was not charged with any crimes by the Grand Jury, but the testimony of Curley and Schultz was regarded as "not credible" (p. 11) in the Grand Jury report. Schultz and Curley were both charged with perjury and failure to report the sexual assault of a minor.

The Freeh Report

Evidence provided in the Freeh report suggests that Spanier, Schultz, Paterno, and Curley had substantial knowledge of the 1998 and 2001 incidents when they occurred and failed to identify and protect past and future victims from Sandusky. The report highlights the following eight critical failures that contributed to perhaps the most damning scandal related to college athletics:

- Profound lack of empathy expressed toward Sandusky's victims by Spanier, Schultz, Paterno, and Curley.
- Failure by the Board of Trustees in 1998 and 2001 to institute proper oversight structures to protect the institution from major risks.
- Failure by the Board of Trustees to demand details regarding the Grand Jury investigation from President Spanier and General Counsel.
- Systemic failure on behalf of Spanier to encourage discussion and debate.
- Lack of knowledge about the Clery Act and whistleblower protection policies.
- Improper handling of Sandusky's retirement from Penn State, which provided him with the resources, platform, and opportunity to continue abusing young boys.
- A football program exempt from participation in some university programs.
- An institutionalized culture of "reverence" toward the football program that existed throughout the Penn State community.

The report also provided 120 recommendations in eight specific domains to the Board of Trustees and university administrators that outlined both structural and policy changes designed to create a safer campus environment for children. However, the report indicated that the most significant threat to the institution's reputation as a progressive institution was its culture called "The Penn State Way," which was described as a heavy reliance on top-down decision making, resistance to diverse perspectives, and overemphasis on intercollegiate athletics. Freeh and his colleagues suggested that making a cultural change would be the most critical but also the most daunting task for the university as it moved forward.

The Ongoing Aftermath

Following the release of the Grand Jury report on Friday, November 4, 2011, Sandusky was arrested and arraigned on 40 criminal counts that Saturday. Sandusky was released after posting $100,000 for bail (Viera, 2011; Boren, 2011a). Over that weekend, the university responded to the Grand Jury report and the arrest by issuing several statements. That Saturday, Spanier issued a statement supporting Schultz and Curley and calling the allegations against Sandusky troubling. An excerpt from his brief statement read:

> I wish to say that Tim Curley and Gary Schultz have my unconditional support. I have known and worked daily with Tim and Gary for more than 16 years. I have complete confidence in how they have handled the allegations about a former University employee. Tim Curley and Gary Schultz operate at the highest levels of honesty, integrity and compassion. I am confident the

record will show that these charges are groundless and that they conducted themselves professionally and appropriately.

(Penn State Live, 2011a)

Later that weekend, Paterno also issued a public statement. He indicated that the allegations were shocking and went on to say that "I did what I was supposed to with the one charge brought to my attention" (Boren, 2011b). The head coach's statement seemed overly concerned with defending the manner in which he handled the situation and less concerned with the pain and damage inflicted on the victims, their families, and the community. Paterno's statement went on to stress that Sandusky was retired and no longer on his coaching staff, suggesting that the responsibility for handling the situation was beyond his control. In addition to the statements that Spanier and Paterno issued, lawyers for Curley and Schultz also issued statements proclaiming their clients' innocence (Penn State Live, 2011b).

In response to the allegations, the Penn State Board of Trustees held an executive meeting on Sunday, November 6, 2011 (VanderKolk, 2011). After that meeting, the university issued its first official public statement. Bill Mahon, the university's spokesman, announced that the Board of Trustees had approved requests from both Schultz and Curley to "step down so they may defend themselves" (VanderKolk, 2011, p. 1). Curley was placed on administrative leave, and Schultz was to return to retirement. Both the chair of the Board of Trustees, Steve Garbin, and Spanier expressed sadness over the allegations, and outlined a four-step plan to address the issue. The university's plan involved: 1) charging a task force to conduct an independent review of the allegations, 2) publicizing the findings of the independent review, 3) reviewing police reporting procedures with administrators, and 4) conducting educational programs on topics related to sexual violence and sexual abuse.

That Monday, both Schultz and Curley surrendered to authorities in Harrisburg, Pennsylvania, where they were arrested and arraigned on charges of perjury and failure to report the sexual abuse of a minor (Associated Press, 2011). Neither was forced to plea, and the judge set bail at $75,000 and required the men to surrender their passports. That same day, the Pennsylvania Attorney General announced that Paterno was not a target of the investigation but declined to indicate whether Spanier was a key target of the case (Associated Press, 2011). At this point, the Penn State story began to receive significant traction in the national mainstream media, and members of the press swarmed the campus. News of the scandal was televised on the NBC Nightly News with Brian Williams, ABC World News with Diane Sawyer, CBS Evening News with Scott Pelley, and other 24-hour news venues such as ESPN, CNN, MSNBC, and Fox News. Additionally, many major national newspapers (*The New York Times, The Washington Post, Philadelphia Inquirer*, etc.) had begun to cover the scandal in significant detail in both their print and online venues. By that Tuesday, the Penn State scandal had usurped all other news stories and became the lead or headline story on most news broadcasts and web pages.

As the frenzy around the scandal continued to build momentum, calls for Spanier's and Paterno's resignations intensified. Many were anxiously awaiting Paterno's weekly press conference on that Tuesday. However, with little notice, the press conference was cancelled (Sanserino, Schackner, & Musselman, 2011). This action only fueled public outcry. Later that day, the media swarmed Paterno, who was with one of his sons, as he was leaving a campus facility. The coach said very little, but his son informed the media that there had been no discussions with the university administration that involved Paterno stepping down (Sanserino et al., 2011). The following day, Paterno released a statement stating that he would retire at the end of the season (ESPN.com, 2011a). The coach made this decision without consulting the institution's Board of Trustees, encouraging them to focus on more pressing issues and "not spend a single minute discussing my status" (ESPN.com, 2011a). In that same statement, Paterno expressed regret about not having done more. That same day, rumors surfaced that Spanier would be fired.

Later that evening, at 10:00 pm, the Penn State Board of Trustees called a press conference to make a public statement about the allegations and the state of the university. John Surma, vice chair for the Board of Trustees, led the press conference, which was nationally televised on most major networks. In his statement, he announced the firing of both Spanier and Paterno, effective immediately. During the press conference, Surma indicated "the best interest of the university is to have a change in leadership to deal with the difficult issues that we are facing" (ESPN.com, 2011b). In addition to remarking on the tragedy and the victims, Surma also stated, "the university is much larger than its athletic teams" (ESPN.com, 2011b). Surma indicated that the defensive coordinator, Tom Bradley, would serve as interim coach, and Rodney Erickson, the executive vice president and provost, would serve as interim university president.

In response to the press conference, students staged a demonstration outside Old Main, the main university administrative building. This peaceful demonstration turned violent as thousands of protestors filled the streets of downtown State College after hearing of Paterno's firing. Light poles were knocked down, a media van was overturned, cars were vandalized, and rocks and fireworks were thrown at law enforcement officials. Nearly 100 police officers were required to bring the riot to a close (Armas, 2011). Pepper spray was used to disperse the crowd, but only after several hours of rioting (Schweber, 2011). A much more peaceful crowd gathered at Paterno's home to express their love for the coach, who greeted the crowd and made a few remarks thanking the students for their support and asking them to pray for the alleged victims.

Sociocultural Context

Sandusky's sexual abuse of young boys is, without question, the most tragic and disturbing aspect of the Penn State scandal. For many, it remains inconceivable that the sexual abuse of young children could go unreported and unobstructed for nearly 15 years even though several of the institution's most senior and visible leaders were, to varying degrees, aware of the situation and had multiple opportunities to intervene. How could this have happened for so long? Although a clear answer to this question may never be offered, examining several of the sociocultural influences that seem prominent in this scandal provides some contextual understanding of how the situation at Penn State spiraled out of control.

It is important to understand that the immense power and influence centralized within Penn State's football program is a major factor in this scandal. The visibility and popularity of the football program, along with its economic value to the institution, made the football program one of the school's most priceless assets. Any negative publicity attached to the football program could have had an impact on Penn State, particularly with regard to revenue and student enrollment. Thus, the football program was an asset to be protected and safeguarded. Equally as valuable to Penn State was Paterno and his legacy. Maintaining Paterno's legacy, reputation, and legitimacy was especially valuable to the institution. To imagine that these considerations did not play a part in shaping the responses of Spanier, Paterno, Curley, Schultz, and the others involved in the scandal would be obtuse. Both Spanier and Paterno invested many years into building Penn State's institutional platform and elite football program. As the Freeh report suggested, both Spanier and Paterno were likely eager to prevent an ugly public relations nightmare that would tarnish "their" institution and personal legacies.

Because of the football program's power and influence, coupled with the fanaticism surrounding the team, if someone were to have a conflict with the football program, he or she could be politically (professionally) and personally hurt. Eyewitnesses (i.e. a university custodian and Mike McQueary) had the opportunity to intervene but did not confront Sandusky or report what they witnessed to the police after conversations with their supervisors yielded insufficient results. The university custodian, Jim Calhoun, opted not to formally report the incident to authorities because he was afraid of losing his job. To most, it may seem a bit illogical or unreasonable to fear losing your job for reporting an act of sexual abuse toward a minor. However, to have such a concern when such a heinous act has been committed speaks volumes about the perceived power and influence of the football program and the culture of pacification at Penn State. Furthermore, given the fanatical culture surrounding the football program, if Calhoun had been fired, he may have found it difficult to find other employment in the area or remain in the region if it were perceived that he personally harmed the institution, Paterno, or the football program. Similar assumptions can be made about McQueary, who was a young graduate assistant at the time. It is possible that he never pressed the matter after he initially witnessed and reported the issue to Paterno in 2001 because of concerns about his career. How would McQueary have landed a job as a coach without the support of Paterno, Curley, and the others at Penn State? Ultimately, McQueary was able to stay at Penn State after the incident and work his way up through the ranks to become the quarterback coach in 2004 (Freeh et al., 2012). Although the Freeh report indicated the McQueary hire was legitimate, it seems appropriate to wonder if what he witnessed in the Lasch Building showers had an impact on his career trajectory at the institution.

At its core this case is about sexual abuse, but it is important to recognize that the same-sex nature of the abuse makes the case more complicated. Might this case have played out differently had young girls been Sandusky's victims? Although this question is uncomfortable to consider, it is worth asking for a number of reasons. In our society, sexual abuse and rape are largely conceptualized in a heterosexual context (Foubert, 1997; Henderson, 1992; Rozee & Koss, 2001). Such an under-developed conceptualization of sexual violence hampers our collective capacity to appropriately address sexually violent relationships that fall outside our socially constructed norms. Additionally, same-sex encounters between men are still taboo subjects, particularly among older men and in conservative environments (Bolton, Morris, & MacEachron, 1989; Donnelly & Kenyon, 1996; Groth & Burgess, 1980).

Paterno, Spanier, Schultz, and Curley's long-standing personal relationship with Sandusky is another factor that must be considered when deconstructing this case. Their relationship with the former coach may have caused these men to conveniently ignore or overlook much of the evidence that implicated Sandusky as a sexual predator. Taking this all into context, the key Penn State administrators, especially Paterno, who probably had the most power, may simply have not known how to appropriately analyze and handle a situation that would have such a tremendous effect on their lives, community, and beloved institution. Although the correct decision in this instance is obvious to most, it may be that the sociocultural realities at the university converged to cloud the judgment of key decision-makers at the university and within the football program.

It is also worth mentioning that the six adults directly involved in this case were also White and presumably heterosexual. Given the lack of diversity among insti-tutional presidents, executive-level personnel, and leaders within athletic depart-ments at traditionally White institutions of higher education, that these men were White should not be surprising. However, this observation seems even more salient when Penn State's turbulent history of homophobia and racism is considered (Cyphers, 2011; D'Augelli & Rose, 1990; Lieber, 2006; Mock, 2011). Certainly, it would be presumptive to suggest that the situation may have played out differently had a more diverse cast of characters been involved. Yet it does seem appropriate to wonder how an administrative group that had been more diverse with respect to gender, sexual orientation, and, perhaps, race would have responded to the situa-tion. Scholarly research indicates that diversity within a group provides multiple perspectives, improves creativity and flexibility, and decreases misconduct and corruption (Ramirez, 2003). Additionally, diversity enhances cognitive complexity and functioning within a group in ways that create positive cultures of scrutiny while decreasing groupthink tendencies (Ramirez, 2003).

Given the evidence pointing to the value of group diversity, it seems reasonable to wonder if a more diverse group of individuals would have botched or mis-managed the administrative response as severely as Paterno, Spanier, Schultz, and Curley did. With more diverse experiences, opinions, and worldviews among key decision-makers, it is plausible that someone would have been more comfortable criticizing the group's handling of the situation or reporting the facts to an outside entity. And perhaps Paterno and Spanier would have been less comfortable crafting or accepting an inadequate administrative response to the incidents in 1998 and 2001 if they had believed the others involved would not stand by and do nothing.

Although Sandusky was the primary perpetrator in the Penn State scandal, the key enablers in this case are not without blame. Sandusky would have been unable to continue his sexual abuse of young boys if one individual had the courage or moral character to simply speak up. To many, it seems implausible that no one had come forward, but when placed within its appropriate context, it is clear that complex, toxic sociocultural influences contributed to one of the biggest scandals in college sports. The immense influence of the football program, the general stigma associated with same-sex male sexual encounters, and the lack of diversity among key decision-makers all had a significant impact on the manner in which the Penn State scandal developed.

Alternate Ending

Penn State's handling of the Sandusky sex abuse scandal was extremely problematic. Without question, the best possible resolution to this situation would have occurred with more substantive action in 1998 or 2001. Unfortunately, this did not happen, and the controversy spiraled out of control. As the final piece of this chapter, we offer an alternate ending that presents another way the university, particularly Spanier and the Board of Trustees (Board), could have approached the situation when Spanier, Schultz, Paterno, and Curley were issued subpoenas by the Pennsylvania Grand Jury in late 2010 to testify in 2011 (Freeh et al., 2012).

Initially, Spanier could have immediately suspended Sandusky's retirement privileges and banned him from campus and university functions. Second, the president should have informed the Board of the subpoenas and pledged to keep them updated on the Grand Jury's investigation of Sandusky. This step seems particularly critical, since the Freeh report suggests Spanier not only failed to keep the Board apprised but also diminished the significance of the Sandusky situation (Freeh et al., 2012). As a third course of action, following the testimony of Schultz, Curley, and Paterno before the Grand Jury in January of 2011, Spanier could have instructed Cynthia Baldwin, Penn State General Counsel, to brief the trustees on all information pertaining to the Sandusky investigation at the Board meeting that occurred in March of 2011. This discussion with the Board could have occurred in a closed session and Schultz, Curley, and Paterno could have been asked to share their testimony with the Board. Additionally, Baldwin could have shared the information she was able to uncover from personal, email, and telephone conversations with current and former Penn State staff that had knowledge of Sandusky's alleged actions.

With this initial information and continued updates, the trustees may have better understood the seriousness of the investigation and its implications for the university. Given the gravity of the issue, the Board could have assumed a more hands-on governance approach and possibly launched an internal investigation and developed a proactive action and communications plan that would help prevent a media firestorm, protect the institution's image, and – most importantly – heal a broken community. The Board's plan could be enacted over several months after commencement in May, but the trustees would need to immediately determine if Spanier would be willing to support and execute their plan or vacate the presidency.

Provided Spanier agreed to cooperate, a small group of trustees, along with Spanier, could meet with Paterno and inform him that the university would like him to retire, effective immediately, in June. Although it would have been difficult to force Paterno to resign since he had not been accused of any criminal wrong-doing, the coach's oversight of the football program while these alleged incidents occurred on campus could have provided the Board with the justification to request he retire. Though it is unknown how Paterno would have responded, upon considerable reflection, his love and admiration for Penn State may have persuaded him to choose early retirement rather than subject his revered institution to the firestorm his firing may induce. With Paterno's agreement, the university could have scheduled a press conference allowing the coach the opportunity to resign publicly, citing health and personal reasons as the impetus. With Paterno voluntarily stepping down during the summer, the possibility of student unrest would be completely eliminated.

Later that summer, or before fall classes began, the Board and Spanier could have placed Curley on immediate administrative leave, pending the results of an internal investigation by the trustees, and refrained from rehiring Schultz in an interim capacity. At that point the university could inform the local community and news media that Penn State is deeply troubled by the allegations, sympathetic to the victims, and will be fully cooperative with the ongoing investigation from the Pennsylvania Attorney General's Office. Moreover, the institution should make a statement suggesting that it will reach out to the alleged victims and provide support to them and other members of the community. Finally, the Board could ensure that Spanier stepped down as president during the fall semester and before the release of the Pennsylvania Grand Jury report in November 2011. This would have been a more graceful departure for Spanier from the institution and enabled Penn State to appear both proactive and responsive in the face of serious allegations. Such actions may have also allowed Penn State to minimize the considerable damage that was done to its reputation.

References

Armas, A. (2011). Penn State trustees fire Paterno, students riot. Retrieved from http://nbcsports.msnbc.com/id/45233483/ns/sports-college_football/

Associated Press. (2011). Tim Curley, Gary Schultz surrender to police as Jerry Sandusky, Penn State abuse scandal widens. Retrieved from www.huffingtonpost.com/2011/11/07/tim-curley-gary-schultz-s_n_1080366.html

Bolton, F. G. J., Morris, L. A., & MacEachron, A. E. (1989). *Males at risk: The other side of child sexual abuse*. Thousand Oaks, CA: SAGE Publications.

Boren, C. (2011a). Joe Paterno on Sandusky charges: "If this is true, we were all fooled". Retrieved from www.washingtonpost.com/blogs

Boren, C. (2011b). Jerry Sandusky arrested on new counts of child sexual abuse. Retrieved from www.washingtonpost.com/blogs

Cyphers, L. (2011). Sandusky case just latest of Penn State. Retrieved from http://espn.go.com

D'Augelli, A. R., & Rose, M. L. (1990). Homophobia in a university community: Attitudes and experiences of heterosexual freshmen. *Journal of College Student Development*, 31(6), 484–491.

Donnelly, D. A., & Kenyon, S. (1996). "Honey, we don't do men": Gender stereotypes and the provision of services to sexually assaulted males. *Journal of Interpersonal Violence*, 11(3), 441–448.

ESPN.com News Services. (2011a). Joe Paterno to retire; president out? Retrieved from http://espn.go.com

ESPN.com News Services. (2011b). Joe Paterno, Graham Spanier removed. Retrieved from http://espn.go.com

ESPN.com News Services. (2011c). Penn State sanctions: $60M, bowl ban. Retrieved from http://espn.go.com

Foubert, J. D. (1997). Effects of a sexual assault peer education program on men's belief in rape myths. *Sex Roles*, 36(3/4), 259–268.

Frantz, J. (2012). Graham Spanier: Jerry Sandusky case took down Penn State president's career. Retrieved from www.pennlive.com

Freeh, Sporkin, and Sullivan, LLP. (2012). Report of the Special Investigative Counsel regarding the actions of The Pennsylvania State University related to the child sexual abuse committed by Gerald A. Sandusky. Retrieved from http://thefreehreportonpsu.com/

Gilliland, D. (2011, November 18). Second Mile CEO made more than $132,000; wife still makes more than $100,000 from charity Jerry Sandusky founded. Retrieved from www.pennlive.com

Groth, N., & Burgess, W. (1980). Male rape: Offenders and victims. *American Journal of Psychiatry*, 137(7), 806–810.

Henderson, L. (1992). Rape and responsibility. *Law and Philosophy*, 11(1), 127–178.

Lavigne, P. (2008, July 27). Has Penn State's on-field progress led to off field problems? Retrieved from http://sports.espn.go.com

Lieber, J. (2006). Harris stands tall in painful battle with Penn State coach. Retrieved from www.usatoday.com

Mock, B. (2011). The other Penn State cover-up: Death threats against black students. Retrieved from http://loop21.com

Murphy, J. (2012a, November 1). Graham Spanier: Former Penn State president's bio and career highlights. Retrieved from www.pennlive.com

Murphy, J. (2012b, January 24). Joe Paterno: A life – A fundraiser supreme. Retrieved from www.pennlive.com

Penn State. (2012a). Penn State's mission and public character. About Penn State. Retrieved from www.psu.edu

Penn State. (2012b). Undergraduate and graduate/first-professional Fall Enrollment 2011 and 2010. Retrieved from www.budget.psu.edu

Penn State Live. (2011a). Trustees announce 2 officials to step down while case is investigated. Retrieved from http://live.psu.edu/story/56238

Penn State Live. (2011b). Statement from President Spanier. Retrieved from http://live.psu.edu/story/56236

Pennsylvania Attorney General. (2011). Attorney General Kelly and PA State Police Commissioner Noonan issue statements regarding Jerry Sandusky sex crimes investigation. Retrieved from www.attorneygeneral.gov

Prato, L. (1998). *The Penn State football encyclopedia*. Champagne, IL: Sports Publishing.

Press Secretary. (2011). Sandusky grand jury presentment. Retrieved from www.attorney general.gov/uploadedFiles/Press/Sandusky-Grand-Jury-Presentment.pdf

Ramirez, S. A. (2003). A flaw in the Sarbanes-Oxley reform: Can diversity in the boardroom quell corporate corruption? *St. John's Law Review*, 77(4), 837–866.

Rozee, P. D., & Koss, M. P. (2001). Rape: A century of resistance. *Psychology of Women Quarterly*, 25(4), 295–311.

Sanserino, M., Schackner, B., & Musselman, R. (2011). News conference cancelled amid reports Paterno departure is near. Retrieved from www.post-gazette.com

Schweber, N. (2011, November 11). Penn State students clash with police in unrest after announcement. Retrieved from www.nytimes.com

VanderKolk, J. (2011). Leaders leave amid alleged Sandusky sex abuse scandal. *Centre Daily Times*, p. 1.

Viera, M. (2011, November 5). Former coach at Penn State is charged with abuse. Retrieved from www.nytimes.com

Wertheim, L. & Epstein, D. (2011). This is Penn State. *Sports Illustrated*, 115(20), 40–53.

21

SEX DISCRIMINATION AND ABUSE OF A FEMALE KICKER ON THE UNIVERSITY OF COLORADO FOOTBALL TEAM

Frank Harris III

It was obvious Katie was not very good. She was awful. You know what guys do? They respect your ability. You can be 90 years old, but if you can go out and play, they'll respect you. Katie was not only a girl, she was terrible. Okay? There's no other way to say it. She couldn't kick the ball through the uprights.

Gary Barnett, Head Football Coach, University of Colorado,
February 2004 in Banda (2004)

Katherine "Katie" Hnida was a student-athlete on the University of Colorado's (CU) football team in 1999. In 2004, she went public with the sexual harassment, sexual assault, and other acts of violence and intimidation that were perpetuated against her by teammates during the year she participated on the team. Gary Barnett, who was the head coach of the CU football team from 1999 to 2005, offered the remarks above to reporters when he was asked about Katie's allegations. While Katie's case is perhaps the most widely known in the CU football scandal, other women were also victimized amid the sexually violent culture that the football program had created. The larger scandal within the CU football program, which reportedly dates as far back as 1997 and persisted throughout the mid-2000s, is largely considered among sports writers to be one of the most egregious acts of negligence and corruption to have taken place in American college sports. At least nine women were reportedly sexually assaulted during this time, and one can only speculate about the number of unreported rapes that occurred. According to a legal brief that the American Civil Liberties Union (ACLU) wrote in 2006, CU fostered an environment where women were repeatedly harassed and assaulted sexually by members of its football program, with little to no accountability imposed on the perpetrators. Reports of football team affiliates hiring escorts and exotic dancers, providing alcohol to minors, and condoning the use of drugs – all in an effort to entice high-profile football recruits to attend the university – are at the heart of the CU football scandal, which is detailed in this chapter.

I begin by offering a detailed account of what occurred in the CU football scandal, focusing primarily on how the wrongdoings were discovered, the stakeholders involved, how they responded to key incidents in the scandal, and how individuals and the institution were held accountable. I then discuss the broader sociocultural implications of the scandal and what it suggests about the larger intercollegiate athletic enterprise. To conclude, I offer an alternative ending to the scandal to illustrate how it might have been handled differently.

The Case

In December 1997, a group of CU football recruits raped a teenage girl, who was in high school at the time the assault occurred, at one of the program's infamous recruiting parties, where booze, drugs, and women were used to attract high-profile athletes. This incident prompted officials from the Boulder County District Attorney's office to meet with CU's leadership to express concern about multiple assaults involving members of the football program. However, these concerns fell on deaf ears. The sexually violent culture that characterized the CU football program only grew more intense and destructive as time went on.

Nearly two years after the 1997 assault, Katie Hnida enrolled at CU. After having a standout football career in high school, Katie was offered a spot as a place kicker on the team by then-head coach Rick Neuheisel and became the first female student-athlete in the program's history. However, Katie never had the opportunity to play for Coach Neuheisel. He left CU before the 1999 season and Gary Barnett was appointed to lead the program as head coach.

Katie's one-year tenure on the football team under Barnett's leadership was tumultuous. At the outset, Katie encountered a climate of harassment and hostility. In a 2004 interview with Rick Reilly of *Sports Illustrated*, Katie recalled her first day of practice, at which five teammates assaulted her verbally, directed sexual remarks toward her, and exposed themselves no fewer than five times. Another teammate "came from behind and rubbed his erect penis against her" (Reilly, 2004). Abuses of this nature continued throughout the year. It was not atypical for Katie to be groped by teammates in huddles or to have footballs randomly hurled toward her head while she practiced placekicking.

Katie considered reaching out to Barnett for support, but ultimately decided against it because "[she] was terrified [and knew he] didn't want [her] around in the first place" (Reilly, 2004). She also feared being kicked off the team. However, Katie's father, Dave Hnida, reached out to Coach Barnett and the athletics director, Richard Tharp, on her behalf when he grew very concerned about the abuse she faced while on the team. According to Mr. Hnida, both Barnett and Tharp did not take his concerns seriously. He described his interaction with Barnett as "like talking to a wall" (Reilly, 2004). In a 2006 interview with ESPN's Jemele Hill, Barnett claimed ignorance of the abuse and harassment Hnida alleged: "Nothing was ever said to me regarding these feelings she had. When I read about it, that was the first time I heard about it" (Hill, 2006).

Matters worsened for Katie during the summer of 2000, when she was raped by a teammate. Katie and the teammate were watching television at his residence. In the 2004 interview with Rick Reilly, Katie described what happened afterward: "He just starts to kiss me. I told him, 'That's not O.K.' Next thing I know he's on top of me. I told him, 'No!' But he just kept going, 'Shhhhh.' I tried to push him off me, but he outweighed me by 100 pounds" (Reilly, 2004).

Katie further explained that he lifted her skirt, pushed her underwear aside, and penetrated her. She somehow managed to break free when he reached for a ringing telephone.

Katie considered pressing criminal charges and pursuing legal action but ultimately decided not to. She was concerned about the victim blaming that often occurs when sexual assault survivors go public (Hill, 2006). She observed it first hand during the Kobe Bryant sexual assault trial, which took place less than thirty miles from Boulder, in Denver, Colorado (Hill, 2006). She left CU after her sophomore year. She did not pursue a second year of football. She knew she would not be welcomed by Barnett and her teammates and could not endure another year of harassment. The trauma she experienced at CU left her depressed and no longer interested in playing football (Reilly, 2004).

After leaving CU, Katie Hnida enrolled in community college and eventually transferred to the University of New Mexico, where she earned a spot on the football team as a walk-on and played for three seasons (Reilly, 2004). Katie became the first woman in history to score a point in a Division I football game. She remained silent about the sexual assault until February 2004, when the CU football scandal became public (Reilly, 2004). It was at this time when Barnett uttered those infamous remarks about Katie and her lack of talent as a football player. For these and other remarks Barnett made about the scandal and the women who were victimized, Elizabeth Hoffman, president of the CU system, placed him on paid administrative leave (Basinger, 2004). Following an investigation of the scandal, Barnett was reinstated in May 2004 (Banda, 2004).

Had the university's leadership acted with greater urgency regarding the concerns that Katie and her father brought to its attention, four reported sexual assaults involving the football program after her departure may not have occurred. Each is summarized in the ACLU (2006) report. In September 2001, a female student who worked as a trainer for the football team was sexually assaulted by a member of the team. One month later, a player on the team assaulted a student and football-recruiting ambassador. One month following this incident, multiple members of the football team sexually assaulted a second student football trainer. Finally, in December 2001, several then-current and then-prospective players who were on a recruitment visit to the campus violated Lisa Simpson, a CU student. One of Lisa's assailants was involved in the aforementioned assault on the football-recruiting ambassador, which further suggests that the university and athletics department did not handle these incidents in a timely way.

According to the account of the American Association of University Women [AAUW] (2005), Lisa and several female friends were socializing over drinks at her off-campus apartment. One of the women (who had been a tutor for the football team) invited a few of her friends from the team to join the gathering. The friends arrived and were accompanied by approximately 16 to 20 others – nearly all were football players or recruits – who had been drinking prior to their arrival. At one point during the gathering, Lisa passed out in her room from intoxication. Shortly thereafter, Lisa awoke to several men removing her clothes, who then proceeded to assault her sexually. Lisa also reported that several other male affiliates of the football program assaulted her sexually that evening and another young woman was also assaulted in the same room on the same occasion.

Lisa reported the assault to the appropriate university personnel. The student-athletes involved in the assault were held responsible for violating the university's code of conduct, but were not punished for committing sexual assault. The consequences for Lisa, however, were significant. She suffered depression, her grades declined, and she eventually withdrew from CU without earning a degree. In 2002, Lisa Simpson and two other women who had been assaulted by members of the football program sued the university under Title IX. Lisa's case was settled for $2.5 million in December 2007 – six years after the sexual assault occurred.

CU, its leadership, and the athletics department were justifiably criticized for their response (or lack thereof) to the sexual assaults. Instead of taking the actions necessary to reel in the football program, the university "adopted a policy of 'plausible deniability,'" by ignoring reasonable evidence that suggested that the program created a hostile environment and posed an imminent risk to women within the CU community (American Civil Liberties Union [ACLU], 2006, p. 26). Concerns about the use of drugs, alcohol, and sex to recruit football players were brought to the attention of Barnett and his staff on multiple occasions. Yet they chose not to address these issues because they were concerned about losing a "competitive edge" in recruitment (ACLU, 2006). In addition, during the investigation of the 2001 sexual assaults, a member of the football coaching staff, who was good friends with a local police officer, reportedly briefed one of the accused players prior to his interview with law enforcement about the assault (Suggs, 2004). Moreover, according to a Boulder police report, Barnett allegedly told one of the women who was assaulted that he would back his player "100 percent" if she were to press criminal charges against him (Suggs, 2004).

As media attention and public concern about the CU football scandal grew, Colorado's governmental leadership intervened. At the urging of Governor Bill Owens, President Hoffman appointed a special committee to conduct a full investigation of the alleged sexual assault on behalf of the university (Basinger, 2004). The special committee concluded that player-hosts used sex, alcohol, and drugs to recruit football players, but it did not determine that athletics and CU officials sanctioned these activities (Banda, 2004). The committee recommended stricter policies for athletics recruitment and greater oversight and accountability of the athletics program. The committee did not recommend that Barnett, Tharp, or anyone else involved in the scandal be terminated. Based on the committee's recommendation, new recruitment and athletics oversight policies were enacted.

Soon after, a full criminal investigation of the sexual assaults, led by the state attorney general, Ken Salazar, began in February 2004. Following this investigation, Salazar determined that it was not feasible to pursue these cases criminally and that none of the recruits or football players allegedly involved in the scandal would be prosecuted.

In the aftermath of the football scandal, other issues that further tarnished CU's reputation emerged. Concerns were raised when a state investigator questioned how "hundreds of thousands of dollars [were] handled by the university, the foundation, and football camps owned by Gary Barnett, the football coach" (Jacobson, 2004a). State officials announced that the department's financial records would undergo a complete audit. These concerns led to Tharp's resignation as CU's athletics director in November 2004.

Four months following Tharp's resignation, controversy arose at CU again after Ward Churchill, a CU professor, wrote an essay in which he compared the victims of September 11, 2001, to victims of the Nazi regime. During the same month, Grand Jury testimony from the 2001 sexual assault investigations was leaked and revealed that, in addition to players and recruits, an assistant football coach had been accused of two sexual assaults (Fain, 2005). Hoffman resigned out of concern that she had become a "distraction," which weakened her ability to lead the university. Finally, in December 2005, Barnett resigned from his position as head coach after reaching a $3 million settlement with the university (Sander, 2007).

To summarize, the CU football scandal spanned nearly a decade and threatened the safety of women throughout the Boulder community. The long-term effects of this scandal are significant. College experiences were terminated, professional careers were lost, millions of dollars were spent, and the reputation of a world-class university was tarnished. While one could justifiably question many of the decisions that were made by those in leadership positions during the scandal and pinpoint these decisions as primary factors that allowed the scandal to persist, the scandal's sociocultural undercurrents also warrant consideration.

Sociocultural Context

The CU football scandal exemplifies the intersection of gender and sports. As is evident from this scandal, the intersection of these two constructs can have a destructive impact on social contexts—college campuses especially. To better understand why this scandal emerged and how it persisted, I discuss its sociocultural undercurrents. In doing so, I highlight the social construction of gender, particularly within the context of sports, and how hegemonic conceptualizations of masculinity shaped the scandal.

Michael Kimmel, Michael Messner, R. W. Connell, and other gender studies scholars have argued that gender is a socially constructed identity – that is, the meanings and expectations that accompany masculinity and femininity are established through social interactions and reinforced in social contexts. They have also contended that there is no single, stable, and all-encompassing definition of masculinity.

Instead, masculinity is a collection of social meanings that defines what it means to be a man and shapes societal expectations of who men are and how they should express gender. Masculinity is also not uniformly experienced the same way by all groups of men. Men who are White, heterosexual, able-bodied, and middle or upper class and have access to desirable material possessions (e.g. cars, jewelry, expensive clothing, etc.) enjoy more social privilege and status than those who are from racial/ethnic-minority backgrounds, are not heterosexual, are physically disabled, and have low socioeconomic status. At the core of socially constructed ideologies of masculinity is Connell's (1995) concept of "hegemonic masculinity." This concept captures the dangers and consequences of traditional social constructions of masculinity. It also challenges us to think beyond binary notions of gender (e.g. man-woman and male-female) by recognizing both the range and fluidity with which gender can be expressed. Hegemonic masculinity is both a concept and a tool for questioning and deconstructing dominant social constructions of gender that prioritize some aspects of masculinity while marginalizing others.

Sport is one of several key social institutions in which hegemonic masculinity and traditional social constructions of gender are reinforced. Just as men and women have clearly defined roles in the home, the same is true in sports. Athlete, coach, reporter, and sportscaster — positions of high visibility and authority — are almost always reserved for men, whereas women are typically relegated to the roles of "sexy props" (e.g. ring girls in wrestling and boxing) or "prizes" for men who succeed in sports (Messner, Dunbar, & Hunt, 2000, p. 383).

Historically, sports have served to separate men from women while simultaneously positioning men as dominant. In sports, men are afforded opportunities to bond in the absence of women, by way of physical contact on the field or the court and through "locker room talk" (Griffin, 1998). Locker room talk primarily entails exchanges of sexist and homophobic jokes and competitive heterosexual narratives in which men share stories of "hooking up" sexually with multiple women (Griffin, 1998).

Given the historical origins and contemporary cultural functions of sport as a space that is shaped for and by men, women's participation can be perceived as invasive and threatening. The consequences are clearly evident in the CU scandal, particularly in Katie Hnida's story. Because Katie dared to participate in college football — a sport and social context that has always been exclusively male — she was subjected to physical and emotional violence perpetrated by men who saw it as necessary to protect a masculine domain. Moreover, given that physical violence is both sanctioned and celebrated within the context of football, it was assumed to be an appropriate tool for putting Katie "in her place."

Katie Hnida also represented what many men — coaches and players alike — have long feared about Title IX and other efforts to bring about gender equity in college sports. Opponents of Title IX have argued that it negatively impacts opportunities for male student-athletes, as institutions have sought to comply with the regulation by cutting men's sports teams (Messner & Solomon, 2007). Opponents have also declared that Title IX is unfair because men have greater interests in playing sports than do women; thus, efforts to bring about gender equity in college sports are unnecessary (Messner & Solomon, 2007). Barnett's indifference to the way Katie was abused by men in his program perhaps reflects a larger perspective he held about the place and appropriateness of women in college sports: that they do not belong. He saw no reason to advocate on her behalf or take the steps necessary to create a safe environment for her. From Barnett's standpoint, Katie's departure was welcomed because, as he stated in his February 2004 remarks to the media, "she was a girl" (Fain, 2005), and girls have no business playing football.

The rash of reported sexual assaults that took place during the scandal can also be explained using the concepts of socially constructed and hegemonic masculinity. The overrepresentation of male student-athletes in reports of sexual assaults on college and university campuses has been widely studied and discussed. Generally, scholars have concluded that there is some correlation between athletic participation and men's propensity to engage in sexually aggressive behavior. For example, Crosset (2000) examined the perpetration of sexual assault among male student-athletes and found that male athletes constituted 3.7 percent of the student population but were responsible for 19 percent of sexual assaults reported to campus judicial affairs offices.

Some scholars argue that the physical aggression and violence that are necessary and rewarded in the context of competitive sports are difficult to compartmentalize and, thus, spill into male student-athletes' personal lives and relationships. Messner (2005) noted that "male athletes' off-the-field violence is generated from the normal, everyday dynamics at the center of male athletic culture" (p. 317). This violence, coupled with a gross sense of entitlement among male student-athletes, could have led the men involved in the CU scandal to conclude that "no," when it came to sex, did not apply to them, and that using force or violence to take what they perceived as rightfully theirs – women's bodies – was acceptable. Sex was used as a tool to recruit football players; these young men were reportedly taken to strip clubs, and female escorts were hired by affiliates of the program to entertain recruits during their visits (Jacobson, 2004b). In reports of the sexual assault involving Lisa Simpson, two recruits allegedly told a then-current player that Colorado was making a "weak case" in its recruitment efforts because they had not "hooked up" with any women at that point (Jacobson, 2004c). Both recruits were alleged to have had sex at Simpson's apartment the night she was assaulted (Jacobson, 2004c). One of the two was among those accused of assaulting Simpson (Jacobson, 2004c). These incidents were perhaps exacerbated with the presence of alcohol. As Hill, Burch-Ragan, and Yates (2001) argued, alcohol abuse is often correlated with incidents of sexual assault and physical violence among student-athletes. We know that Simpson's assailants had been drinking alcohol prior to her assault. The extent to which alcohol was involved in the other reported assaults is unknown.

Finally, the manner in which state and university system leaders responded to the CU football scandal deserves some attention in this discussion. There were reports that the football players and recruits were assaulting women sexually as early as 1997. Yet effective intervention did not occur. Richard Byyny, then-chancellor of the CU Boulder campus, enacted new recruitment guidelines and sought to strengthen procedures for the university's handling of sexual harassment and assault. But these efforts were ineffective. President Hoffman convened a task force to conduct a full investigation of the football program but did not do so until Governor Bill Owens got involved. Owens's intervention, to some, was fueled by his own political aspirations (Jacobson, 2004a). Tharp and Barnett showed little regard for the women who were victimized and resisted the type of actions necessary to reduce the likelihood that more women would be harassed and assaulted by football players.

My previous critique of President Hoffman notwithstanding, some recognition of and sensitivity to the precarious position that she was in while presiding over the CU system during the scandal is warranted. Historically, American higher education has prioritized and protected the interests of men (Harper & Harris, 2010), and women in leadership positions often face challenges that can be attributed to gender dynamics and politics. Perhaps nowhere is this more evident than in big-time college sports. For Hoffman to act in the best interests of the women meant openly challenging patriarchal values and holding men in positions of power and authority accountable for acting in ways that advanced sexism and patriarchy. While Hoffman held positional authority as president of CU's system, her identity as a woman likely complicated, if not constrained, the actions she could take to address the systemic patriarchy that was the catalyst of the scandal and allowed it to persist. Had she taken a heavy-handed approach, such as suspending the program and immediately firing Barnett, she likely would have been viewed by some as advancing a feminist agenda. A more measured approach (which she appeared to take) required cooperation, trust from the larger CU community, and a greater level of transparency on the part of Tharp and Barnett. As evident in the way the scandal ultimately played out, a measured approached was time-consuming and costly. More women were assaulted, more acts of impropriety in the football program were discovered, and Hoffman was forced to resign from her post as system president.

Alternate Ending

Having discussed the CU football scandal in detail and explored its sociocultural undercurrents, in this section I offer an alternative ending to the scandal. The question that guides this part of the discussion is: How might matters have played out differently had institutional and athletics leaders at CU handled this situation in a more responsible and socially just manner?

It is spring 1999. Gary Barnett has just been named head football coach. On his first morning of work, Barnett meets with Athletics Director Tharp, Chancellor Byyny, and President Hoffman. Together they devise a set of performance goals and expectations for the football program during its first three years under Barnett's leadership. Among these goals are target grade point averages, graduation rates, and, of course, team wins, conference championships, and bowl games. During the meeting, Hoffman, Byyny, and Tharp also inform Barnett about recent behavioral incidents involving players on the football team. Barnett also learns that there was a spike in the number of reported sexual assaults in the past two years and that football players were named as perpetrators in a disproportionate number of these incidents. Hoffman and Byyny decide that Tharp and Barnett should meet with the vice chancellor for student affairs, the director of the women's center, the campus police, and the director of judicial affairs to get more insight about these and other issues of concern with respect to football players. From these meetings, Tharp and Barnett decide to invite a guest speaker to that year's football camp to talk with players about sexual assault. Beyond the speaker, no other interventions are enacted.

Tharp, Barnett, and the athletics department's Senior Woman Administrator (SWA) also meet with Katie Hnida. The purpose of the meeting is to formally welcome her to the team and to provide an opportunity for her to bring forth any questions or concerns she has. They all acknowledge that there will likely be challenges to welcoming Katie and making her feel like part of the team. However, they assure Katie she has their unconditional support and that they will take proactive steps to make sure she is safe, treated fairly, and has a positive experience on the team.

One year later, in spring 2000, Barnett, Hoffman, Byyny, and Tharp meet for Barnett's annual performance review. The team was 7–5 and won a bowl game in Barnett's first year. While this is slightly worse than the previous season in which the team was 8–4 and won a bowl game, they agree that this is respectable given the program's leadership transition. They also revisit the behavioral concerns that were raised in last year's meeting and review campus crime and student conduct data that had been prepared for the meeting at Byyny's request. They learn that reported sexual assaults did not decrease significantly from the previous year. Again, Tharp and Barnett reach out to their colleagues in student affairs for their expertise and support. A more careful review of the data reveals that many of the reported sexual assaults and other incidents involving the football team have occurred during recruitment visits. Thus, they enact new policies to get a better handle on recruitment activities. Barnett decides that current players and recruits who do not abide by the new policies will be removed from the program or no longer be recruited. Barnett and his staff also participate in professional development activities related to gender (not just gender equity) in college sports throughout the year. For students, the gender component of the athletics department's Champs/Life Skills program is enhanced to cover critical issues related to gender and college sports beyond gender equity. Tharp enacts new protocols for reporting sexual assaults in the athletics department, including granting more authority to the SWA.

The aforementioned efforts and policy enhancements result in a significant decrease in the number of reported sexual assaults by CU students in general and the football program in particular. While Tharp, Barnett, and the university's leadership are pleased with the decrease, they understand that the majority of sexual assaults that occur on college and university campuses are not reported. Thus, they recognize the need to continue to enact policies and practices to reduce the number incidents of sexual assault that occur at CU. For example, in partnership with the division of student affairs, the athletics department sponsors a comprehensive campaign to encourage men to intervene as bystanders when they witness situations that can lead to sexual assaults. Moreover, when a football player is accused of sexual assault, Tharp and Barnett allow the Office of Judicial Affairs, campus police, and local law enforcement to conduct a full investigation of the incident. They do not intervene or use their political prowess to influence the outcome of the investigation. As a result of these, and other, actions, CU becomes a much safer campus for women than it has been in past years.

References

American Association of University Women (AAUW). (2005). Lisa Simpson, et al. v. University of Colorado. Retrieved from www.aauw.org/act/laf/cases/simpson.cfm

American Civil Liberties Union (ACLU). (2006). *Simpson v. University of Colorado – Amicus Brief.* New York: ACLU.

Banda, P. S. (2004, May 27). Colorado reinstates Barnett, plans changes to athletic department. Retrieved from www.usatoday.com

Basinger, J. (2004). How one president fielded a football crisis. *The Chronicle of Higher Education,* 50(29), A1–A28.

Connell, R. W. (1995). *Masculinities.* Berkeley: University of California Press.

Crosset, T. (2000). Athletic affiliation and violence against women: Toward a structural prevention project. In J. McKay, M. A. Messner, and D. F. Sabo (Eds.), *Masculinities, gender relations and sport,* pp. 147–161. Thousand Oaks, CA: Sage.

Fain, P. (2005). Under fire on 2 fronts: U of Colorado chief resigns. *The Chronicle of Higher Education,* 51(28), A1–A27.

Griffin, P. (1998). *Strong women, deep closets: Lesbians and homophobia in sports.* Champaign, IL: Human Kinetics.

Harper, S.R., & Harris III, F. (2010). Beyond the model gender majority myth: Responding equitably to the developmental needs and challenges of college men. In S. R. Harper and F. Harris III (Eds.), *College men and masculinities: Theory, research, and implications for practice,* pp. 1–16. San Francisco: Jossey-Bass.

Hill, J. (2006, December 8). Hnida finds peace in telling her story. Retrieved from http://sports. espn.go.com/espn/page2/story?page=hill/061208

Hill, K., Burch-Ragan, M., & Yates, D. Y. (2001). Current and future issues and trends facing student-athletes and athletic programs. *New Directions for Student Services,* 93, 65–80.

Jacobson, J. (2004a). Athletics chief quits troubled program. *The Chronicle of Higher Education,* 51(15), A29.

Jacobson, J. (2004b). Sex and football. *The Chronicle of Higher Education,* 50(25), A33–A34.

Jacobson, J. (2004c). Panel blasts U. of Colorado for handling of scandal. *The Chronicle of Higher Education,* 50(38), A1–A35.

Messner, M. A. (2005). Still a man's world? Studying masculinities and sport. In M. S. Kimmel, J. Hearn, and R. W. Connell (Eds.), *Handbook of studies on men and masculinities,* Thousand Oaks, CA: SAGE.

Messner, M. A., Dunbar, M., & Hunt, D. (2000). The televised sports manhood formula. *Journal of Sport and Social Issues,* 24(4), 380–394.

Messner, M. A., & Solomon, N. M. (2007). Social justice and men's interests: The case of Title IX. *Journal of Sport and Social Issues*, 31(2), 162–178.

Reilly, R. (2004, February 23). Another victim at Colorado: After being verbally abused and molested by teammates, former kicker Katie Hnida says she was raped by one of them. Retrieved from http://sportsillustrated.cnn.com

Sander, L. (2007). U. of Colorado settles lawsuit over alleged gang rapes. *The Chronicle of Higher Education*, 54(16), A20–A21.

Suggs, W. (2004). Colorado's coach-cop coalition. *The Chronicle of Higher Education*, 50(26), A33–A35.

22

GENDER DISCRIMINATION AND RETALIATION UNDER TITLE IX AT FRESNO STATE

Jennifer Lee Hoffman, Jacqueline McDowell, and Valyncia C. Raphael

The Case

On Monday, July 9, 2007, Linda J. "Lindy" Vivas, former women's volleyball coach at California State University, Fresno (Fresno State), was awarded $5.85 million in a Title IX gender discrimination and retaliation lawsuit. At the time, it was the largest amount ever granted to a coach suing for retaliation under Title IX. Not only was the award a record-setting amount, but the jury also awarded $1.7 million more than Vivas asked for in the case. The jury found that she was discriminated against based on her gender, her marital status, and her perceived sexual orientation. The jury also found that Fresno State took retaliatory action against Vivas when she spoke up about gender equity for female student-athletes at the university. This verdict was the first of several Title IX settlements and verdicts at institutions in the state of California, and specifically at Fresno State.

On October 11, 2007, Diane Milutinovich, former Fresno State Associate Athletics Director and Senior Woman Administrator (SWA), settled a discrimination lawsuit with Fresno State. Milutinovich sued the university in 2004, claiming gender discrimination and retaliation after advocating for gender equity in women's sports. Milutinovich received $3.5 million, but Fresno State admitted no wrongdoing in the case.

Margie Wright, Fresno State's women's softball coach, filed a Title IX complaint in fall 2007 with the Office for Civil Rights (OCR) claiming retaliation for advocating for equal treatment of the women's softball program. At the time of the complaint's filing, the softball program was twenty-fifth in the national rankings. The OCR complaint cited that a decline in the softball budget left inadequate funds to pay for uniforms for all female softball players. Subsequently, Wright was awarded $605,000 in a July 2008 settlement with Fresno State, which prevented any other large-scale gender discrimination lawsuits against the university from going to trial.

Stacy Johnson-Klein, Fresno State's former women's basketball coach, was fired mid-season in 2005. She sued the university for retaliation after she complained about inequitable treatment of female student-athletes and sexual harassment directed at her. Fresno State contended that she was fired for erratic behavior, inappropriate conduct with student-athletes and assistant coaches, and NCAA violations. Just five months after the record-setting award for Vivas, Johnson-Klein topped that record and was awarded $19.1 million for wrongful termination, sexual harassment, and gender discrimination. Although the judge later reduced the award to $6.6 million, the Johnson-Klein case represents another large-scale lawsuit from a current or former female coach at Fresno State.

Fresno State and Gender Discrimination in Athletics

Fresno State's troubles were first known as early as 1991, when the institution was not in compliance in 11 of 13 Title IX categories. A settlement in a prior lawsuit included several benchmarks that the Fresno State athletic department agreed to, including funding for women's athletics programs within 10 percent of enrollment, grants in aid to women within 5 percent of enrollment, and a biennial review of compliance (Vivas v. Board of Trustees, Trial Brief, 2007). Despite this agreement, Fresno State continued its pattern of "discriminatory and unlawful practices" in violation of Title IX, including:

- Failure to offer female students opportunities to participate in intercollegiate athletics substantially proportionate to the percentage of women enrolled as students;
- Reducing the number of female student-athletes and women's programs, coaches, and staff;
- Withholding adequate support for existing female student-athletes and their programs, replacing female coaches with men, failing to hire assistant coaches for women's teams, and providing women coaches with inadequate and unequal compensation;
- Neglecting to provide female athletic teams with adequate publicity and recruiting resources; and
- Denying female athletes necessary facilities, practice opportunities, and opportunities to compete at higher levels.

To address these compliance issues, Fresno State submitted a Corrective Action Plan to the OCR, which added two women's sports, increased the percentage of women participating in sports, improved and constructed new women's sport facilities, increased the portion of athletic expenditures devoted to women's sports, and provided equal radio and television coverage for women's sports. There was also a directive to promote women's volleyball through marketing equal to men's sports and moving women's matches to the Save Mart Center, the university's main arena, where men's programs regularly competed.

The Vivas trial documents revealed an athletic department under tremendous financial strain and infected with a discriminatory culture. Budget cuts made women's and men's programs fear loss of funding or program elimination all together. Perhaps exacerbated by the budgetary issues, there were problems among the women's programs' staff, administrators, and coaches. The resentment for women's athletics was not limited to the athletic department. In 1995 a local radio station, KMJ, which held the contract for promotion of Fresno State athletics, broadcast a three-hour, anti-Title IX show (Steeg, 2008). In April 2000, Fresno State's athletic director, Scott Johnson, and other men from the athletic department celebrated "Ugly Women Athletes Day," with posters featuring vulgar cutouts of women's bodies, topped with men's heads.

Despite these attitudes toward women's athletics, in 2002 the women's volleyball team, under Vivas, had the best season in school history. The team posted a 23–7 record and made its third NCAA appearance in her 12th year as head coach; they had done so twice in the previous five years. The team also appeared in the National Invitational Volleyball Championship (NIVC) post-season tournament three times under Vivas. Three volleyball players were named to the All-West Regional team. Two sophomores received first team honors and one senior received an honorable mention award. Coach Vivas was also honored as Western Athletic Conference (WAC) Coach of the Year for the third time in 2002 (previously winning in 1992 and 1997). During the 2002 season the women's volleyball team won its 450th match, and Vivas won her 100th game as head coach at Fresno State. At the start of the 2003 season, Coach Vivas was approaching 300 career wins.

Yet things took a turn, revealing deeply held views about female coaches and staff in the department. At the end of the 2004 volleyball season, the team posted a 15–13 overall record. Just three years following the best volleyball season in school history, the women's volleyball coach, Lindy Vivas, did not have her contract renewed. In December 2004, Scott Johnson announced a national search for a new women's volleyball head coach. Although Vivas led the team to three NCAA Tournaments and a 263–167 record in 14 years, her firing was cited as being a consequence of the university not having a nationally competitive program.

The women's basketball program experienced a similar turn of events. When the women's basketball head coach, Stacy Johnson-Klein, arrived in spring 2002, she immediately turned the basketball program around. The women's basketball program improved from 9–20 in the 2001–02 (the year before she arrived) to 21–13 in 2002–03. Under Johnson-Klein, the team made its first post-season appearance since 1990, advancing to the Women's National Invitational Tournament (WNIT) quarterfinal. The team dipped to 13–16 in 2003–04, but during the 2004–05 season the team posted another winning record of 20–11 and first round appearance in the WNIT. Despite these successes and only three years as head basketball coach, Johnson-Klein was fired in 2005 by Fresno State, which alleged deceptive and improper fiscal management, NCAA violations, and inappropriate conduct with student-athletes and assistant coaches. Johnson-Klein sued Fresno State for disparate treatment, a hostile work environment, and retaliation for her complaints over inequity for women's athletics (Johnson-Klein v. The Board of Trustees, 2007).

According to trial documents, Johnson-Klein alleged that she received unwanted sexual advances from the athletic director and was sexually harassed by her supervisor who, she said, made demeaning remarks about her appearance and clothing. In 2004, Fresno State's human resources director alerted university officials, including President John Welty, that Johnson-Klein was considering Title IX and whistle-blower complaints over her treatment in the athletic department. After filing a formal complaint of sexual harassment in January 2005, she was fired on February 5, 2005 (Daily Journal, 2008).

Scott Johnson resigned as athletic director in 2005, in the wake of the lawsuits, but he was retained as the special assistant to the university's president (USA Today, 2008). Fresno State's president, John Welty, and Charles B. Reed, the chancellor of the California State University system, remained in their positions.

Fresno State and Athletics Discrimination in California Higher Education

Starting with a Title IX complaint filed with the OCR in 1991, in which Fresno State was found out of compliance, the list of lawsuits and OCR complaints filed against Fresno State shows a long history of troubles with gender equity. However, Fresno State is not the only institution in the California State University (CSU) or University of California (UC) systems that has been involved in lawsuits for gender discrimination and retaliation against coaches. In January 2007, Michael Burch, former wrestling coach at University of California–Davis, received a $725,000 settlement from the University of California system. He was fired after advocating that female student-athletes have the opportunity to wrestle on the men's team. In July 2007, Karen Moe Humphreys, Olympian and former University of California–Berkeley women's swimming coach, was awarded $3.5 million in a gender discrimination case. Ms. Humphreys, who was laid off in 2004, accused Berkeley of firing her for complaining about a hostile work environment for women in the athletic department. Finally, Deena Deardurff Schmidt was awarded $1.45 million in a September 2008 settlement. The former swimming and diving coach was fired in July 2007 from San Diego State University (SDSU) after filing a gender discrimination lawsuit that cited mistreatment and sexual harassment by an SDSU booster. These settlements show that other campuses failed to learn from Fresno State's noncompliance.

The Fresno State jury verdicts and other Title IX whistleblower cases in California universities have caught the attention of state policy-makers. In 2007, the California State Senate appointed the *Select Committee on Gender Discrimination and Title IX Implementation* to investigate all CSU and UC schools. California State Senate President Don Perata and other state legislators were interested in finding out if a pattern of discrimination in women's athletics existed in California public universities. Senator Dean Florez chaired the committee and held two hearings in summer 2007 to examine whether and to what extent patterns of discrimination

(Araiza, 2007) and bias against female athletes existed (Jones, 2007). The five-member committee interviewed administrators, coaches, athletes, and the president's office at all UC campuses and CSU campuses to gauge how well the schools complied with Title IX (Jones, 2007). In convening the hearings, Florez said, "These are public universities, and the question is: Why are we paying such large amounts when we should be complying with Title IX in the first place?" (Jones, 2007).

Senator Florez also noted that, despite some then-recent advances in Fresno State's women's participation rates in intercollegiate athletics, the pattern of lawsuits and size of the verdicts and settlements indicated that those gains have "yet to change a culture of discrimination" (Burke, 2007). Furthermore, by investigating all CSU and UC institutions, the committee sought to "send some sort of signal of confidence to women throughout California that their claims will be taken seriously" (Burke, 2007).

Sociocultural Context

The Fresno State cases represent the complex mix of federal Title IX law,[1] state gender-equity law, and legal protection under Title IX for whistle-blowers. The Vivas and Milutinovich cases illustrate three important components of gender equity in intercollegiate athletics. First, the cases demonstrate the application of new protections, granted in 2005 under federal Title IX law, for gender-equity advocates, following the Supreme Court's establishment of a precedent in Jackson v. Birmingham Board of Education (2005). In 2001, Roderick Jackson, a Birmingham, Alabama, physical education teacher and high school girls' basketball coach, was fired after complaining about inequitable treatment of the girls' basketball team. His suit against the school board for discriminatory retaliation under Title IX went all the way to the U.S. Supreme Court. As a result, his case has extended the shield of Title IX to advocates, such as coaches or administrators, who are retaliated against for their efforts to stop or reverse gender inequities in athletics.

Second, there is, as the cases highlight, an additional layer of state oversight of gender equity in athletics, complimenting federal Title IX law. California is among the few states that have state gender-equity laws or guidelines and an active state legislature that monitors gender equity in athletics. Third, Fresno State blamed Vivas for the low attendance at its women's volleyball meets because, Fresno State contended, she failed to schedule top-25 opponents and, therefore, no games were played in the Save Mart Arena. According to trial documents, "Fresno State refused to allow Vivas to schedule volleyball matches in the Save Mart Center, although it allowed similarly situated coaches to do so, thereby making it impossible for her to schedule matches with top ranked teams and to generate income from attendance" (Vivas v. Board of Trustees, 2007). Should the women's volleyball team have played in the larger venue and invited top-25 teams when they had fewer fans to help promote the team so the stands filled, or should they have waited until the team generated a larger fan base and then moved to the larger facility? The former supports a commonly used mantra in the Title IX discourse: If you build it, they will come. Such a mantra suggests that investing in and building up women's teams will encourage better play, more fans, and better competition.

These three issues illustrate critical aspects of gender equity in intercollegiate athletics that have emerged since Title IX was mandated by federal law in 1972. Unfortunately, similar gender discrimination and Title IX lawsuits occur at higher education institutions throughout the United States, but the Fresno State cases are unusual in that the university had a history of repeated Title IX violations, OCR complaints, and related lawsuits in a fairly short period of time. Moreover, instead of the athletic director or president being fired from Fresno State, as is common in other high-profile athletics scandals, Fresno State retained both individuals who were in these positions at the time of the scandals.

The analysis of Fresno State's gender discrimination and Title IX lawsuits reveals two central themes in intercollegiate sports: these sports are a harbor for gender inequity, and there are negative ramifications for colleges and universities when these institutions lack control of their intercollegiate athletics. The following paragraphs expound on these two themes and some of the underlying reasons why the compliance with Title IX and adherence to gender equity in intercollegiate athletic departments is encumbered with complexities.

Collegiate Sports as a Harbor for Gender Inequity

The Fresno State cases provide clear examples of an institution that has not embraced gender equity. Despite federal and state laws mandating gender equity in college sports, the majority of collegiate sports environments continue to serve as a harbor for gender inequity due to the limited commitment on the part of key stakeholders in collegiate sports and at the institutions. Although most athletic departments proclaim their commitment to the goals of Title IX, for some, this commitment still remains unfulfilled. In the most recent Office of Civil Rights Annual Report to Congress, there were 16 complaints filed alleging discrimination in athletics on the basis of sex at post-secondary institutions (United States Department of Education, 2007). Many institutions attempt to lay the blame for their Title IX incompliance on economic reasons. Institutions assert that they lack the funds to achieve gender equity or that they would have to cut men's programs to achieve this goal. These assertions are partially true, as the vast majority of athletic departments operate in the red (French, 2004). However, research suggests that, despite sufficient funds, gender equity would remain an issue, as less money is typically allocated to nonrevenue sports and more money is distributed inequitably to men's (revenue-generating) sports (Clotfelter, 2011).

This inconsistent commitment to supporting and embracing gender equity in collegiate athletic departments is further caused by the NCAA's and OCR's inadequate monitoring and enforcement of Title IX violations (Setty, 1999). Many men in leadership positions do not support Title IX statutes, as they feel that male athletes have lost opportunities because of the legislation. Furthermore, prominent practices of noncompliance with diversity management strategies in collegiate athletic departments further limit the integration of leaders who support gender equity (Fink, Pastore, & Heimer, 2001). Organizations at the low end of the compliance continuum do very little to attempt to comply with federal or state legislation on diversity, as members tend to view diversity as a liability to their organization (Cox, 1991; Doherty & Chelladurai, 1999; Fink & Pastore, 1999). Thus, what emerges is a gap between the formally stated goals of Title IX and the values actually adopted in the department. Title IX policies opened up some previously unavailable opportunities for women, but these policies are only truly effective if "they are backed up by transformation of informal interpersonal values and processes within the organization" (Bond & Pyle, 1998, p. 137). It is unsurprising that, without this transformation, few collegiate athletic programs are in compliance with Title IX, and many senior administrators, primarily men, strive to silence those with dissimilar values who advocate for gender equity.

Lack of Institutional Control

The Fresno State cases also highlight the lack of institutional control over intercollegiate athletics. In many higher education settings, athletic departments function unlike other academic departments. James Duderstadt, former University of Michigan president, noted that athletic departments operate under "management values and cultures that depart quite significantly from those of the academic core of the university" (Duderstadt, 2000, p. 87). Further, although the president has an influence on other academic units, "it is rare that the chief executive officer will make decisions specifically affecting the operations of the institution's athletic program" (National Collegiate Athletic Association, 1997, p. 1). Moreover, the NCAA committee states that senior administrators, such as the athletic director, usually delegate compliance duties and responsibilities to subordinates. Therefore, the onus of Title IX compliance is moved farther down the chain of command, resulting in the failure of many presidents and athletic directors to actively monitor athletic programs' compliance with Title IX and to proactively take steps to advocate for and enforce gender equity. For example, it was not until 2007, approximately five years after the first OCR complaint was filed and in light of the state investigation, that President Welty established a gender equity plan task force (USA Today, 2008). The Fresno State cases provide clear examples of an institution that failed to fix a broken system.

Alternate Ending

This case would have turned out differently had the California State University Board of Regents announced in July 2007 the termination of President John Welty in a statement like the following:

> The recent verdicts and settlements in gender discrimination and the testimony given at yesterday's hearing underscore the limitations in Dr. Welty's

leadership for supporting non-discrimination values that are central to our educational mission. California State University is committed to fostering an environment that will meet the needs of our citizenry in the 21st century. There is no room for gender discrimination in any of our institutions. We cannot serve the future needs of our state in an environment where discrimination is tolerated or where those that speak up against discrimination are in jeopardy. Students, faculty, and staff can be assured that we take seriously the commitment to values of fairness in all aspects of California State University.

In addition to firing President Welty and issuing a statement, publicly committing to working with the state's gender discrimination and Title IX implementation officers, as well as establishing a confidential unit on campus for faculty, staff, and students to report gender harassment and discrimination, likely would have yielded a different outcome at Fresno State.

Note

1 Title IX states, "No person in the United States shall, on the basis of sex, be excluded from participation in, be denied the benefits of, or be subjected to discrimination under any education program or activity receiving Federal financial assistance" and provides protection from gender discrimination against women students in 10 areas of education, including intercollegiate athletics (U.S. Department of Labor, 1972).

References

Araiza, A. (2007, July 20). Pressure on Fresno State President John Welty is heating up. Retrieved on July 4, 2012 from http://abclocal.go.com/kfsn/story?section=archive&id=5465224

Bond, M. A., & Pyle, J. L. (1998). Diversity dilemmas at work. In R. Forrant, J. Pyle, W. Lazonick, and C. Levenstein (Eds.), *Approaches to Sustainable Development: The Public University in the Regional Economy*, pp. 119–148.

Burke, G. (2007, July 12). State legislators to review gender bias at public universities. Retrieved from www.csun.edu/pubrels/clips/July07/07-13-07J.pdf

Clotfelter, C. (2011). *Big-time sports in American universities*. New York: Cambridge University Press.

Cox, T. (1991). The multicultural organization. *Academy of Management Review*, 5(2), 34–47.

Daily Journal. (2008, February 1). Johnson-Klein v. The Board of Trustees of the California State University. Verdicts & Settlements Supplement. Retrieved from www.dailyjournal.com/public/pubmain.cfm

Doherty, A. J., & Chelladurai, P. (1999). Managing cultural diversity in sport organizations: A theoretical perspective. *Journal of Sport Management*, 13(4), 280–297.

Duderstadt, J. (2000). *A university for the 21st century*. Ann Arbor: University of Michigan Press.

Fink, J. S., & Pastore, D. L. (1999). Diversity in sport? Utilizing the business literature to devise a comprehensive framework of diversity initiatives. *Quest*, 51(4), 310–327.

Fink, J. S., Pastore, D. L., & Heimer, H. A. (2001). Do differences make a difference? Managing diversity in Division IA intercollegiate athletics. *Journal of Sport Management*, 15(1), 10–50.

French, P. (2004). *Ethics and college sports: Ethics, sports, and the university*. Lanham, MD: Rowman & Littlefield.

Jackson v. Birmingham Board of Education. 416 F.3d 1280 (2005).

Johnson-Klein v. The Board of Trustees of the California State University, Verdict & Settlement Summary. Superior Court of California, Fresno County, WL 4592759 (2007).

Jones, C. (2007, August 23). State Senate panel gauges equity between sexes in college athletics. Retrieved from www.sfgate.com/sports/article/State-Senate-panel-gauges-equity-between-sexes-in-2524843.php

National Collegiate Athletic Association. (1997). Principles of institutional control as prepared by the NCAA committee on infractions. Indianapolis, IN: Author.

Setty, S. (1999). Leveling the playing field: Reforming the Office for Civil Rights to achieve better Title IX enforcement. *Columbia Journal of Law and Social Problems*, 32(4), 331–358.

Steeg, J. L. (2008, May 13). Lawsuits, disputes reflect continuing tension over Title IX. Retrieved from http://usatoday30.usatoday.com/sports/college/2008-05-12-titleix-cover_N.htm?csp=34

U.S. Department of Education. (2007). *Annual Report to Congress of the Office for Civil Rights: Fiscal Year 2006*. Washington, D.C: Author.

U.S. Department of Labor. (1972). Title IX, Education Amendments of 1972. Retrieved from www.dol.gov/oasam/regs/statutes/titleix.htm

USA Today. (2008, May 13). Timeline of gender equity issues at Fresno State. Retrieved from www.usatoday.com/sports/college/2008-05-12-fresno-timeline_N.htm

Vivas v. Board of Trustees of the California State University, Defendant, Trial Brief. Superior Court of California, Fresno County, No. 06CECG00440 (2007).

EDITORS AND CONTRIBUTORS

Editors

Shaun R. Harper is the Clifford and Betty Allen Professor in the Rossier School of Education at the University of Southern California. He is also Executive Director of the USC Race & Equity Center and President of the Association for the Study of Higher Education. Dr. Harper has published 12 books and over 100 peer-reviewed journal articles and other academic publications. He has authored papers on death in college athletics, Black male student-athletes at community colleges, racial inequities in revenue-generating intercollegiate sports, and student-athlete engagement in educationally purposeful experiences beyond athletics. Professor Harper has served on the USC Provost's Oversight Committee for Athletics Academic Affair. He was previously a tenured professor at the University of Pennsylvania and an assistant professor at Penn State University. He taught an undergraduate course at Indiana University on college sports and a graduate course at Penn on athletics administration. The New York Times, Washington Post, Sports Illustrated, and over 11,000 other media outlets have quoted Dr. Harper and featured his research. He has been interviewed on ESPN and CNN. His Ph.D. in Higher Education is from Indiana University.

Jamel K. Donnor is an Associate Professor in the School of Education at the College of William and Mary. Professor Donnor's research focuses primarily on race and equity in education, the schooling experiences of Black male students, and college sports. *Teachers College Record, Race, Ethnicity and Education, Education and Urban Society*, and *Urban Education* are some peer-reviewed journals in which his research is published. His 2005 journal article, "Towards an Interest-Convergence in the Education of African American Football Student Athletes in Major College Sports," is one of the most widely cited publications on African American male student-athletes. Dr. Donnor earned his Ph.D. from the University of Wisconsin-Madison. His dissertation was on the racialized experiences and outcomes of African American football players. His books include: *The Resegregation of Schools: Education and Race in the Twenty-First Century* (Routledge, 2013), *The Education of Black Males in a "Post-Racial" World* (Routledge, 2012), and *The Charter School Solution: Distinguishing Fact from Rhetoric* (Routledge, 2016).

Contributors

Ross D. Aikins is on the faculty in the Graduate School of Education at the University of Pennsylvania, where he serves as an administrator for the Higher Education Division. Aikins specializes in student health research, including alcohol consumption and performance-enhancement drug use in academic and athletic contexts.

James Soto Antony is on the faculty in the Graduate School of Education at Harvard University, where he serves as director of the Higher Education Program. He previously served as Professor of Higher Education, Associate Vice Provost and Associate Dean for Academic Affairs in the Graduate School, and Co-Director of the Center for Leadership in Athletics at the University of Washington.

Albert Y. Bimper Jr. is an Assistant Professor in the Ethnic Studies Department at Colorado State University. He also serves as the Senior Associate Athletic Director for Diversity, Inclusion and Engagement for Colorado State's Department of Athletics. Bimper played on the Indianapolis Colts Super Bowl XLI Championship team.

Horatio W. Blackman is a Ph.D. student in the Graduate School of Education at the University of Pennsylvania, where he serves as a research associate in the Center for the Study of Race and Equity in Education. Blackman also earned a bachelor's degree in Policy Analysis and Management from Cornell University, where he was a member of the football team.

Scott Bukstein is on the faculty in the College of Business Administration at the University of Central Florida, where he serves as the Assistant Director of the DeVos Graduate and Undergraduate Sport Business Management Programs. In addition, he is an Adjunct Assistant Professor in the Goizueta Business School at Emory University as well as an Adjunct Instructor in the College of Business at the University of South Florida.

Marc E. Christian is a doctoral candidate in the Graduate School of Education at the University of Pennsylvania and Assistant Coach of Swimming and Diving at the University of Pittsburgh. He previously coached men's and women's swimming at Penn. Christian was a student-athlete on three NCAA Swimming and Diving national championship teams at Kenyon College.

Langston Clark is on the faculty in the Department of Kinesiology in the College of Education and Human Development at the University of Texas at San Antonio. His research examines the integration of collegiate sports in the Deep South, the racial and academic identity of successful student-athletes, and the academic self-concept and athletic identity of adolescent student-athletes.

Eddie Comeaux is an Associate Professor in the Graduate School of Education at the University of California, Riverside. He is the co-founder of the *Research Focus on Education and Sport* Special Interest Group of the American Educational Research Association. Comeaux's books include *Introduction to Athletics in American Higher Education* (Johns Hopkins University Press). He played professional baseball for the Texas Rangers.

Emil L. Cunningham is a Senior Research Associate with a private consulting firm. Since 2004, he has worked in several capacities in undergraduate education and student affairs. His Ph.D. in Higher Education and M.Ed. in College Student Affairs are from The Pennsylvania State University, and his bachelor's degree is from Vassar College. Cunningham's research focuses on campus climate, the college experiences of underrepresented students, sense of belonging, and institutionally designated safe spaces.

Charles H.F. Davis III is Assistant Professor of Research at the University of Southern California Rossier School of Education. He is also Director of Research in the USC Race & Equity Center. His Ph.D. in Higher Education is from the University of Arizona. His bachelor's and master's degrees are from Florida State University and the University of Pennsylvania.

Justin L. Davis is an Associate Professor of Strategic Management at the University of West Florida. His research focuses on topics related to organizational management and sport gambling market inefficiencies.

Timothy Davis is the John W. and Ruth H. Turnage Professor of Law at Wake Forest University School of Law. He recently co-authored the third edition of *Sports Law and Regulation: Cases, Materials and Problems*, and has published numerous articles and books that examine sports- and contract-related issues. Professor Davis serves on the Review Board for the United States Anti-Doping Agency. He is a former chair of the Law and Sports Section of the Association of American Law Schools.

Christopher Faison is Coordinator of Men of Color Engagement in the Center for Student Success and Academic Counseling at the University of North Carolina at Chapel Hill. He also collaborates with the Assistant Athletic Director for Student-Athlete Development and the Academic Support Program for Student-Athletes to provide programming for male student-athletes.

Joy Gaston Gayles is an Associate Professor of higher education in the Department of Leadership, Policy and Adult and Higher Education at North Carolina State University. She was previously an Assistant Professor at Florida State University. Gayles' research agenda focuses on college student access and success, particularly for student-athletes and women and underrepresented minorities in STEM fields. Gayles is a former student-athlete. She previously worked as an academic advisor and coordinator of student-athlete advising at The Ohio State University.

Whitney N. Griffin is a graduate of the Educational Psychology Learning Sciences Program at the University of Washington. She is currently a postdoctoral fellow at the University of California, Riverside, where Dr. Eddie Comeaux is mentoring her. Griffin's research draws on several different domains in fields such as neuropsychology, mild traumatic brain injury, revenue-generating college sports, and race. Her dissertation investigated how Black football players with concussions and/or learning disabilities cope with negative stereotypes of athletic and academic performance.

Frank Harris III is a Professor of Postsecondary Education and co-director of the Minority Male Community College Collaborative (M2C3) at San Diego State University. Before joining the San Diego State faculty, Harris worked in student affairs administration, student crisis support and advocacy, new student orientation programs, multicultural student affairs, academic advising, and enrollment services. His doctorate in Higher Education is from the University of Southern California. Harris has coached youth sports in San Diego since 2011.

C. Keith Harrison is an Associate Professor and Associate Director of the DeVos Graduate and Undergraduate Sport Business Management Programs in the College of Business Administration at the University of Central Florida. Additionally, he is an adjunct faculty member in the Goizueta Business School at Emory University and the Department of Communication at Boise State University. During his tenure on the Sport Management Program faculty at the University of Michigan, Harrison founded the Paul Robeson Research Center for Academic and Athletic Prowess.

Louis Harrison Jr. is a Professor in the Department of Curriculum and Instruction at the University of Texas at Austin, where he also serves as Research Director of the African American Male Research Initiative (AAMRI). Harrison has focused his academic research on the influences of race and African American racial identity on sport and physical activity choices and performance. He was recently inducted as a Fellow into the National Academy of Kinesiology.

Jennifer Lee Hoffman is an Associate Professor at the Center for Leadership in Athletics in the College of Education at the University of Washington. Her research examines educational policies and practices in intercollegiate athletics from a critical equity perspective. She has presented research on the retention and turn-over of NCAA Division I FBS leaders, including presidents, athletic directors, and head football coaches, to the Knight Commission on Intercollegiate Athletics and at several academic conferences.

David Horton Jr. is an Associate Professor in the Higher Education and Student Affairs program at Ohio University. Horton's research centers on the curricular and co-curricular experiences of marginalized groups at the community college, with a special focus on student-athletes. Additionally, he has conducted research on graduation rates for student-athletes and the impact and influence of coaches on Black male student-athletes' academic success at Historically Black Colleges and Universities.

Jacob Houston is a specialist with Google, via Xtreme Consulting Group. He earned his Ph.D. from the College of Education at the University of Washington in 2014. During his time at the university, Houston examined the academic and career development of undergraduates, particularly college student-athletes. Additionally, Houston worked with the Center for Leadership in Athletics, an organization that develops effective leaders and leadership practices, while maximizing the positive educational impact of sports.

Neal H. Hutchens is an Associate Professor in the Higher Education Program at Penn State University, where he is also a Senior Research Associate in the Center for the Study of Higher Education. He previously served as a faculty member at the University of Kentucky and the Barry University Dwayne O. Andreas School of Law. His scholarship centers on law and policy issues in higher education.

Willis A. Jones is an Assistant Professor of Higher Education at the University of Kentucky. Jones earned his Ph.D. in Higher Education Policy and Leadership from Vanderbilt University. His research examines issues related to the economics of intercollegiate athletics and the educational experiences of student-athletes. Jones has also published on the topics of Historically Black Colleges and Universities, college rankings, college student interactional diversity, retention, and faculty governance.

Jacqueline McDowell is a faculty member in the School of Recreation, Health and Tourism at George Mason University. Her research focuses on diversity and inclusion in sport and recreation, with a focus on identity issues as well as structural, social, and psychological factors that impact the experiences and opportunities of underrepresented populations. McDowell is particularly interested in investigating how women of color construct and negotiate their organizational identity in the workplace and the role of sports in reducing health risks and disparities.

Demetri L. Morgan is an Assistant Professor in the School of Education at Loyola University Chicago. His experience in athletics includes serving as a Five-Star

Basketball Camp counselor to some of the top prep basketball players in the Southeast as well as consulting projects for the Gulliver Prep High School basketball team and the Athletics Department at California State University, Northridge. Morgan earned his B.A. from the University of Florida, master's degree from Indiana University, and Ph.D. from the University of Pennsylvania.

Andrew Howard Nichols is Director for Higher Education Research and Data Analytics at The Education Trust in Washington, DC. Nichols previously served as Director for Research and Policy Analysis at the Maryland Higher Education Commission, a Senior Research Analyst at the Pell Institute for the Study of Opportunity in Higher Education, and a research assistant in the Center for the Study of Higher Education at Penn State University. Nichols earned his bachelor's degree from Vanderbilt University, master's degree from the University of Southern California, and Ph.D. from Penn State University.

Valyncia C. Raphael is a 2016 graduate of the Educational Leadership and Policy Analysis doctoral program at the University of Wisconsin-Madison. She also is a 2013 graduate of the University of Wisconsin Law School. While pursuing her bachelor's degree in English and Political Science at UW-Madison, Raphael played four years on the women's softball team. She joined the University of Wisconsin Athletic Department Academic Services staff in 2009 as an intern assisting with CHAMPS/Life skills, diversity and inclusion programming, and advising and mentoring freshman student-athletes.

Mercedes Rosado is a graduate of the University of Kentucky, where she earned a bachelor's degree in Kinesiology with an emphasis on Health Promotion in 2013. Rosado is also a distinguished graduate of Air Force ROTC and serves as an officer in the United States Air Force.

Kenneth L. Shropshire is the David W. Hauck Professor at the University of Pennsylvania Wharton School. He is founder and director of the Wharton Sports Business Initiative, a consultant to the Miami Dolphins Foundation, and a trustee of the Women's Sports Foundation. Additionally, he leads the research efforts of the Major League Baseball On-Field Diversity Task Force. Shropshire's books include *Agents of Opportunity: Sports Agents and Corruption in Collegiate Sports*.

Edward J. Smith is a Ph.D. candidate at the University of Pennsylvania, where he serves as a research associate in the Center for the Study of Race and Equity in Education. He previously worked as a Senior Policy Analyst in the Research and Policy Institute at the National Association of Student Personnel Administrators, a Research Analyst at the Institute for Higher Education Policy, and an instructor at the University of the District of Columbia Community College. His bachelor's and master's degrees are from Penn State University.

Martin Smith received his bachelor's and master's degrees from the University of California, Berkeley. At Berkeley, he played point guard for four years on the basketball team. Martin started his own business, Phil Smith Basketball Camps, and taught at San Diego Community College after completing his master's degree. He also has international experience running his own basketball clinics in China and the Philippines. Currently, he is an assistant professor at Duke University. His Ph.D. is from the University of Texas at Austin.

Karen Weaver is an Associate Professor at Drexel University, where she teaches in the Undergraduate and Graduate Sport Management Programs. She also teaches courses on intercollegiate athletics for the Higher Education Division at the University of Pennsylvania. Weaver has written extensively about financial issues facing higher education and athletics. Weaver spent 16 years as a collegiate head field hockey coach. Her teams made five postseason appearances and won one NCAA National Championship. She served as the broadcast announcer and assistant producer for men's and women's field hockey at the 1996 Centennial Olympic Games in Atlanta.

Collin D. Williams Jr. works in Social Responsibility and Player Programs at the National Basketball Association. He previously worked as Assistant Director of Player Engagement for the Baltimore Ravens. Williams earned his bachelor's degree in Sociology and Ph.D. in Higher Education from the University of Pennsylvania. His research explores how undergraduate students' social experiences and participation in intercollegiate athletics influence engagement, academic performance, and post-college outcomes.

Timothy Zimmer is an Analyst at Manhattan Strategy Group, a management consulting firm that specializes in research and technical assistance for federal clients, including the U.S. Department of Education. Zimmer was a student-athlete at Northwestern University, where he graduated with a B.A. in Psychology. He was the 2009 Illinois Gatorade Soccer Player of the Year. He earned his master's degree in Higher Education from the University of Pennsyvania.

INDEX

Taylor & Francis eBooks

Helping you to choose the right eBooks for your Library

Add Routledge titles to your library's digital collection today. Taylor and Francis ebooks contains over 50,000 titles in the Humanities, Social Sciences, Behavioural Sciences, Built Environment and Law.

Choose from a range of subject packages or create your own!

Benefits for you

- » Free MARC records
- » COUNTER-compliant usage statistics
- » Flexible purchase and pricing options
- » All titles DRM-free.

Benefits for your user

- » Off-site, anytime access via Athens or referring URL
- » Print or copy pages or chapters
- » Full content search
- » Bookmark, highlight and annotate text
- » Access to thousands of pages of quality research at the click of a button.

REQUEST YOUR **FREE** INSTITUTIONAL TRIAL TODAY	**Free Trials Available** We offer free trials to qualifying academic, corporate and government customers.

eCollections – Choose from over 30 subject eCollections, including:

Archaeology	Language Learning
Architecture	Law
Asian Studies	Literature
Business & Management	Media & Communication
Classical Studies	Middle East Studies
Construction	Music
Creative & Media Arts	Philosophy
Criminology & Criminal Justice	Planning
Economics	Politics
Education	Psychology & Mental Health
Energy	Religion
Engineering	Security
English Language & Linguistics	Social Work
Environment & Sustainability	Sociology
Geography	Sport
Health Studies	Theatre & Performance
History	Tourism, Hospitality & Events

For more information, pricing enquiries or to order a free trial, please contact your local sales team:
www.tandfebooks.com/page/sales

 Routledge
Taylor & Francis Group

The home of
Routledge books

www.tandfebooks.com